CW00351328

e-Music

e-Music

Finding, playing, recording, and organizing digital music

James Maguire, Brandon Barber, Lara Gifford, and Steve Allen

SAMS

201 West 103rd Street, Indianapolis, Indiana 46290

Sams Teach Yourself e-Music Today

Copyright © 2000 by Sams Publishing

International Standard Book Number: 0-672-31855-5

Library of Congress Catalog Card Number: 99-69262

Printed in the United States of America

First Printing: October 2000

03   02   01   00   4   3   2   1

Trademarks

Warning and Disclaimer

Acquisitions Editor
Jeff Schultz

Development Editor
Damon Jordan

Managing Editor
Charlotte Clapp

Project Editor
Dawn Pearson

Copy Editor
Sean Medlock

Indexer
Erika Millen

Proofreader
Daniel Ponder

Team Coordinator
Amy Patton

Software Development Specialist
J.G. Moore

Interior Design
Gary Adair

Cover Design
Jay Corpus

Table of Contents

PART I

What's What

CHAPTER 1

What Is E-Music?

Talkin' About a Revolution

A music revolution is upon us. Like the '50s genesis of rock-and-roll, the British invasion, and the punk scene of the '70s, this revolution has music consumers, record companies, and recording artists "all shook up," to quote the king. But this revolution isn't in just one genre; it affects *every* musical genre. This revolution is e-music, and you can join it with a few clicks of your mouse.

This chapter will tell you what e-music is, give a brief overview of the most popular e-music formats, tell you how you can listen, and explain why you'll want to.

What Does *E-Music* Mean?

It's hard to avoid e-music these days. In fact, you might have dabbled in e-music without even knowing it. Have you ever gone to a news site and clicked on an audio clip, or listened to an online greeting card? Then you've already entered the world of e-music. E-music is anything you listen to on your computer—even if it's not music at all. Comedy monologues, political speeches, even talk radio on the Internet fall under the heading of e-music because they can be recorded, saved, or played on your computer as audio files.

What You'll Learn in This Chapter:

▶ What *e-music* means

▶ What you need to get it and play it

▶ What all the MP3 fever is about

▶ Other common audio files you'll find on the Internet

▶ How e-music stacks up against CDs

Talk radio stations like this one in Portland, Oregon hope to increase their listener base by transmitting their programming live to the worldwide audience on the Internet.

Can I Listen to E-Music Now?

You don't have to be George Jetson to listen to e-music; in fact, you don't even have to be George Jefferson. The equipment is standard and relatively cheap. If you purchased your computer within the last two or three years, chances are that everything you need is within your reach.

To play audio, your computer needs a sound card, speakers, and some free space on the hard drive to save audio files and small software programs. If your computer doesn't have these items, you're missing out in a big way! It's time to go computer shopping to enhance your online experience. (Find out more about buying sound cards and other equipment in Chapter 6, "Equipment Check.")

Next, you're going to need one of those small software programs that allow you to listen to audio files. Your computer might already be loaded with some of these programs. If not, most of the software is available free of charge on the Internet. Chapter 7, "Choose Your Weapons Wisely—Software Matters," will guide you through finding and installing these programs.

What's an MP3, and Why Is Everyone Talking About It?

There are several different formats you can use to listen to or record e-music, but the one everyone is talking about these days is MP3. MP3 files are unique because of their small size. Audio files used to be huge. One song or sound bite could take up a good-sized portion of your computer's memory, which in turn slowed down the computer and allowed fewer applications to run. But MP3s are different. All the information that used to bog down computers has been compressed into tiny files that are one-tenth the size. This makes them easy to download off the Internet and store on your computer by the dozen. A good rule of thumb with MP3s is that one minute of music takes up 1MB of memory. This means that you can store about 100 average-length songs in the space it would take to store and run a typical computer game.

That's great news for the average computer user, but it's not why people are talking about MP3s. The big news is that MP3s are changing the way that knowledgeable computer users acquire music. Instead of paying $17 for a new CD, music fans are downloading their favorite songs from the Internet as free MP3 files, sometimes even before the CD reaches store shelves! Given this, it's no big surprise that MP3s are a huge source of discontent for the record industry. The Recording Industry Association of America (RIAA) is doing everything in their power to hold back

MP3s and the new music revolution, filing suit against Web sites that function as clearing houses for free (but often copyrighted) music. But the record industry isn't having much luck stemming the flow of illicit music to computers everywhere. There's just too much of it out there and too many ways to scoop it up (you'll learn how in Chapter 10, "The Lowdown on Downloading").

Streaming Audio and WAV Files

MP3 files aren't the only audio files you'll discover as you search the Internet for music. You can also expect to find streaming audio and WAV files. *Streaming audio* files aren't saved to your computer; instead, they simply stream into your computer much like a radio signal. Just as with radio, you can't pause, rewind, or fast-forward a streaming file. However, new software allows you to record these streaming files and then convert them to MP3 (see Chapter 7).

WAV files function more like MP3 files, but be warned that they take up a *lot* more space. You can rewind, fast-forward, pause, and play them, and most importantly, you can edit them. If you're a musician, you'll be using WAV files frequently to alter and perfect your songs (see Chapter 22, "Gather the Right Stuff"). WAV files can be played on a regular CD player; MP3 files can't. So if you want to listen to your MP3 files on a regular CD player, you'll need to convert them to WAV format first (see Chapter 7). For more on e-music formats, see Chapter 3, "Fun with Formats."

E-Music vs. CDs: Why Make the Switch?

For over a decade, the CD has been the standard for music quality. It delivers the cleanest, crispest sound available, and its lifespan is longer than the LP and the cassette tape. But CDs have their own set of drawbacks. They can be scratched easily, causing them to skip (or cease to function altogether). A bumpy car ride or a jog around the park can take its toll, rendering a song or even an entire CD unplayable.

E-music has none of the problems associated with CDs, and its sound quality can rival that of any compact disc. Because e-music is stored in your computer as a data file, it can't be scratched like an LP or CD, it can't melt like a tape, and it can't be broken, nicked, or otherwise physically harmed. An e-music file is like any other computer file—a series of 0s and 1s that tells your computer to act in a certain way. The 0s and 1s in an e-music file tell your computer to produce certain sounds. E-music files can be copied and transferred to small, portable devices that you can hook up to headphones or your car stereo. Unlike CD players, these devices have no moving parts. They simply read and execute the file information, providing a music experience that's clear, crisp, and skip-free.

CDs vs. E-Music: The Power of Choice

As a music lover, quality was my main concern when I switched from CDs to MP3s. But as my MP3 collection grew, I found some interesting additional benefits that would forever change the way I experienced music. Let's take a close look at a CD I used to listen to frequently and contrast it with how I listen to e-music by the same artist. After reading this book, you'll be able to complete each of the New E-Music Options outlined below.

- **My old CD:** *Simon and Garfunkel's Greatest Hits*. Contains 14 songs, only 12 of which I actually like.

- **New E-Music Option #1:** I could take my *Greatest Hits* CD, convert the 12 songs I like into e-music, and forever have a custom-made version of the CD on my computer. This option is similar to the Skip function on my CD player, except I'll never have to reprogram my computer to skip the two other songs.

- **New E-Music Option #2:** Why limit myself to songs deemed greatest hits by a record company? One of my favorite Simon and Garfunkel songs, "The Big Bright Green Pleasure Machine," isn't included on their *Greatest Hits* album, but I own the CD where it appeared. In fact, I own a

Stop the Scratching:

No matter how wonderful e-music is, CDs aren't going anywhere. In fact, later in the book you'll learn how to burn your own CDs.

The best way to avoid scratching a CD is to properly store it in a jewel case. But if you have loose CDs lying around, make sure you place them upside down on a clean surface. All the digital information is written on the bottom of the CD, so one little scratch can ruin it.

CD of every album Simon and Garfunkel ever recorded. This means I can convert all of my favorite songs into e-music and listen to them in any order I want. It's the power of choice!

- **New E-Music Option #3:** With the small amount of space my MP3s take up on my computer, I can convert all of my Simon and Garfunkel CDs to e-music files, along with the rest of my CD collection. Then I can create personal playlists for any occasion, time of day, or musical mood. Although the song "Bookends" doesn't rank on the Greatest Hits playlist I've created, it can be found on my Mellow Music Mix playlist or the Discontented Couples I Relate To playlist.

Are You a Mix Master?

This book will teach you everything you need to know about compiling the perfect mix CD or playlist. Well, not everything...it's up to you to determine what kind of songs will set the right tempo or capture just the right mood.

This last option is a significant improvement over CDs for more than one reason. First, you can organize MP3s any way you want them, much like creating your own musical compilations on a dual tape deck. (Who's ever heard of a "mix CD"?) Second, MP3 playlists don't waste any space on your hard drive. They're simply road maps to your music collection. I have two physical copies of "Mrs. Robinson" on CD (one on the greatest hits compilation and one on the soundtrack for *The Graduate*), but I only need one MP3 of the song, even if I put it on multiple playlists.

Wrapping It Up

Here's what you learned in this chapter:

- E-music includes any audio file stored on a computer.

- You don't need a lot of special gizmos to listen to e-music; you should have everything you need on your computer already.

- The three main types of audio files you'll encounter on the Internet are MP3s, WAVs, and streaming audio files. The most popular type, MP3s, are notable because their compact size makes them easy to copy, download, and save.

- The sound quality of MP3s rivals CDs, but you can do cool things with MP3s that you can't with your CD collection.

CHAPTER 2

Fun with Formats

The Gravity of Formats

As digital music begins to realize its potential, one thing has become obvious: The consumers are way, way ahead of the curve. In fact, they're setting it, which is an extraordinary thing. The industry is forced to keep previously established consumer habits in mind, not as mere market suggestions, but as lines drawn in the sand that cannot be crossed. As companies scurry about, searching for profitable ways to distribute and secure their music, they're being guided by a natural system of checks and balances that, for the most part, protect the consumer.

Software makers, hardware makers, and record companies are acutely aware of this reality. They move incrementally, constantly gauging public reaction as they introduce new rules for digital music. Part of the reason that no single standard for delivery or payment has emerged is that the industry knows that if consumers aren't happy with it, they'll go somewhere else to find it. Any standard that emerges is going to have to lure them away from their comfort zone and convince them to jump through a set of hoops and part with their hard-earned dollars to get what they were previously getting for free. It's this tenuous consumer relationship that makes the industry in-fighting so fierce. Whoever strikes the balance between consumers and the industry will win big.

What You'll Learn in This Chapter

▶ Why digital audio formats matter

▶ The difference between open and closed formats

▶ Who is trying to make formats pay

▶ A little audio format history

▶ The who and what of MPEG

The Format Framework

At the center of the billion-dollar bickering are the digital audio file formats—the vehicles for the music itself. A file format is really just a particular arrangement of digital bits that conveys music. There are many candidates for the throne. MP3, the file format explored most thoroughly in this book, has captured the lead, but there are other formats that offer higher compression and better audio quality.

It all began with standard digital audio files like WAV and AIFF. These large, uncompressed audio files can be found throughout your PC and the Internet. Both of these file types are based on Pulse Code Modulation (PCM), a generic format for storing uncompressed audio that can be read by multiple platforms, including CDs and DATs.

Here's a breakdown of standard audio file types:

- **AIFF**   Apple Computer developed this audio file format for storing high-quality sampled audio and musical instrument information. Although it's primarily used by Macintosh systems, it's compatible with PCs. AIFF is also used by Silicon Graphics and is included in several professional audio packages. Compressing these files can affect interoperability between Windows and Macintosh platforms.

- **AU**   This is the standard audio format for Sun Microsystems and UNIX boxes. UNIX has a stronghold on Internet technology, so most browsers will support the AU format.

- **WAV**   WAV files were an early standard for waveform audio files used by Windows. Remember that nightmarishly loud system crash sound that made you spit your morning coffee all over that new PC? That was a WAV file. These files usually carry great audio quality, but they're uncompressed and, subsequently, very large.

Digital Alchemy: Turning Formats into Gold

Standard digital audio files have been used as the building blocks to formulate new formats that are considerably smaller in file size and truer in audio quality. Some of the new formats, like the

It's All About the Benjamins:

According to leading industry analysts Jupiter Communications, the recording industry is really a $100 billion market restricted to $40 billion by the Big Five record companies (EMI, BMG, Sony, Universal, and Warner). The other $60 billion could be unleashed by the rapid growth of digital music over the next few years. As fun as that might sound to you and me, it's got the big guys in cold sweats, because no one is certain exactly *who* will be claiming the rest of the bounty.

MPEG family, were developed out of a desire to regulate the quality of audio used on the Internet. Others were developed to capture a slice of the ballooning digital audio market and profit from it.

There are numerous companies that are using the MP3 technology to *close* the standard, or make it proprietary. The resulting format types attempt to lock the files down with a particular set of secure business rules so that the artists, labels, and enablers can profit from the music's consumption. However, proprietary formats have a tough row to hoe. The MP3 phenomenon is fueled by a need to experience common things in new ways, and proprietary formats run counter to that impulse. There's some question as to whether consumers will stand for them.

Some of the most notable names in the business of creating proprietary formats are Liquid Audio, Mjuice, Apple's QuickTime, and AT&T Lab's a2b format, all of which are built on an MP3 backbone. Microsoft Audio 4.0 and VQF are two proprietary formats that claim to have better audio quality and compression than MP3, but they have yet to make significant headway into the popular digital music market.

Here's a look at some of the most noteworthy MPEG-based proprietary formats:

- **a2b**   Developed by AT&T Labs to secure the rights to digital audio files, this format uses proprietary compression algorithms based on MPEG-AAC codecs. a2b significantly encrypts the audio files to protect copyrights and limit illegal usage. It also includes digital rights management (DRM) software that protects and manages the rights and interests associated with digital information, and ensures any payment scheme is coordinated and fulfilled with a backend financial institution. Lately, a2b has been lagging behind in the race to capture the market. Like its main competitor, Liquid Audio, a2b requires a special player to play its files.

- **Apple QuickTime**   This is Apple Computer's standard for multimedia. It's used to store audio, video, and graphics files. Although it was originally developed for Macintosh systems, it can now be used on Windows machines as well.

- **Liquid Audio** Liquid Audio files are encrypted for copyright protection and layered with a DRM to manage royalties. Liquid also requires you to download the Liquid Audio player in order to play back files. The player allows significant personalization (cover art, notes, links, etc.) and plays several other file types, including Dolby Digital (AC-3), AAC, and MP3.

- **Mjuice** Mjuice creates proprietary encrypted MP3s that can be played on popular player software such as the Winamp player.

Real Cool, Real Fast

The default audio technology used by most high-traffic media sites for sampling, live performances, and one-time plays is RealAudio, created by RealNetworks. This proprietary format allows you to listen to the audio as the data streams into your computer, instead of waiting for an entire download. The immediacy and consistency of RealAudio provides clear benefits to users who are looking for a quick, one-time-only listening experience such as a radio broadcast or news sound bite. However, an audio stream can't be stored for playback at a later time without stripping the encryption from the file.

Playing By Their Own Rules

There are a number of digital file formats that draw from original codecs that aren't based on MPEG technology. Their fight for ubiquity has been tough. However, one of the main competitors, MS Audio, is gaining momentum and will have vast resources to draw upon once Microsoft puts its weight behind it.

Here are some popular proprietary formats that aren't based on MPEG:

- **Dolby Digital, or AC-3** This is the home audio version of the digital surround sound that you commonly find in theaters. AC-3 has been chosen as the official sound format for digital TV, and it's already encoded on many DVDs and laserdiscs.

- **MS Audio 4.0** Built on Microsoft's Active Streaming Format (ASF), MS Audio claims to carry higher-quality sound and a higher compression rate than MP3. MS Audio has an encryption scheme for securing file copyrights. This file format is most frequently used in conjunction with the Microsoft Windows Media Player that comes bundled with most PCs.

- **VQF** Developed by NTT Human Interface Lab, this format offers superior compression and audio, but longer encoding times. This format has very little supporting software at this point.

Table 3.1: Audio File Extension Key

The audio formats discussed in this chapter carry the following file extensions when they appear on your computer:

Type	Extension
AIFF	.aif, .aiff
AU	.au
MP3	.mp3
MS Audio	.asf
QuickTime	.mov
WAV	.wav
VQF	.vqf
RealAudio	.ra

Meet the MPEGs

Because Dr. Karlheinz Brandenburg got a jump on the competition with the revolutionary open MP3 codec, and because of its inherent lack of restrictions on the consumer, it has developed a substantial lead over other digital audio formats. MP3, the favored son of the MPEG family, is currently supported by multiple platforms, operating systems, software packages, and (of course) consumers.

MPEG (Moving Pictures Experts Group) is a consortium of technology and media concerns pioneered by Leonardo Chiariglione (head of the Multimedia Services and Technology Research Division of CSELT, the corporate research center of the Telecom Italia group, and executive director of SDMI) and Hiroshi Yasuda (University of Tokyo Engineering Professor and consultant to Nippon Telegraph and Telephone Public Corporation). The organization includes heavy-hitters like Fraunhofer-Gesellschaft of Germany, Thompson Multimedia, and Dolby Labs (the latter two of the United States). The product of their considerable expertise is the MPEG family of interoperable file formats, including MPEG-1, MPEG-2, and AAC. (MP3 is part of MPEG-2.) The audio facet of these formats is based on the science of psycho-acoustics, which eliminates extraneous sounds that human beings can't hear.

Since the group's inception in 1988, it has met several times a year to devise new standards for encoding audio. Each version of MPEG includes a video and graphics standard as well, but we'll leave that for someone else's book. Because such a large number of parties are involved in defining each stage of the technology, it often takes years to come up with a new version.

Here's a look at the various phases of the MPEG audio file formats:

- **MPEG-1**   Released in 1992, MP1 offers less compression and supports mono and stereo audio, but fails to deliver surround sound.

- **MPEG-2**   Released in 1994, MP2 offers five-channel surround sound and bass enhancement. MP3 is actually a component of the MP2 release called Layer III. Its hallmark is it's excellent compression and high audio quality.

- **AAC**   Part of the MP2 release, Advanced Audio Coding (AAC) has improved sampling rate versatility. Although it offers some advantages over MP3, it's more expensive to license, so its widespread use has been limited.

- **MPEG-4**   Released in 1998, MP4 was developed to handle the entire spectrum of audio applications. Visual data can also be added to MP4 files.

- **MPEG-7**   Currently in development, MP7 has been dubbed Multimedia Contents Description Interface. It will support interactivity such as content search and digital rights management.

Wrapping It Up

Let's review, shall we?

- Right now, consumers rule. Early adapters of digital music technology have established firm ground rules that have limited corporate greed. This is a good thing.

- Developing a standard file format for digital audio that satisfies all parties involved—hardware and software makers, consumers, record labels, and artists—means big, big business. Whether it's even possible is another question.

- Early digital audio standards sounded great but were far too large for distribution. Recent digital audio file formats reduce file size enormously and retain great audio quality.

- MP3 is an open, non-proprietary digital audio file format derived from the MPEG family. It currently constitutes the lion's share of the digital music market.

- There are a number of proprietary formats out there, all vying for the same piece of pie. At this time, there is no clear winner.

CHAPTER 3

Layers of Players

As poet Gil Scott-Heron said, and my man Chuck D quoted, "The revolution will not be televised." The e-music revolution won't be broadcast on your boombox either (unless you set it up to, but we'll get to that in Chapter 15, "Your PC Wants to Be Your Stereo—So Let It"). You're going to need some new equipment to join the e-music revolution, and it all starts with an e-music player. This chapter will give you a quick overview of your choices, and highlight the key features of some of the most popular players out there.

Decisions, Decisions

If you want to join the e-music revolution, the first thing you need is an e-music player. Like e-music itself, an e-music player isn't a physical object but rather a computer program. That means you can download one from the Internet right away, and most of them come free of charge.

There's no shortage of players on the Internet today. In fact, the challenge isn't finding one, but deciding which one of the hundreds of choices is right for you. This chapter will break the choices down for you. Then, if you want to move along to installing one, turn to Chapter 7, "Choose Your Weapons Wisely—Software Matters."

Choose Your Poison

When you're choosing an e-music player, the first thing you need to decide is what you want to do with it. If you just want to listen to your MP3 collection, your best bet is a *standalone* player. But if you want to convert your CD collection to MP3s, you'll need to get a *ripper and encoder*. You can download a ripping/encoding program that functions separately from your player (see Chapters 7 and 19, "Let 'er Rip! (Make CDs into MP3s)"), or you can opt for an all-in-one player that rips, encodes, plays, and organizes your music. Oh, and if you want to play RealAudio files (and why wouldn't you?), you also need to pick up one of the RealAudio products described in this chapter.

Standalone MP3 Players

These utilitarian standalone players really get the job done—when the job is just playing digital music. They don't do a whole lot more than that, but they do it efficiently. Standalone MP3 players work a lot like CD players. You can play, pause, stop, fast-forward, and rewind your MP3s, and most players have a shuffle function that plays your MP3s in random order. Any standalone worth its weight will also have a *playlist* function, which allows you to group songs to your liking and save the grouping for future use. This feature is essential for the serious e-music listener because it lets you quickly recall small musical groupings from your ever-growing music collection.

For the techie in all of us, standalone players have many sound levels to adjust. You can raise the bass, change the pitch, and tweak a host of buttons, bars, and knobs to your heart's content.

What standalones lack is editing functions and ripping/encoding technology. You might be asking yourself why you would want a player with fewer functions than the all-powerful all-in-ones (which we'll talk about later). The answer is that those functions take up space and slow down your computer. If you don't need them, stick with a sleek, no-nonsense standalone player. You'll have an easier time learning what it does, how it does it, and how to make it really snap, crackle, and pop.

This section will describe a few of our favorite players, which not only snap but sizzle. Then you'll look at some other contenders in the pack that are widely used, but not widely recommended.

The Sonique Standalone

This player looks a little like a science fiction prop; maybe that's why its creator, Lycos, claims it's "Made by Aliens." These aliens know their stuff—they've taken a straightforward approach to designing the controls. The player is easy for new users to understand, and it has some cool bells and whistles. You can download it now, free of charge, at www.sonique.com.

This player's best feature is its versatility. It's not limited to playing MP3s; it can also handle WAVs, CDs, and a plethora of other audio formats. Also, it has three different modes. The large square window mode takes up about 1/6 of your screen and is easy to read. The medium-sized, double-bubble mode looks the coolest and is functional without being a space hog. The minimalist mode is barely a blip on your screen, so it only shows the most important features, like the Play button.

Those wacky aliens and their double-bubble Sonique player!

Sonique has an easy, straightforward interface for making playlists. In just a few steps, you can make as many as you want (see Chapter 14, "Make Killer Playlists"). And Sonique not only lets you make great lists, but it helps you add to them with music from the Sonique site. If you're online while using the player, click the links on the player to go to pages with free music recommended by those wacky alien creators. You'll also find other useful stuff on the site, such as help files and plug-ins that give you more control over the sound output.

Oh, and there's one other cool feature of Sonique that must be
noted—the visual mode. Sonique gives you several different
visual programs to choose from, which will show splashes of
color synched to your musical selection. In the double-bubble and
large window modes, you can see the colors move around with
more precision than a marching band, and you can also go full-
screen with the effects. Some other players do this too, but
Sonique does it best.

Try It Yourself ▼

To find and use these players, follow these steps:

1. Go to the Web address listed with each player.

2. Look for a button or link that prompts you to "download
   now," and follow the instructions for downloading.

3. When a player downloads to your computer, remember to
   note where it's being saved on your hard drive so you can
   install it.

4. The installation program will guide you through setup, but
   there are several options, including if you want a shortcut on
   your desktop. Select this option for now; it will make the
   player easy to find and use.

5. You may also encounter an option that asks if you want to
   make this program your default player. If you choose this
   option, the player will start automatically whenever you click
   on an audio file.

6. To use the player after installation, click on its shortcut on
   your desktop, or click on any audio file on your computer.
   The default player should pop up and play the file.

▲

7. Need more help? Get detailed instructions in Chapter 7.

Winamp

Winamp is said to be the most popular standalone player on the
Internet today; I know it's by far the most popular in my circle of
geeky computer friends. It's been around longer than most other
players, which means you'll encounter fewer program bugs.
Because Winamp has an *open source* code, many computer hob-
byists have built their own helpful plug-ins for the player. You can

download these plug-ins and the latest version of Winamp, free of charge, at www.winamp.com.

The most compelling features of Winamp are its equalizer, and playlist options. The ten-band graphic equalizer and preamp (which boosts the audio signal before it's sent to the equalizer) can be adjusted and saved as a preset for all play, or you can customize and save presets for individual songs. There are more sliders and buttons on the Winamp equalizer than you could ever possibly use (unless you're a real guy's guy), but it's nice to have the options anyway.

Plug It In, Plug It In:

A plug-in is a small computer program that enhances or alters another computer program. Plug-ins for MP3 players often give users more audio-adjustment options or visual accompaniments, such as bursts of colors timed to the music.

Look at all the plug-ins you can snag at www. winamp.com!

The Winamp interface is simple. The EQ button opens the equalizer, and the PL button lets you create or open playlists.

Pressing the PL button on the right side of the player takes you to the playlist options, which are pretty straightforward. While Winamp is open, you can open a file containing all your MP3s and drag and drop the files you want to play. You can also direct Winamp to play a whole directory of songs, or even give it an Internet address.

RealPlayer

This isn't the best player when it comes to MP3s, but it does one
thing the other standalones can't...it plays RealAudio files. You
can download it at www.real.com. If you spend much time on the
Internet, this is something you've just gotta have. There's a lot of
information out there in RealAudio format, and you'll miss it
without this free player.

However, resist the temptation to make the RealPlayer your
default player. You'll do better with Sonique or Winamp because
they're sleeker and not as clunky. This is because the RealPlayer
is a "corporate" player, if you will. RealAudio has many corporate partners that want to force their content onto your desktop via
the big, 1984-esque telescreen that appears each time you try to
play a tune. Because of the logos, mini-banner ads, and other
extraneous content that weighs down this player, it takes up three
times the space on your desktop as Winamp. Plus, it takes longer
to load. So using it as your default player is a bad idea. However,
not using it at all is a worse one. The fact is, a sizeable amount of
audio content on the Internet is in RealAudio format, making the
RealPlayer a necessity.

*The RealPlayer
keeps getting big-
ger and bigger
without offering a
lot more than
your typical
player.*

Yahoo Player

At the time of this writing, only the beta version of this player is available. This means a few bugs still need to be worked out, and some program revisions are likely. But even as a beta, the Yahoo Player is an impressive piece of work. It can handle your MP3s, CDs, and video clips. When you insert a CD, it automatically logs on to the Internet and looks up title, artist, and song information.

If you're looking for new, interesting audio content on the Internet, Yahoo makes it easy. Since Yahoo is a major player in Internet content, the player has links to Internet radio stations and pages with free MP3s. Since this is a beta version, the audio and playlist features could change substantially between now and the official release date. In general, though, the player seems to mimic Winamp's style: functional yet simple. This could be a major player in the coming years. It's available free of charge at www.player.broadcast.com/.

Testing, Testing: *Beta version* is a term used by computer folks to indicate that the product is still being tested and tweaked, with the official release date still looming.

Windows Media Player

This program has all the style and pizzazz you'd expect from Bill Gates...that is, almost none. This is Microsoft's own beauty school reject, the simple worker bee of MP3 players...the Windows Media Player. If you've got a Windows-based operating system, you may have already seen this player pop up when you play an audio file. It starts out as Windows' default player, but that doesn't mean you have to settle for it. Bigger, brighter options abound. However, if you really want to use this program and you don't have it on your computer, you can always pick it up free of charge by visiting www.microsoft.com and typing "Windows Player" in the search window.

The Rest

There are literally hundreds of other standalone players out there. The preceding have been the most popular, but your choices certainly aren't limited. Typing "mp3 player" into any search engine will turn up many results, so feel free to explore the options and find the one that suits your needs best.

Give Me Some Skin:

Skins are small programs that change the look of a player without changing how it functions. Techies design them to fit different interests or themes. Odds are that you'll find a skin to match your inclinations, especially if your inclinations happen to be anything gothic, sci-fi, or tech-oriented. My personal favorite was a skin that looked just like my pet hedgehog (it was created by a computer-capable friend). Feel free to switch skins time and again—after all, they're only skin-deep (sorry, I had to) and won't affect the operation of the player.

All-in-One MP3 Players

So you want it all? Who doesn't? If you want to rip your CD collection into MP3s and play them using the same program, it's time to snag an all-in-one player. In Chapter 19, you'll learn all about converting CDs to MP3s, and we'll even tell you about standalone ripping and encoding programs that you can use instead of all-in-ones. But here, we'll focus on a few great programs that can serve as E-Music Central. With these programs, you can create, convert, manage, and play all your e-music files.

When you're looking for an all-in-one player, there are a few ripping and encoding features to look for. First, if you're going to *burn* your own CDs, you need to make sure the player supports the CD burner you own. Check the player's system requirements, or read its FAQ page on the Internet to see what types of CD burners it supports.

Next, make sure your all-in-one copies CDs at fast rate without sacrificing sound quality. Pay special attention to something called the *bitrate*. This refers to the quality of the recording and indicates how crisp and clear it will be. CD-quality is 128Kbps or above. If you're getting less, you're losing out. The higher the bitrate, the better the quality…although higher bitrates also take up slightly more space on your hard drive. Often, all-in-one players offer you great sound for a small fee, or less-than-great sound if you download the free version. If music is as important to you as it is to me (and I bet it is), you won't want to settle for less. And you won't have to…

MusicMatch Jukebox

Brava Software has developed one of the best applications known to music fans. Not only does it rip and encode CDs (see Chapter 19 for more information), but it also functions as a database of MP3 files and a playlist editor. You're going to want this program, so download it at www.musicmatch.com. It doesn't cost anything for the standard version, which allows you to record unlimited near-CD-quality MP3s. For $29.99, you can upgrade to MusicMatch Jukebox Plus, which lets you record MP3s and new CDs at a faster rate. Plus, you get a few cool graphical features, like a program that prints out album covers for your CD's jewel case.

The MusicMatch Jukebox takes up a lot of screen space, but hey, it does a lot more than the average player.

The designers at MusicMatch call their playlist editor The Jukebox, and it looks like something you'd see in a '50s restaurant. The jukebox does everything that typical playlist editors do, but it also lets you save lyrics and liner notes. You can even customize it to show album covers or other art you want to associate with the album. You'll learn more about these options in Chapters 7 and 12, "Be a Jukebox Hero."

RealJukebox

From the same people who brought you RealAudio, the RealJukebox is quickly becoming the all-in-one player to contend with. Just like MusicMatch, there's a free version and a $29.99 version, but this time the price difference affects sound performance. RealJukebox Plus gives you CD-quality sound at 320Kpbs, as well as a 10-band graphic equalizer. The free version gives you sub-CD-quality sound and no equalizer. Get either version at www.real.com.

Like MusicMatch, RealJukebox has elaborate playlist options and a built-in ripper and encoder. And if you like your gratification instantly, RealJukebox lets you listen to music as you record it. But perhaps the most important feature that sets the RealJukebox apart from the rest is that it plays RealAudio files. As mentioned earlier, you'll find RealAudio clips all over the Internet, whether it's a sound bite or a complete radio broadcast. Only products from the RealAudio family (RealPlayer, RealJukebox, and RealJukebox Plus) can handle this format, so it's convenient—dare we say necessary—to have one on your computer.

Playing Music on a Mac

There are two hot choices when it comes to MP3 players on
Macintosh computers: MacAmp's Macast and Audion by Panic.
The latest version of Macast is available for $24.95, but you can
try it out for 30 days free of charge. You can also download
Macast Lite, which has fewer visual and sound adjustment features and costs $15. Both versions play CDs, MP3s, and stream-
ing audio in the form of Shoutcast and Icecast files, and they're
both available for download at www.macamp.net.

The better deal for Mac users is probably the Audion, available
for $17.95 at www.panic.com/ppack/audion/. It includes many
features that are less common on PC players, like an easily
adjustable interface that allows you to create your own keyboard
shortcuts or control window text. Audion also offers an alarm
clock feature that lets you wake to your e-music collection, and a
karaoke feature that mutes out the vocals on your favorite songs
so you can sing along. Would you expect anything less from a
Mac program?

Wrapping It Up

Now you know some of your options when it comes to e-music
players. Let's recap, shall we?

- There are two main types of players to meet your e-music
  needs: standalones and all-in-ones.

- If you just need to do some old-fashioned music listening,
  you're safe with a standalone player. Consider Sonique or
  Winamp.

- If you want something that will rip and encode your CDs as
  well as play MP3s and other music files, go with an all-in-
  one player like RealJukebox or MusicMatch.

- You need a RealAudio product on your computer to play
  RealAudio files. Go with either the RealPlayer or
  RealJukebox.

- Mac users have fewer options, but many Mac players come
  with cooler features than their PC alternatives.

CHAPTER 4

Pirates and the Musical Mutiny

So, as you're sailing the digital seas in search of a little music, you come across a Yanni fan site that has a rare MP3 that you've been dying to get your hands on. You proceed to download it. Freeze! Have you weighed all of the ramifications of that mouse-click? Odds are that you haven't. Think about this: What about Yanni's record label? How's his manager supposed to keep himself in Ferraris if you don't cough up some dough for the track? What about Yanni's royalties? Mousse ain't cheap, ya know.

What You'll Learn in This Chapter:

▶ Discretionary downloading

▶ A little legal background

▶ How the recording industry is getting secure

And you thought I was kidding. Most major artists, even Yanni, have numerous Web shrines created by fans.

Don't feel bad, because you're not alone. You came, you saw, you downloaded a bit of digital information that caught your eye. For the most part, it's a disembodied transaction that seems about as sinister as opening email or sending your friend a link to a news article. However, there are those who would like to jail you for cutting Yanni's label out of the loop, and they're spending millions of dollars to do so.

Let's take a look at some of the most interesting areas of this debate so you can speak confidently about Yanni's fate at your next cocktail party.

Good versus Evil

There are two types of MP3s—legal and illegal. Legal files are those that are offered for free as promotions or for sale on any of the major MP3 sites such as MP3.com, Emusic, Amazon, and the like. Many record labels are getting into the act by distributing their artists' music online as well.

The rest are illegal, or at least they're looked upon as such by governing bodies and big-money watchdog groups like the Recording Industry Association of America (RIAA) and the Alliance of Artists and Recording Companies (AARC).

According to the International Federation of Phonographic Industries (IFPI)—which includes the big-five record labels EMI, BMG, Sony, Universal, and Warner, as well as 1,400 record producers and distributors in 70 countries—there were somewhere in the neighborhood of 1 million illegal files on the Net by the end of 1999. By all estimations, the IFPI had it easy back then. Today, you'll find more than half a million songs listed on the controversial Napster.com alone, and most of them are obtained illegally. Because it's so darn easy to make an MP3 and even easier to pass it along, expect the number of illegal music files on the net to grow exponentially.

Cyber Cops:

The RIAA is the trade association devoted to protecting the creative content of the recording industry. Their members produce, manufacture, and distribute 90 percent of the music purchased in the United States. And they want to keep it that way.

Illegal MP3s: Born Bad, or Just Made That Way?

Let's take a look at what makes an MP3 illegal. Although most of the MP3s that you find on the Internet aren't posted for financial gain, in many cases they're the intellectual property of someone else. Copyright laws that grant the holder sole distribution, reproduction, modification, and public performance rights for their work protect intellectual property. This means that by downloading it without accessing a particular set of business rules (payment, for instance), you're in violation of their copyrights and, therefore, screwed. The Digital Millenium Copyright Act

(DMCA), passed in 1998, reinforces artists' rights to their intellectual properties and sets some guidelines for how music is to be distributed online.

However, there are loopholes in the current system due to a lack of clear legislation regarding how PCs are used as audio devices. Although you're still not off the hook if you download copyrighted music from the Internet, you can convert your personal CD collection into MP3s free of the long arm of the law. According to a section of 1971's Copyright Act called the Doctrine of Fair Use, you can make copies of prerecorded music as long as they're intended for personal use only and not for distribution.

Regulating the use of copyrighted music on the Web has become an extremely contentious area of the law. There have been several high-profile cases brought against companies that are trying to create businesses around digital music. When the RIAA recently filed suit against MP3.com, the association successfully put new limits on the Doctrine of Fair Use. The case revolved around two key features that MP3.com was offering its users, Instant Listening and Beam-It. Using these programs, a listener could prove ownership of a copyrighted CD by placing it in the CD-ROM drive for MP3.com to scan. Once ownership was proven, the listener could access the same music online at any time, from any computer, by visiting a personalized "musical locker" on the MP3.com site.

Users may have seen this service as the Doctrine of Fair Use made easy, but the RIAA saw it as a threat. It asserted that since users aren't actually copying their own CDs onto their own specific areas of MP3.com, but instead are given access to a digital music library of over 45,000 albums owned by MP3.com, the service was illegal. The courts agreed in a ruling issued in May 2000. Yes, you can upload your CDs onto your desktop. Yes, you can upload them to the Internet so that you and you alone can access them from any computer. But you can't get any help with it—at least not from MP3.com, or whichever company the RIAA targets next.

Getting into the Act:

U.S. Copyright Act (Title 17)—This 1971 law grants artists exclusive rights over the distribution of the music they create. Also, any permitted distribution of their copyrighted property will result in royalty payments. The Copyright Act also sets limits for professional public use of their product.

But the RIAA doesn't win *all* its battles. One of the most signifi-cant wins for a digital music company was the case of RIAA vs. Diamond Multimedia in June 1999. The RIAA claimed that the creators of the popular Diamond Rio personal media player were destroying the digital distribution strategy of the recording indus-try because it plays both legal and illegal files. However, an appeals court judge in California ruled that an MP3 player isn't subject to government restriction because it's a playback-only device. The judge also ruled that the Diamond Rio player was merely a method of *space-shifting*, or moving music from one device to another. The precedent for this finding was established in a 1984 case in which the sale of videocassette recorders was validated due to their role as *time-shifters*.

The RIAA has spent a consider-able sum putting a friendly face on their aggressive reputation, including this snappy and youth-ful Web site.

But the biggest court battles these days revolve around a little program written by 19-year-old Shawn Fanning. This program, which he wrote after reading a beginner's guide to computer pro-gramming, launched the Internet startup company Napster (dis-cussed in more depth in Chapter 5). Napster allows users to swap MP3 files with incredible speed and efficiency. Users search for MP3s within other users' collections, eliminating broken Web links and speeding up searches considerably. Although Napster

doesn't host any of the files itself, the RIAA charges that Napster
is guilty of "contributory copyright infringement" due to its role
as a conduit between users. In this ongoing court battle, the first
round has gone to the RIAA. A U.S. district judge in San
Francisco ruled that Napster's assertion that it was "a mere conduit" would not suffice in court, and that the company could be
held liable in the case.

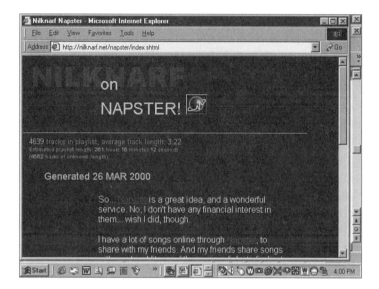

*The legal atten-
tion Napster is
attracting has
only made it more
popular. Napster
fan sites like this
one have popped
up all over
the Web.*

But the RIAA isn't the only group that's legally sticking it to
Napster. Heavy metal stalwarts Metallica are heading off to court,
claiming Napster is guilty of copyright infringement and racke-
teering for listing the availability of purloined Metallica songs.
Drummer Lars Ulrich, who appears to be leading the battle of the
band, got a jump on the court case in May 2000 when he gave
Napster the names of 300,000 users he claimed were illegally
offering Metallica songs. A written disclaimer on the Napster site
warns that users who exchange illegal copies of music risk ban-
ishment from the site, so Napster quickly banned those users. The
move satisfied, but did not soften, Metallica's anti-Napster fervor.
The lawsuit is still pending, along with another from rap artist
and producer Dr. Dre, who has collected user names as well.

Not all artists are anti-Napster or anti-MP3. Public Enemy's Chuck D has come out strongly in favor of Napster, and rock band Limp Bizkit joined forces with the company to present a free summer tour.

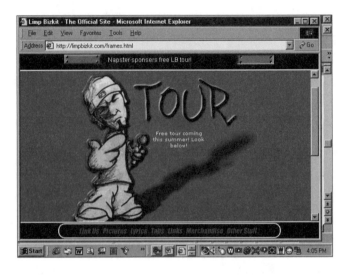

Getting the Boot:

The Napster users who were kicked off the system in The Great Metallica Boot of 2000 were supposed to be banned for good. Instead, many were back within minutes of the sweep, using new names... and instructions they gleaned off Napster's own site. You can jail a revolutionary (or at least his user handle), but you can't jail a revolution.

Although the RIAA's litigation tends to be aimed at companies, individuals have also been ensnared in its anti-MP3 agenda. In November 1999, an Oregon University student was sentenced to two years of probation, limited Internet access, and periodic urine tests (relevance?) for violating the No Electronic Theft (NET) act by distributing copyrighted MP3s. The penalty was actually far less severe than what the student *could* have received.

Universities have also become an RIAA target. Carnegie-Mellon and the University of South Carolina have been singled out by the RIAA because their students possess and trade illegal MP3s. As the prevalence of digital music continues to grow, we can only expect more legal rumblings from the recording industry.

There's No "I" In "Team"

At this point, these legal shenanigans constitute almost the entirety of the recording industry's digital music strategy. To bring an end to this chaos, clear, logical standards must emerge. The first real attempt at a unified set of standards for labels, software makers, and hardware makers is the Secure Distribution of Music Initiative (SDMI).

SDMI is a concerted effort by more than 150 music, electronics, and software companies to find a way to distribute digital music across multiple platforms using an agreed-upon rights management system. The task is a dizzying one, for a couple of reasons. First, these industries aren't really known for sharing their toys. These are ego-laden industries, and most of the players involved didn't get where they are today through cooperation.

Second, they're up against a phenomenon that's defined by its ease of use. You find a music file, you click on it, and you're done. Any solution they come up with will have to be equally simple, or users will hit the bricks.

The first phase of SDMI requires manufacturers of portable digital music players (Diamond Rio, RCA Lyra, Yepp, and so on) to implement several security components, foremost among them a digital rights management (DRM) system. This will allow record labels to securely distribute and track files as they're transmitted over the Net and onto portable players. Basically, a DRM includes encryption to secure the files, a "clearinghouse" to monitor the distribution of files and process transactions, and a software solution that connects PCs to the clearinghouse. Several companies have stepped up to offer the definitive DRM, including InterTrust, Microsoft Reciprocal, and Magex.

The second phase of SDMI will attempt to establish a secure format for incorporating licensing information into files. The hope is that once all players use the same DRM that recognizes the agreed-upon secure format, piracy will lose its foothold.

This could be a foolhardy plan. Even if companies like InterTrust and Microsoft succeed in creating an easy-to-use distribution system, there will always be someone creating a workaround for any encryption scheme. Hackers have already broken through both Microsoft's Media format and the movie encryption scheme for DVDs (which took five years to develop).

As the record industry begins to evaluate the different DRM systems and other technologies over the next year, there's a strong possibility that each and every record label, hardware maker, and software maker will choose a different system to distribute and play digital music. Ultimately, the resulting confusion will drive users back to their old ways.

Safety NET:
NET is a 1997 amendment to the U.S. Copyright Act that further defines the term "financial gain" as the receipt of anything "of value." This includes file trading, posting, and so on. In effect, if you illegally receive a copyrighted MP3, you've willfully received something of value and are bound by the laws that govern it.

Wrapping It Up

Let's recap, shall we?

- Even Yanni has fans.

- Think before you click. Most of the files that you come across are copyright-protected, even though you might think they're free-and-legal.

- Even though copyright law has been tailored to the Web, there's still a lot of controversy over how it's to be enforced.

- If you plan to create a tiny Internet company that brings the all-powerful recording industry to its knees, don't forget to budget for a legal team.

- SDMI is an attempt by the recording industry to stem the flow of illegal music files into the marketplace. Its success will depend on the level of cooperation between its traditionally feisty members.

- A Digital Right Management (DRM) system encrypts, tracks, and monitors digital music files.

CHAPTER 5

What's Next?

How you obtain, save, and play e-music is changing all the time. A few years ago no one knew what an MP3 was, and in a few years maybe no one will remember what it was. An even zippier, smaller, more-streamlined, better-sounding music format might come along, and we'll all say "MP-*what*?" The digital landscape is like that—rapidly changing, and usually for the better.

In this chapter, I'll speculate on the new directions that e-music may take in the coming months and years. You'll learn a bit about what to expect in the future, who's going to make it happen, and where you can turn to keep pace with the changes.

Seeds of Change

The end of 1999 will go down as a turning point for e-music because it brought us Napster, a revolution in acquiring and sharing tunes. Before Napster, e-music belonged to an elite club of determined computer geeks and musical bounty hunters. Finding it could be laborious, and there wasn't much of it out there. The world needed a new working model to make e-music palatable.

Nineteen-year-old Shawn Fanning knew this. He knew he needed a place where all his friends could share their MP3 collections with each other. Shawn probably hadn't even heard of the term "distributed aggregation model," but he spent all his college free time creating one. He called it Napster, and it opened the world of e-music to the masses.

Shawn's circle of MP3-swapping friends multiplied and exploded after Napster appeared on the scene. Friends told friends, college students told their older brothers, office computer geeks told anyone who was interested... and *everyone* was. Soon, music news sources like MTV, *Rolling Stone*, and *Spin* were reporting on this

What You'll Learn in This Chapter:

- ▶ Which current trends will make it in the future and which won't
- ▶ The business models that record companies are considering for the future
- ▶ Where to keep up-to-date in the rapidly changing world of digital music

A program that brings users together to share and copy their e-music files is called a *distributed aggregation model*. Napster, Gnutella, and FreeNet all use this model to link users all over the world into one gigantic network.

new e-music revolution, and consequently, Napster experienced even more explosive growth. Around the same time some lawsuits hit the company, inspiring the development of new programs. These programs delivered the same goods but didn't face the same threats.

Gnutella and FreeNet led the pack of Napster knockoffs. These programs are even more enticing to users. By the same token, they're more worrisome to record companies because, unlike Napster, they don't have a centralized, corporate-funded backbone. In other words, there's nobody to sue.

File Sharing Will Expand

By going after Napster full-force, record companies and artists are attempting to cut off the world's main route to file sharing. However, other thoroughfares have been built and are expected to expand. Traffic is increasing every day, and no determined driver will abandon his vehicle just because one road is blocked—he'll just find another.

Gnutella and Freenet are expected to be those main arteries if Napster is ever blocked. These programs let users share not only e-music, but also software programs and video files. Expect the motion picture industry and the software industry to try to stop these programs as well, because large corporations stand to lose big in an information-free-for-all. But just *how* these industries will stop a free program with no operator, and no center, is questionable. Users could be tracked and sued, but this would force media companies to sue media consumers, and that might be even worse for business than a free-media-grab culture.

Courts and corporations are slow. Computer renegades, programmers, hackers, and geeks are fast. If Gnutella or FreeNet go away, expect other file-sharing programs to pop up.

The Record Industry Has to Change

There's just no way around it; the record industry is in for a change. The buying public is changing, technology is changing, and it's time for them to get on with it and change too. Eventually, they'll have to accept that the public is embracing digital music, and act accordingly.

There are several ways they may change their business practices to get in line with the new world of e-music. They could actively distribute e-music to consumers just like they do CDs, but at a significantly reduced price. The industry would save considerably on distribution and production (no package to make, no shipping to pay), and consumers would enjoy a more direct path to their favorite tunes. Copyright infringements would decrease as consumers turned to corporate sites for inexpensive, digitally protected, top-quality audio. Smaller record labels like Atomic Pop are already trying this at their Web sites, but major labels have yet to jump on board.

Another business model that the industry is considering right now is the subscription-based e-music system. Listeners would pay a monthly fee (the equivalent of a premium cable channel bill) to record companies. This would grant them access to any music they wanted to hear. In this scenario, you wouldn't own physical copies of the music, but you could tap into a massive, comprehensive library of tunes and listen to what you want, when you want, as much as you want. In this model, the monthly fees would be distributed to artists and record companies according to how often their songs were selected.

Is Traditional Music Media on Its Way Out?

Every time I visit Seattle, I pop in and out of the funky stores along University Street. On my last trip, the e-music wave really hit me as I entered a used record shop. The place was a ghost town. CDs and band posters covered the shop, but there wasn't a customer in sight. Where was the usual Seattle crowd of purple-haired girls and pierced boys? Then I saw the sole employee stationed at an amber-colored computer screen, and I recognized the program he was using: Napster. This went a long way in explaining why one lone tourist inhabited his shop. This employee was consorting with the enemy, downloading songs off the Internet as the cash register read $0.00.

Record stores in wired towns like Seattle and San Francisco are already feeling the effects of e-music. Although the record industry reports that CD sales are up over previous years, a recent study of record stores in college towns, where Napster is the most popular, showed significantly decreased sales. As more people discover all the possibilities of e-music, we'll undoubtedly see the trend expand. CD and tape purchases will suffer, as will music stores.

However, traditional music media won't go away. E-music won't be embraced by everyone, and those who *do* embrace it won't necessarily shun CDs altogether. There's just something about those neatly packaged liner notes and artwork that make you want to spend your money at the CD store and not on more hard drive space. However, the more you turn to the Internet for music, the more you tend to forget the appeal of CDs. The ease of acquiring digital music replaces the benefit of the CD.

For the Record:

At the beginning of the year 2000, the Federal Trade Commission ruled that record companies were guilty of price inflation and that they had to lower the prices on CDs. If the prices go low enough, digital music lovers might still visit record shops.

The record industry might lure consumers back to the CD by adding extras that you can't get on the Internet. Expect to see albums come out with trading cards or posters, which you just can't get over a phone line. Another route that record companies may take is simple but radical: price reduction. The law of supply and demand makes this inevitable. Few people will pay $17.99 for a CD they can get for free on the Internet, but they might jump back into the buying market if the price tag was, say, $9.00.

E-Music Is Eternal, But MP3s Are Not

Digital music will be around forever, but count on MP3s to go the way of the LP someday. Right now the MP3 format is great, even remarkable. Everyone who's downloaded one is impressed at the audio quality it delivers in such a small package. But we won't be in the future. We'll think of MP3s as large, clunky relics. The computer geeks of the world will unite in their love of good music and small file sizes, and they'll create an even more efficient format. We'll undergo many incarnations of digital music standards, each one more compressed and with better audio quality. It's hard to say just what the new format will be called, what it will consist of, or who will make it. But right now, there are computer kids all around the world poised behind their keyboards, looking for the answer.

Equipment Will Improve

Today's digital music equipment is impressive, but tomorrow's will be fantastic. As far as music players for your desktop computer, today's music jukeboxes point to the future. Expect more complex organizational tools to start popping up, as well as more visual features. Want to see the music video to your favorite song at the click of a button? You will.

And what about portable players? Watch as prices go down and performance increases. Right now the best-selling Diamond Rio lets you carry about an album's worth of music, Sony's new product doubles that, and the trend will continue. Players now hold enough music for a trip to the mall, but soon they'll hold enough music for an all-out road trip. Speaking of road trips, you'll also see home and car stereos built to play and save digital music. It will be the standard because the market demands it.

Revisionist Radio

Are you a picky person? Then you must love the Internet. With all the choices it provides and all the niches it serves, it lets you be as picky as you want to be. Music fans can locate the music they want more easily than ever before. So, with all the options on the Net, why settle for the radio, with its limited playlists and endless prattle of DJs?

More and more people will ask themselves this question as they discover Web radio stations. These stations, managed by ordinary music fans, will grow in popularity as they serve musical niche markets that traditional radio ignores. Britpop fans won't have to settle for broad-reaching "alternative" stations in their area, Garth Brooks fans can tune into all-Garth stations instead of wading through country station lineups, and rap fans can listen to their music undistilled and free of radio edits. As music fans jump ship from traditional radio, those stations may adopt talk-oriented formats or rely more heavily on syndicated programming.

No matter the format, all radio stations will eventually broadcast their signals to the Internet. Most have already embraced this audience-expanding option. Local radio on the Net will give you even more e-music choices, and you can listen to the rhythm of your hometown without actually flying back.

The specialized music stations at this site are brought to you free-of-charge by other music fans. If you don't see your brand of fun, you can create your own station.

Not Available in Stores!

Right now, the record industry keeps reminding e-music listeners that they just can't duplicate the CD experience with their computers. The industry cites the lack of packaging and the compression problems with MP3s. These people want you to believe that they have something that you can't get on the Internet. What they don't tell you is that there are some things the Net gives you that they never can.

There are many special music mixes and remastered songs floating around the Internet that have never been on store shelves, and never will. Music fans and artists make these mixes on their home computers and then distribute them for free on the Internet. Some files are completely original, some aren't. Some are new versions of copyrighted songs by popular artists like Eminem, or mixes of several different songs by popular artists blended together. A Tupac Shakur/Phil Collins mix is one example that's very popular, while an all-Madonna mix, which blends six different Madonna hits into one long-playing song, also has its fans.

As music fans discover the ease of altering and mixing sound files, expect more of these Internet-only songs to pop up. In high school hallways, talk will turn from "Did you hear that new song on the radio the other day?" to "You'll never guess what I found on Napster the other day." Music fans with sound editing programs may make names for themselves by creating mixes of other people's work. Meanwhile, expect artists to keep putting out their own e-music-only tracks, hoping for their songs to sweep the world and become playlist favorites.

Keeping Up with the Trends

If you're afraid of technology slipping by right under your nose, take comfort because you're not alone. There's just so much of it appearing so quickly that it's hard to know which developments to take seriously and which to ignore. When it comes to e-music trends, there are a few news sources that can help. My two favorite spots for technology news of all kinds are C|Net (*www.cnet.com*) and ZDNet (*www.zdnet.com*). Both have sections dedicated to e-music that review and link to software and hardware updates and digital music download sites. ZDNet also reports on digital music news. If there's a court decision about Napster, you'll find it there. MP3.com is also an excellent source for news and product developments. While you're scooping up legal MP3s from the site, keep yourself informed with their message boards and news pages.

ZDNet.com has its own digital-music area.

If you like to do your in-depth reading offline, as I do, pick up magazines like *PC World* and *Yahoo Life*. Every issue of these magazines touches on some aspect of digital music. If you already read magazines like *Newsweek*, *Rolling Stone*, or *Spin*, you can look for their sporadic but helpful digital music updates. As the e-music revolution spreads, these magazines will introduce regular features to satiate the needs of the wired world.

Wrapping It Up

The recent past of digital music only proves how volatile and exciting the future will be. I know many computer geeks who hit themselves over the head when they think about Napster, because it's so simple and they wonder why they didn't come up with it first. What other simple, lifestyle-altering notions are out there, undiscovered? What will be the next digital music milestone that's unturned?

Nobody knows the answers to these questions right now, but you've learned a few things about the future of digital music:

- File-sharing programs will expand and change.

- We *hope* the record industry will eventually get in step with the times by adopting a new business model.

- The future will still have traditional music media, but radio stations will be a lot different and MP3s will give way to something better.

- There are news sources you can use to track the ever-changing landscape of digital music.

PART II

Get Loaded

CHAPTER 6

Equipment Check

MP3 devices are proliferating at an incredible rate. You can buy portable players, players for your car, and players for your home stereo. In the very near future, there will be MP3 devices that can download files without a computer.

For the time being, though, the term "MP3" usually means "music played on a computer." A computer is needed to surf the ever-expanding universe of MP3 Web sites. Portable players require a computer to load music files. And despite the growing popularity of MP3 devices, most people enjoy MP3 music on computers, and only on computers. So, what kind of computer do you need?

Computer Basics

There are several factors that affect a computer's performance and its capability to play or record MP3 files. These are processor speed, memory, and hard disk size. You've probably seen computers advertised with specifications like "450MHz, 64MB RAM, 6GB."

The first number, 450MHz, refers to the clock speed of the processor, expressed in megahertz and abbreviated as MHz. The processor is the most important part of the computer and is where the actual computing is done. You may also see a processor referred to as a CPU (central processing unit). The higher the clock speed, the faster the computer can process information. For good MP3 operation, this figure should be at least 166MHz. A slower computer may be able to play MP3 files, but it will have difficulty encoding (recording) them.

The second number means that the computer has 64 megabytes of random access memory. This type of memory, abbreviated as

RAM, is the temporary memory where programs and files are stored while they're being used. More RAM allows you to run several programs simultaneously, and it also lets you open larger files. These days, 64MB is standard. 128MB is even better, especially if you're running Windows 2000.

Finally, 6GB refers to the size of the hard drive, expressed in gigabytes. A gigabyte is one million bytes, or one thousand megabytes. Just a couple of years ago, most hard drives were measured in megabytes and a 540MB drive was considered quite large. Hard drives have come a long way, though, and today even 20GB drives are relatively cheap.

Regardless of what kind of computer you have, you'll need plenty of space on your hard drive if you plan to start collecting MP3 files. Although MP3s are compressed to one-tenth the size of uncompressed formats such as WAV, AIFF, or CD tracks, they still take up about one megabyte for every minute of music. A typical album converted to MP3 will occupy around 64MB of space, so it's easy to see how you could fill up a hard drive in short order. Get the largest drive possible that fits your budget.

Another feature to look for is called a USB (Universal Serial Bus) port, which is found on all newer computers. Included on both Windows and Macintosh machines, USB ports can be used to connect printers, monitors, modems, and many other peripheral devices. The better portable MP3 players now use USB connections to transfer files from the computer.

File transfers through a USB connection are much faster than those made through a parallel port. The parallel port is where you attach your printer, so if your portable MP3 device uses the parallel port, you have to detach your printer first. Windows users should know that Windows 95 and Windows NT don't support USB; Windows 98, 2000, and Me work just fine, though.

The good news is that almost any computer purchased within the last three years or so can play MP3s and has a USB port. For PCs, this means a Pentium processor or better, and preferably 166MHz or better. Most Power Macs and all iMacs can play MP3 files just fine. If you have an older computer that uses a 486 processor, you probably need to upgrade. Any PC that can run

Windows 95 or higher, or any Mac that can run System 7 or higher, can play MP3 files.

To amass a large collection of MP3s in a hurry, you need a fast connection. If you're lucky enough to live in an area where cable modems or DSL connections are available, it may be worth the charge of approximately $50 per month.

Holy Wars

So which is better, a PC running Windows or a Macintosh? This question is only slightly less contentious than Middle East politics. Mac enthusiasts, especially, are almost religious in their loyalty. Traditionally, Macs have been the choice of the creative community, while PCs have been seen as business machines. Graphics and multimedia software were created mostly for Macs. In recent years, however, the sheer number of PCs in operation has meant that the latest software is available for them first, with Macintosh versions released later.

This is certainly true for MP3 software. Many of the most popular programs aren't even available on the Macintosh platform. Therefore, if you're buying a new computer and you want to use it for MP3s, a PC is probably the best choice. This is *not* to say that PCs are superior to Macs. Does anyone remember the Sony Betamax? That videotape format was superior to VHS, but it lost out in the marketplace because the major manufacturers lined up behind the VHS standard.

Alternatives

Of course, there are other operating systems besides Windows and Macintosh. The most promising of these are Linux and the other operating systems based upon UNIX. Another is BeOS, a free operating system designed especially for Internet and multimedia applications. For most computer users, though, the overwhelming choice will be Windows, with Macintosh a distant second.

Sound Considerations

Most people don't consider sound when purchasing a computer. After all, computers traditionally have been business machines. But with Internet audio becoming more popular and computer

games becoming more sophisticated, computer makers are finally
equipping their models with good sound cards and speakers.

As any audiophile knows, speakers are the most important part of
any audio system. We've come a long way from the days when
"computer speakers" meant a pair of cheap plastic speaker cabi-
nets with one tiny speaker each. Better systems use separate
speakers for treble and bass, called *tweeters* and *woofers*. Many
also come with a separate sub-woofer for handling the very low
frequencies.

A good alternative to speakers are headphones, which are often
cheaper than high-end speakers and can deliver incredibly good
sound. This is an especially good option if you want to listen to
music in noisy environments or don't want to disturb others.

As for sound cards, the one that came with your computer is
probably adequate for handling MP3s or other sounds. One of the
most popular sound cards is SoundBlaster Live!, which is
included with many systems. This is adequate for almost any situation and is a good replacement for a cheaper card. If you intend
to do commercial-quality audio editing, you should consider a
high-end card from Turtle Beach, Guillemot, Echo, Digital Audio
Labs, or Ensoniq.

Getting the Best Sound from Your Present System

If you already have a computer, you probably don't want to go
out and buy another one just for playing MP3s. Even if you have
a newer computer and spend a bundle on computer speakers, they
probably won't sound as good as even a modest home audio system. The solution? Just connect your computer to your stereo.

Option One: Analog Connection

The most common way of connecting a computer to an audio system is through an analog connection. This is accomplished by
connecting the sound card's output to a line input on the audio
system. You'll need a cable with a 1/8" (3.5mm) stereo mini-plug
on one end and twin RCA plugs on the other. MusicMatch recognizes the advantages of this, so the retail version of MusicMatch
Jukebox comes with such a cable. You can also buy one at most
any electronics store, such as Radio Shack.

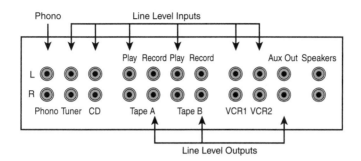

Typical analog stereo connections.

In order to connect your stereo in this manner, you'll need a system with line inputs. These are found on true component systems but may not be available on all-in-one stereos. Line inputs may be labeled in various ways, including "auxiliary" or "AUX", "line in", "tape in", "tuner", or "CD". It doesn't matter which you use, but you'll need to select the appropriate source on the audio system when you want to listen to music from your computer. Do *not* use a phono input.

The other end of the cable is connected to your sound card's line output, usually labeled "line out". Do *not* use the speaker outputs because this will result in distorted sound.

> Sometimes, old technology works just fine. Many new stereo systems don't have input and output jacks, but older ones do.

If you don't have an appropriate stereo system, you can do what I did. Find an old but good stereo receiver for about $40 in a pawn shop and use it as your computer sound system.

Option Two: Digital Connection

The preceding example used an analog connection. If you have both a high-end sound card and a home theater system or top-of-the-line stereo, you may be able to make a digital connection between the computer and the sound system. Digital signals are cleaner than analog ones because they're transmitted as bits of data instead of electrical voltage.

There are several types of digital connectors, but the most common is called S/PDIF. This connector resembles an RCA jack, but

one connector carries both audio channels. Other digital connectors use fiber-optic cables. If your audio system and sound card
use similar connections, you're in luck!

Learn to Use Your Volume Control and Mixer

On Windows PCs, a volume control usually appears in the lower-right
corner of the screen. If it doesn't, in Windows 98, select Start, Settings,
Control Panel, Multimedia, and then check the box labeled Show volume control on the taskbar. Not only does this let you adjust the output
of your sound card, but double-clicking on the volume control icon will
bring up a mixing panel that lets you adjust the volume of CD sound,
MIDI, Line In, WAVE Out, etc.

For best results, turn the volume levels on the microphone, line-in, and
CD all the way down, unless you're using those devices. Leaving them
turned up will increase the noise level.

Note that some sound cards will replace the standard Windows mixing
panel with one of their own. For example, Creative Labs SoundBlaster
cards have a mixer that's opened from Audio HQ.

Portable Players

Although most people still listen to MP3 music on their computers, the home audio market is awash in new MP3 devices. The
most popular are the portable players, which work like portable
CD players and enable you to take your music anywhere. Unlike
CD players, MP3 players have no moving parts, so the music
never skips.

There are so many portable players being brought to market that
it's difficult to list them all. What follows is an overview of the
more popular ones.

Diamond Rio

Diamond Multimedia shook up the music industry in October
1998 when it introduced the first portable MP3 player, the Rio
PMP 300. The recording industry, seeing a threat to their domi-
nance and alleging possible copyright infringement, challenged
Diamond in a lawsuit. Diamond pressed on, and Rio players are
now seen everywhere, from college campuses to corporate board-
rooms.

The Diamond Rio 500 is an updated version of the original portable MP3 player.

Diamond has now released the second-generation Rio 500. This is the first player to work with either Mac or PC, and music transfer is done using the extremely fast USB port that comes on newer computers. Its small size and choice of trendy colors makes for a cool-looking unit.

The Rio 500 is extremely compact, weighing only 2.75 ounces and measuring 3.59×2.46×.74 inches (you can do the metric conversions yourself). One AA battery powers the unit for up to 13 hours of play. The built-in 64MB of memory is good for storing up to two hours of music, according to the manufacturer. However, if you record your MP3s in true CD-quality, storage is limited to a little over an hour. Additional memory flash cards can be ordered from Diamond in 16MB ($59.95) and 32MB ($99.95) sizes.

The unit includes software for ripping songs from CDs to MP3 format and transferring them to the player. PC users get RioPort Audio Manager with a built-in Web browser, while Mac folks get the excellent SoundJam MP by C&G. The PC version I reviewed was very easy to use. One nice feature is the ability to create folders within the software, which are then transferred to the player. This allows you to organize your music into categories, album names, etc. Also included are a cable for attaching the unit to the computer's USB port and a carrying case.

The controls are very simple. There are just four buttons on the front, one on each side, and a multi-function wheel that controls volume, equalization, selection of songs and folders, and repeat/random play functions. The built-in EQ function features preset levels for jazz, rock, and classical music, as well as a custom setting that lets you manipulate bass and treble on a 1-10 scale. The Bookmark button is handy for spoken-word files, such as those available from Audible.com.

The audio quality is extremely good. The included in-ear earphones deliver nice sound, but you may prefer headphones that are more comfortable and deliver even better response.

The Rio 500 retails for $269.95. As of this writing, I've found street prices as low as $240. Many PC users will opt for the older 300, since it's now available for around $100.

Creative Nomad

The Nomad from Creative Labs stands out as one of the sleekest and most feature-laden of all portables. With its unique titanium case and the convenience of an FM tuner and memo recorder, the original Nomad set a new standard. In late 1999, Creative rolled out its next-generation Nomad II. It has everything the original Nomad had, plus a lot more.

The cool-looking Creative Nomad.

The original Nomad connected to a computer via a parallel port. This meant the user had to unplug the printer in order to transfer files. The new version uses the USB port, which is not only more convenient but much faster. Other improvements include a backlit LCD and separate controls for bass, treble, and gain. The FM tuner with 20 presets means that you may not need another portable music device.

The Nomad II uses a 64MB memory card, just like the original Nomad. This holds about one hour of CD-quality music. Unlike some other players, there's no onboard memory, so 64MB is the maximum.

The NOMAD II plays files in the MP3 and WMA (Windows Media Audio) formats, and it can be upgraded to support future audio compression standards and digital rights management technology, including SDMI compliance (a protection scheme developed by the recording industry to protect files from unauthorized copying). These updates will be available for download from *www.nomadworld.com*.

The styling on the Nomad II is different from the original. It may strike some as more conventional. If you liked the look of the original, wait for the Nomad II MG later this year.

RCA Lyra

RCA was the first well-known consumer electronics maker to offer a portable MP3 player. Available in 32MB or 64MB versions, the Lyra uses CompactFlash memory cards.

RCA's Lyra Plays RealAudio and MP3 files.

Although the Lyra isn't as flashy as some, it's still a handsome player. It plays both MP3 and RealAudio G2 files, which is convenient for listening to Webcasts. It can also be upgraded to support future music formats.

A modified version of RealJukebox is included. File transfers are done through a parallel port. More information is available at *www.lyrazone.com*.

Pine D'Music

Priced at $149, Pine Technology's model SM-320V is a great value. It has 32MB of built-in memory and takes 32MB memory cards. It also does voice recording and doubles as a portable hard drive. Some models have an FM radio tuner.

The versatile Pine D'Music.

The D'Music can store most formats, allowing for storage equivalent to 21 floppy disks. It uses a parallel port interface for file transfers. Further information can be found at *www.pine_dmusic.com*.

I-Jam

The I-Jam player includes an FM tuner and features separate bass and treble controls. Offered in a variety of cool colors, this unit is designed to fit comfortably in your hand. It ships with two 16MB SanDisk memory cards.

I-Jam, for those who like it loud.

The I-Jam player claims the highest audio output of all portable MP3 players, 60mW versus 5mW. If listening to loud music has not already damaged your ears, this little beauty will do the job!

More information is available at *www.ijamworld.com*.

Rome

Most portable players look rather similar, even if some are more stylish that others. The Rome MP3 player is different. It looks just like a cassette tape (except for the buttons on the side), and it doesn't weigh much more. In fact, this is the smallest and lightest player on the market.

Rome looks like a cassette tape, but stores and plays MP3s.

It works like a cassette tape, too. You can pop it into your car stereo or Walkman and use the play, fast forward, and other controls. Some other MP3 portables come with adapters for cassette decks, but the Rome is ready to go as is. You can also use the included earphones and take the Rome with you anywhere.

Unitech Electronics, best known for motherboards and other computer components, manufactures the Rome in Korea. It comes with 32MB of flash memory. One nice feature is its rechargeable battery, which yields about six hours of playing time per three-hour charge. Files are downloaded through the computer's parallel port. The included software does a good job, although it's not as feature-rich as some.

The memory cannot be expanded, so you can load only about a half-hour of music. Also, the lack of a display is an inconvenience. It just has an LED indicator that flashes cryptic messages to indicate its status. Luckily, the manufacturer promises to address both of these issues in the next version of Rome.

The unit may be purchased on the Web for $249.95, plus shipping.

Sony Memory Stick Walkman

Sony is perhaps the best-known name in electronics, so you would expect its portable MP3 player to be first-rate. The Memory Stick Walkman uses 64MB Memory Stick flash media cards for storage, and files are transferred via USB.

Sony's Memory Stick Walkman doesn't play ordinary MP3 files.

Unfortunately, this is not a true MP3 player at all. It plays ATRAC III, which is a Sony-developed, secure digital music format used in their MiniDisc products.

The player is compliant with SDMI (Secure Digital Music Initiative). According to Sony, this "enables the secure storage and playback of digital music content while protecting the rights of copyright holders." This means that before you can load your MP3 files into it, first you need to use the included software to convert them to the ATRAC III format. This is an inconvenience, and the design is obviously influenced by the fact that Sony is both a consumer electronics company and a music company. Music companies see MP3 as a threat because they don't profit from the free exchange of files. The music company side must have had a big say in the development of this product.

eGo

eGo portables are colorful and fun. More importantly, you can get one with huge amounts of memory. In addition to conventional 32MB, 64MB, and 96MB models, eGo offers a 340MB model! The smaller models use compact flash memory, but the 340MB version uses an IBM microdrive.

eGo players can hold hours of music.

A microdrive is basically a very small hard drive. This new technology is beginning to be used in many devices, including digital cameras. Whereas flash memory cards require very little power to operate, microdrives are much more power-hungry. Therefore, the 340MB eGo is recommended for car or home use only.

In addition to the microdrive, the eGo boasts other high-end features, such as three processors, an upgrade-ready operating system, and a USB port. See *www.i2go.com* to learn more about this player.

Portable PCs

Many handheld computers, also called PDAs (Personal Digital Assistants), can play MP3 files. Any device that uses the Windows CE operating system and has sound capability can be used for MP3s. All you need is software such as the Hum player from Utopiasoft (*http://www.utopiasoft.com/*).

Examples of suitable portable computers include the Cassiopeia E-100 and the Hewlett Packard Jornada 430se, which comes with Hum preloaded. Who says these devices are just for business?

Other Portables

As previously mentioned, new players are being brought to market at an incredible rate. Other portables include the raveMP (*www.ravemp.com*) , PONTIS Mplayer3 (*www.pontis.de*), Audiovox MPDj (*http://www.audiovox.com*), DAP MP3 player (*www.righttechnology.com*), jazPiper (*www.jazpiper.nl*), MPMan (*www.mpman.com*) , VAROMAN PLUS (*www.varovision.com*), and Samsung's yepp (*www.yepp.co.kr*) .

You can find an excellent and continuously updated list of portable players at *http://portablemp3players. activebuyersguide.com*. This site allows you to search by specific model or compare players by price and features.

Car and Home Players

MP3 players for home and car use are the newest consumer electronics frontier. This area is exploding, and it shows that the potential for digital music is truly limitless.

These devices vary in size, cost, and complexity, but they can be divided into two basic types: those that use flash memory or hard drives to store the music files, and those that use regular CDs. The latter are basically CD players that have a built-in MP3 decoder.

One of the first companies to offer a car MP3 player was Empeg.com. Priced at over $1,000, this player is intended only for those who like to be on the cutting edge. It uses an internal hard drive to hold the music. The standard model uses a 4GB drive; other models offer up to two 18GB drives. Even the smallest model can hold around 1,000 MP3 files. Visit their Web site at *http://www.empeg.com/* to learn more.

Just coming to market are car and home CD players with added circuitry to decode MP3 files. The advantage to this is that a CD full of MP3s can play for over ten hours, while a regular CD lasts an hour or less.

Wrapping It Up

With all the flashy new hardware available today, it's easy to forget that the music is all that matters! In order to make the sounds, though, you need some basic technology. This chapter taught you the following:

- What kind of computer is needed to download and play MP3 files.

- How to make a computer sound better by connecting it to a stereo.

- The expanding world of MP3 players that let you take music anywhere—for a walk, a drive, or whereever you are. With all these options, there's no reason to ever be without your favorite music!

CHAPTER 7

Choose Your Weapons Wisely—Software Matters

All new computers can play MP3 files. Windows includes Media Player, and Mac machines have QuickTime. Both are designed to play a variety of audio and video formats. Although these will do, you're much better off using software that's designed specifically for MP3. This chapter will introduce you to essential software that any music enthusiast should have, and it will also explore the many options for taking your musical experience to the next level.

Is It Really Free?

All of the software discussed in this chapter can be downloaded from the Internet and comes in four flavors: freeware, shareware, retail, and trialware. Much of the software available on the Internet is *freeware*. You don't have to pay for it, and you can keep it as long as you like.

Shareware is usually developed by independent programmers. They make the product available to the public, but they expect to be paid. Shareware can be used for a limited time, usually 30 days, before you must pay for it or stop using it. Most of the time, the software will continue to function and the payment is on the honor system. In many cases, though, the programmer includes *nag screens* that remind you to purchase the product. After you purchase it, you'll be sent a code number to remove the nag screen.

A good place to find music shareware and freeware is at Shareware Music Machine (*www.hitsquad.com/smm*). They offer a variety of players, encoders, and other music-related utilities.

You can find programs to convert RealAudio to MP3, MIDI to WAV, AIFF to WAV, etc.

Retail software is also sold on the Net. In many cases you can order the boxed versions, but it's usually cheaper to just download these programs. You won't get the printed manuals, of course, but many companies include extensive electronic documentation.

Most commercial software is also available as *trialware* that you can download from the Web site of the software company. This allows you to see how the product works on your computer before you commit to spending any money.

In some cases, trialware isn't fully functional and only demonstrates the product's features. In most cases, though, the software is fully functional but limited to 30 days of use or less. After the time limit expires, you'll have to purchase the regular version or enter an unlock code to continue using it.

Which software should you consider? The following are the more popular programs, but there are hundreds available and more are being created all the time.

Winamp

MP3 was just an obscure compression scheme known only to scientists and hackers before Winamp made it accessible to a mass audience. The free Winamp player is something every Windows user should have. If you don't have it, go to *www.winamp.com* and download it for free!

Winamp is the most popular MP3 player for Windows and is used by over 10 million people. In addition to MP3, the current version plays CD audio, WMA, and several other formats.

Winamp popularized the concept of *skins*, which allow you to customize the program's appearance. Over 10,000 Winamp skins are available, and you can make your own using a bitmap editor such as PC Paint, Photoshop, or Corel Photo Paint. Available skins range from basic designs that look like brushed aluminum or wood to some really bizarre creations. Skins change the way the program looks on your screen, but they don't affect its functionality.

*Winamp with its
basic skin.*

The player's functionality can be augmented by *plug-ins*. Some
are visualization plug-ins that display light shows synchronized
with the music. Others add effects to the music, such as echo,
equalization, etc. One of the most useful plug-ins is the crossfade,
which automatically fades between songs like a DJ.

Winamp includes separate windows for the player, playlist manager, equalizer, and minibrowser. The equalizer is helpful for fine-
tuning the sound, giving you control over a range of frequencies
from bass to treble. If you want to take the time, you can even a
record equalization profile for each song that's automatically
recalled each time the song is played.

Other Players

There are literally hundreds of MP3 players, so a definitive list
would be a moving target. A good place to go for the latest
releases is MP3.com's software section, *software.mp3.com*. I will
briefly mention two of the more interesting options, Sonique and
UltraPlayer.

Sonique

This free MP3 and media player for Windows claims to have better sound than Winamp and other players due to Stardust, its MP3
decoding engine. Tests have confirmed that this player is especially good with tracks encoded at lower bitrates.

Night 55's Sonique is also one of the most radical-looking players, with an interface like no other. It does take some getting used
to. If you tire of its look, you can always use its extensive skins
collection.

Sonique also includes a playlist editor and plug-in support, along
with controls for adjusting pitch and a 20-band equalizer. You can
download it from *www.sonique.com*.

UltraPlayer

This extremely cool-looking player for Windows 95/98/NT/2000 handles MP3, WMA, WAV, CD Audio, and streaming audio. Like Sonique, the design borders on the extreme, but it's still easy to use. You can customize it with Deeply-Dynamic skins, save files to WAV format, use the 10-band EQ, and more. The product is free, but it displays brief advertisements. Get it at *www. ultraplayer.com*.

UltraPlayer's design is radically different from ordinary players.

Jukeboxes

Winamp and its imitators were designed to play MP3 files only, and they do this single job very well. For this reason, you should use Winamp or another simple player as your default player for MP3 files. In other words, when you click on a file in Windows Explorer, Winamp (or your chosen substitute) will automatically pop up and play it.

MP3 players are constantly evolving, with new features being added to each new version, but they don't offer the flexibility of *jukebox* software. Also called an *all-in-one* player, a jukebox includes a player, ripper (for making MP3s from CDs), encoder, and advanced features for creating and organizing playlists.

Playlists are a great way to organize and catalog your music. You can program hours of continuous music or create custom lists to fit your mood. Also, the same songs can be used in several playlists. In other words, once your music is in MP3 form, you have tremendous flexibility that would not be possible if the music was still on CDs.

Most jukeboxes can also load MP3 tracks to portable players such as the Rio, Nomad, etc.

The two most popular jukeboxes are RealJukebox and MusicMatch. Here's how they compare.

RealJukebox

Real Networks (*www.real.com*), makers of the popular RealPlayer for streaming audio, offers two flavors of RealJukebox: Basic, which is free, and Plus, which costs $29.95. The free version is all you really need for most purposes. The Plus version offers faster CD ripping, changeable skins, and a few other features.

RealJukebox comes from the company that invented RealAudio.

RealJukebox has the reputation of being very user-friendly, and the controls are rather simplified. Advanced users may find it a bit *too* simple. RealJukebox's default setting is to encode CDs in RealAudio format. To change this to MP3, select Options, Preferences, Recording Options, Encoding Options and set it to MP3.

If you want to make RealAudio recordings that can be streamed, this product is a good choice.

MusicMatch

MusicMatch, available at *www.musicmatch.com*, calls itself "The world's first and best jukebox software program." As with RealJukebox, there's a free version and a $29.95 Plus version.

Also like RealJukebox, earlier releases of the free version limited MP3 encoding to 96Kbps, or near-CD quality. To get higher fidelity, you had to purchase the Plus program. However, the free software now encodes at rates up to 160Kbps, which is better than the 128Kbps CD-quality standard.

The Plus version offers faster recording performance, jewel case printing, and a more advanced equalizer. The free version is so good, though, that most users will be quite happy with it.

MusicMatch is the most popular MP3 jukebox.

One of the coolest features of MusicMatch is its ability to make CDs from MP3 files. (All jukebox programs can make MP3s from CD tracks, but very few can go the other way.)First, the files must be converted to uncompressed WAV files. MusicMatch makes this process transparent by offering one-button control. Simply drag the MP3 tracks to the upper-right pane and click the Record button to make a custom CD that can be played in any CD player.

Another useful feature is the ability to record from the sound card's line-in jack, allowing you to make MP3s from records or tapes. Just connect your stereo's line out jack to the line-in jack of the sound card, and then play the record or tape while recording to MP3 with MusicMatch.

Previously limited to Windows users, MusicMatch has just released a version for the Macintosh.

SoundJam MP

Speaking of Macintosh, SoundJam MP (*www.soundjam.com*) is described as "the first full-featured, all-in-one MP3 player and encoder for the Macintosh." The free version has unlimited play-back capability but is limited to 14 days of MP3 encodings, or 30 total files.

SoundJam allows you to view and sort your playlists by a variety of criteria, including album, artist, title, date, and genre. It also has a nice equalizer that can store presets for individual songs, and it can be customized with skins and third-party plug-ins.

RioPort Audio Manager

This player/CD ripper for Windows comes free with the Diamond Rio 500 and includes an MP3 browser. The downloadable version, available from *www.rioport.com*, lets you make 50 MP3s for free. Upgrades range from $9.95 to $18.95. It isn't as full-featured or intuitive as MusicMatch, but it's good for downloading to Rio portable players. The latest version can make audio CDs.

RioPort Audio Manager was made to work with Rio portable players.

Siren

This is a great new jukebox product from Sonic Foundry. The simple interface allows for fast and easy encoding, CD ripping, or sending to portable devices. The full version, which can write MP3 files to a CD, is $39.95. A free version, called Siren XPress, is available at *www.sonicfoundry.com*.

Media Box

This all-in-one Windows program from England features automatic normalization and a text and photo editor. One nice feature is that you can select a portion of an MP3 file to convert to WAV. The basic version is free, and registration is $19. Their site can be found at *www.e-soft.co.uk*.

Mixers

Besides players and jukeboxes, mixers should be mentioned here. These are programs that let you load two or more songs at once and cross-fade them like a DJ. With MP3s becoming the medium of choice for college students, DJs armed with mixers and a disk full of MP3s are replacing the more traditional mixmasters armed with turntables and CD players.

Visiosonic PCDJ Phat

More than a jukebox, this cool tool can play two audio or video files at once, and you can mix them like a DJ! Set up a playlist of MP3 files and it will automatically cross-fade them. This software is free; you just have to provide an email address. Go to *www.visiosonic.com* for further information.

MixMeister

This automated mixing tool detects the BPM (beats per minute) of your MP3 files and produces a fully automated mix, with fades between songs. A fully-functioning demo version is available for free download, and the commercial product is scheduled to be released for $29.95. Learn more at *www.mixmeister.com*.

Liquid Audio

If you've cruised the Net looking for MP3 files, you've probably encountered Liquid Audio. It's a compression format similar to MP3, but it can be played only with the free Liquid Audio Player. What sets it apart is the built-in copy-protection scheme. This is popular with music companies who provide music for a fee.

Liquid Audio is like MP3, but you can't share files with your friends.

You can download a Liquid Audio file to your computer, but it cannot be copied. As you can see, the Liquid Audio player also displays a picture and information about the artist.

Wrapping It Up

Regardless of which software you choose, you'll quickly discover why MP3 is so popular. No longer are you limited to playing songs in the order they were placed on the CD. You can mix and match to your heart's desire. More than ever before, *you* are in control of your music.

CHAPTER 8

Users, Start Your Engines

Have you ever looked for a specific song on the Net? You could spend a lot of time visiting MP3 Web sites, but the best way to find a particular tune is through a search engine that looks for files on many sites at once.

You've probably used search engines like Yahoo!, but did you know there are search engines just for finding MP3 files?

Downloading Basics

Before you begin, you need to know that there are two rather different ways of downloading files. The first uses HTTP, just like your Web browser. This is by far the easiest way. Just remember that when you visit Web sites offering MP3 or other music files, clicking on the link downloads the file to a temporary directory and then plays it. After the song plays, the file goes away.

To save a file rather than playing it, don't simply click on the link. If you use Windows, click with the right mouse button, and if you use a Mac, Command+click on the filename. This will bring up a menu allowing you to "save target as" or 'save link as." You can then specify a directory on your hard drive in which to save the file.

The second method of downloading files is through File Transfer Protocol, or FTP, which was originally used to transfer files between Unix workstations. It's still the standard way of transferring files over the Internet.

Most Web browsers can be used to download files via FTP, but their functions are limited. Most importantly, you can't upload files through a browser. It's much better to use a true client such as WS_FTP (download it from *ipswitch.com*, or download the free version from *www.csra.net/junodj/ws_ftp.htm*) or CuteFTP

What You'll Learn in This Chapter:
- ▶ The two basic ways to download files
- ▶ How to use FTP
- ▶ The best search sites
- ▶ Why legal issues make downloading difficult

(*www.cuteftp.com*). Mac users may use Fetch, available from Dartmouth College at *www.dartmouth.edu/pages/ softdev/fetch.html*.

These programs will give you access to the *ratio* sites that require you to upload files before downloading anything. Many FTP sites also require you to enter a username and password, which can be found on many search sites. Full instructions on using FTP may be found on the AudioGalaxy Help page, at *www.audiogalaxy.com/info/help_page03.php3#ftp*.

FTP programs can be quite confusing for first time FTP users. Below are step-by-step instructions for two of the more popular Windows FTP clients, CuteFTP and WS_FTP.

Using CuteFTP

1. Open CuteFTP. If the FTP Site Manager window appears, click Exit. Click View and then click Quick connect bar. (Or just press Ctrl+F4.)

CuteFTP is free, but it displays ads.

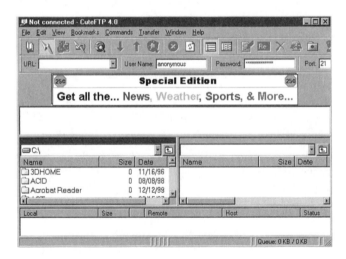

2. Copy the IP address of the desired site into the Host Address box. (This will be a series of numbers separated by periods into four segments, such as 209.143.212.20.)

3. Fill in the User ID and Password boxes.

4. Change the login type to Normal.

5. Click the Advanced tab and enter the port number into the Port box.

6. Click OK to connect.

Using WS_FTP

1. Open WS_FTP.

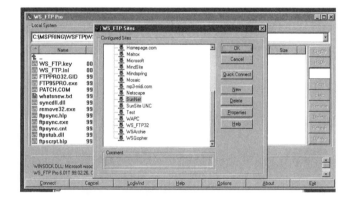

WS_FTP comes in several flavors. This is the main screen of WS_FTP Pro.

WS_FTP comes with several built-in addresses. To add your own, click New, give it a name, and then select Next.

2. Copy the IP address of the desired site in the Host Name/Address box.

3. Copy the logon name into the User ID box and the password into the Password box.

4. Uncheck the Anonymous box.

5. Click OK to connect.

Even if you follow these instructions correctly, the site may fail to connect. This may be due to one of several problems, but the most common one is that the server is simply too popular to support all the requests it's receiving. Also, you may have entered an incorrect username and password. The username/password combination is often given on search sites, but not all of them include this information.

In addition, FTP sites usually carry pirated files, so they often
move around or exist for only a short time. The connection log
window above the directory listing will give you a clue about why
the site isn't responding.

Major Search Sites

Now that you've learned how to download files, you need to
know how to find them. Search sites are so numerous that it's
pretty hard to enumerate them all, but what follows is a list of the
more established or notable ones.

AudioFind (*www.audiofind.com*) offers a clean interface that isn't
cluttered with excessive ads or extraneous information. It provides fast, elegant, and comprehensive searches for MP3s and
multimedia files. Searches can be made by artist, genre, or date.
This site searches only Web sites, not the harder-to-use FTP sites.

*AudioFind's lean,
clean main screen.*

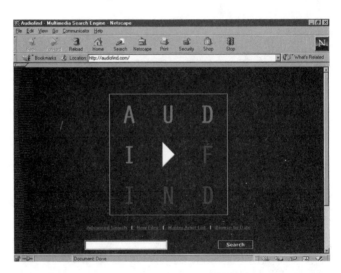

AudioFind also notes which files need to be renamed with
the .mp3 extension. Because the music industry is always searching for sites that carry illegal MP3 files, some Webmasters delib-
erately mislabel their files. So instead of files that end with .mp3,
you may encounter extensions like .zip, .doc, or most anything
else.

AudioGalaxy.com locates MP3s and multimedia files on FTP
sites, and it allows you to filter out ratio sites. One nice feature is

the percentage of how likely it is that you'll be able to access the site. Special sections feature new bands. Artists can create their own Web pages using a simple template and are offered 25MB of space. Other sections of this site explain how to use FTP and ratio sites.

MP3Bot Search Engine (*www.informatch.com/mediabot/*) finds more files than most, and the links are usually reliable. It saves your searches and displays new results upon your return. You can also enter your email address and be informed of new files that meet your search criteria. For example, if you search for files by the Goo Goo Dolls, you'll receive an email every time a new song by them is added to the directory.

Another MP3Bot feature allows you to download all files listed in your search results, or to try each link until one is successful. Banner sites, which require you to click on banners before downloading, are identified. This site searches mostly Web sites, but it indicates if the link is from an FTP site.

Oth Net, also called Kermit Search (*www.oth.net*), is clean and returns results incredibly fast. This FTP search utility displays the results as links that allow you to download files directly from a browser. The filenames are usually the same as the song titles, but not always.

> Many sites that offer free MP3 files also bombard you with annoying *pop-up* ads. These are extra browser windows that open when you enter or exit the site. The solution? Just go to any search engine and type "kill pop-up ads" to find several free utilities to end this irritation.

With a database of over a million files, Lycos MP3 Search (*mp3.lycos.com*) claims to be the world's largest MP3 site. However, you may find many dead links. This ancillary area of Lycos, one of the more established general Web search sites, is proof that MP3 has forced major sites to acknowledge its presence. Included are a reliability guide and basic information on MP3.

Listen.com (or its sister site Listen.About.com) is a great place to find legal files. At first glance it looks similar to MP3.com, but it doesn't contain any file archives. What it does have is a nice search engine listing Web sites that carry MP3, Liquid, RA, and other audio formats, and it states whether the files are free or require a fee. It also includes a Featured Artist section with news about the performers.

Scour.net searches for MP3s, video, RealAudio, and other media files. Some downloads require their free Scour Exchange, which features a Hotlist that keeps track of users with similar tastes.

Want more? A comprehensive listing of MP3 search engines may be found at mp3.about.com/msub21.htm. Happy hunting!

Why Is This So Complicated?

If you've spent much time searching for files, you've probably encountered a fair number of dead ends, bad links, sites that force you to view ad banners, or FTP sites that appear to be private clubs you cannot join. Why is this so difficult?

The simple fact is that the vast majority of MP3 sites are posting commercial files illegally (see Chapter 5, "Pirates and the Musical Mutiny"). Copyright law allows an individual to make a copy of a commercial recording for personal use, but not for distribution to anyone else. In other words, it's okay for you to make MP3 files from your CDs so that you can use them in your portable player, but it's illegal to post them on the Internet or give them to anyone else, even if you're not charging anything for them.

Since the sites that carry MP3s of commercial music are doing so illegally, they're constantly being pursued by record companies and threatened with legal action. Therefore, many of them change addresses frequently, or exist for only a few days.

Some sites add disclaimers, such as

- If you download a sound file, you must delete it from your hard drive in 24 hours.

- You must already own these CDs to legally download the sound files.

- This site is for promotional purposes only.

- Please support the artist and buy the CD.

It doesn't matter. Under current copyright laws, these disclaimers
in no way absolve the site owners of responsibility. A full expla-
nation of this, along with the top ten myths of copyright law, may
be found at *www.soundbyting.com*.

The overwhelming popularity of the MP3 format has forced
record companies and established Internet sites to make some
rather comical attempts to embrace it while still condemning its
illegality. For example, the popular Web search engine Lycos
offers a disclaimer that includes such phrases as this: "The content in those files is determined entirely by other parties who
make those files available on the Internet and those other parties
are solely responsible for such content."

In other words, major companies condemn the illegal use of MP3
technology, but it's so popular that they also want to be in on it!

You can avoid the hassle of dead links by relying on *Listen.com*,
but you must be prepared to pay for many of the tunes you find.

CHAPTER 9

Content Mining

By now you realize that Web and FTP sites offer thousands of music files. You could spend countless days surfing these sites and collecting tunes. As incredible as it seems, these sites are only part of the picture. This chapter explores other ways to find and share MP3s over the Internet: newsgroups, IRC, and direct file sharing.

Before we begin, let me offer a word of caution. No matter which method you use to download files, be sure to have an up-to-date anti-virus program installed and running on your computer. Although viruses aren't quite as common as the news media would have you believe, they do exist and they can greatly harm your computer.

Newsgroups

To most people, the terms *Internet* and *World Wide Web* are synonymous. Indeed, the Web has made surfing the Net so easy that older protocols are rarely encountered anymore. (Do you remember Gopher?) However, one of these older areas is still very much alive. In fact, it's one of the most dynamic areas of the Net. It's called *Usenet* (short for *users' network*), and it consists of tens of thousands of *newsgroups* that are organized into various topics. The terms *Usenet* and *newsgroups* are often used interchangeably.

Usenet began in late 1979 when two graduate students at Duke University, Tom Truscott and Jim Ellis, hooked computers together to exchange information with the Unix community. Steve Bellovin, a graduate student at the University of North Carolina, put together the first version of the news software and installed it on the first two sites, called *unc* and *duke*.

What You'll Learn in This Chapter:

► What Usenet is and how to find MP3 files in newsgroups

► Which Usenet software to use

► How to use IRC to chat or find music

► How to use Napster to share files

► Alternatives to Napster

Since that time, Usenet has been greatly refined and the software has become more sophisticated, so that thousands of people around the world use newsgroups every day.

Despite the name, you won't find much news in most of these groups. Newsgroups are like bulletin boards on which anyone can post a message. You'll often encounter lively discussions, debates, and nasty arguments taking place.

Why visit a newsgroup if you're seeking MP3 files? Well, you may find useful information about Web or FTP sites. You can also exchange messages with fans or share information about concerts. But more importantly, newsgroup messages can contain MP3 files posted as attachments.

A word of caution before you jump in: While newsgroups can be a valuable resource, they're also the most controversial area of the Net, and often the most frustrating. Exercise caution in giving children access to Usenet because many newsgroups are of a sexual nature, and some rather bizarre things can be found there. Even though the newsgroups are organized into specific topic areas, there's nothing to prevent someone from posting something inappropriate to a newsgroup. Operators of adult-oriented Web sites and other sex-related businesses also *spam* the newsgroups with ads for their services, and they often include explicit images. Also, many people can be quite rude and obscene in their posted messages.

However, if you're willing to dig deep enough, you can find a lot of useful information, MP3 files, and music programs in the MP3-related newsgroups.

The best place to begin is *alt.binaries.sounds.mp3*. This is by far the largest group, and a wide variety of music is posted there.

There are many subcategories for various types of music. Some contain lots of files, others only a few. Here's just a sampling:

alt.binaries.mp3.zappa

alt.binaries.sounds.country.mp3

alt.binaries.sounds.mp3.1950s

alt.binaries.sounds.mp3.1960s

alt.binaries.sounds.mp3.1970s

alt.binaries.sounds.mp3.1980s

alt.binaries.sounds.mp3.1990s
alt.binaries.sounds.78rpm-era
alt.binaries.sounds.mp3.alternative-rock
alt.binaries.sounds.mp3.bootlegs
alt.binaries.sounds.mp3.brazilian
alt.binaries.sounds.mp3.classic-rock
alt.binaries.sounds.mp3.comedy
alt.binaries.sounds.mp3.dance
alt.binaries.sounds.mp3.heavy-metal
alt.binaries.sounds.mp3.indie
alt.binaries.sounds.mp3.jazz
alt.binaries.sounds.mp3.latin
alt.binaries.sounds.mp3.reggae
alt.binaries.sounds.mp3.requests
alt.binaries.sounds.mp3.zappa (Yes, Frank Zappa rates two newsgroups)

Alt.music.mp3 is a more traditional "bulletin board" group where people post questions and opinions. If you need help, try posting a question here.

Language-specific groups include *it.comp.musica.mp3*, with postings in Italian, and *japan.comp.mp3*, a small group with postings in Japanese and English.

When you're setting up your newsreader, don't enter your real email address unless you want to receive tons of junk mail. Spammers extract addresses from newsgroups.

Newsreaders

How do you view newsgroups and download the files you find there? Web browsers work rather well, and Microsoft's Outlook Express email program also includes newsgroup-browsing capability. For serious newsgroup junkies, though, a program called a *newsreader* works much better.

Newsreaders include Agent and its free cousin, Free Agent, available for download from *www.forte.com*.

Free Agent in action. The number of newsgroups it displays is controlled by your Internet Service Provider.

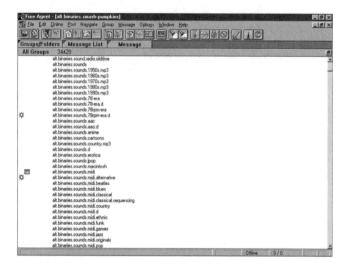

WinVN is a public-domain newsreader for Microsoft Windows and Windows NT. It can be found at *www.ksc.nasa.gov/ software/winvn/winvn.html*.

Pine is a free newsreader offered by the University of Washington's Program for Internet News and Email. This multiplatform client works with Unix, DOS, Windows, VMS, and Amiga. You can download it at *www.ii.com/internet/messaging/pine/*.

One newsreader that's preferred by many Macintosh users is MT NewsWatcher. It's derived from an earlier program called simply NewsWatcher by John Norstad of Northwestern University, but it greatly enhances that program's feature set. This is available for free at *www.best.com/~smfr/mtnw/mtnewswatcher.html*.

No matter which program you choose, you will find that Usenet is a window into a vast, exciting, and sometimes frustrating world.

IRC

Another way to find files is through *Internet Relay Chat* or *IRC*, which existed long before AOL chatrooms. As the name implies, IRC is a method of chatting in real time over the Internet. You can also share files this way.

To get started, you first need a software program called an *IRC client*. There are many to choose from, but the most popular is probably mIRC. You may already have this on your computer. If not, just download it from *www.mirc.com.*

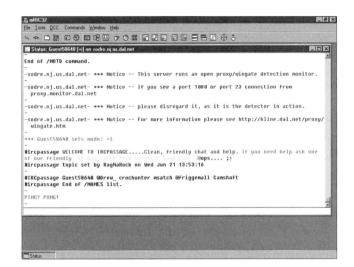

mIRC is the most popular Internet Relay Chat program.

After installing the program and following the steps for setting it up, instruct it to connect to a random DALnet server. Then join a channel by typing in a forward slash, the number sign, and the name of the chatroom. An example is /join #mp3.

Besides #mp3, good rooms include #mp3z, #cmp3, #mp3alternative, #mp3party, and #mp3addicts. You'll probably discover more, and you can always ask if anyone has suggestions. Type in /list to list all active channels, but be prepared for a very big list!

It takes a while to get used to IRC. Messages fly by so fast that you may need to pause the screen to read it all. Many of the messages and commands may appear cryptic at first, but you'll learn more through practice.

Users will advertise the files they have and tell you what to type in order to receive them. This is usually an exclamation mark followed by the name of the file.

Keep in mind that you cannot initiate a download. The person with the file must offer it to you. If he offers, a screen will pop up asking if you want to download the file. Click Get! and the transfer will begin.

If you're having trouble, try sending a message to an operator (the person listed at the top, with an @ symbol at the start of his name) by double-clicking on the name. You can find a helpful list of Frequently Asked Questions (FAQ) on IRC in general at *mirc.com/ircintro.html*. The FAQ for specific mIRC issues is at *mirc.com/faq.html*.

Some people claim that IRC is the most reliable method of sharing files, but it does take some getting used to. If you master IRC, you can call yourself a true power user!

Direct File Sharing

What if you could share files with other computer users around the world? Although you may have searched the Net in vain, surely *somebody* has the music you want. These thoughts must have been going through Shawn Fanning's mind when he got the idea for Napster. At the time, he was an 18-year-old college student. He probably didn't realize how radically his invention would affect the music world.

Napster: The Program That Shook the Music Industry

Few music software programs have attracted as much attention, or generated as much controversy, as Napster. This program allows users to share MP3 files over the Net with other Napster users. They describe it as "a completely new way of thinking about music online" and an alternative to search engines that often yield broken links. You can search for music files among logged-in users or join one of the chatrooms and interact with others.

With Napster, you actually get files from other users' computers. Each person logs onto a Napster server and specifies which files they want to share. You don't have to offer any files to participate, but thousands of users do, and this is what makes the system work.

Napster is so popular, especially among college students, that many campuses have banned its use. Students were downloading so many files that the universities' servers became overwhelmed! Also, there is growing concern over copyright issues.

Some little-known facts about Napster: It's named after creator Shawn Fanning's nickname in middle school. Fanning met cofounders Sean Parker and Jordan Ritter while chatting on IRC. The company was started with seed money from Fanning's uncle.

Napster's copyright policy page states that "Napster respects copyright law and expects our users to do the same... You should be aware that some MP3 files may have been created or distributed without copyright owner authorization." They further state that the company will terminate the accounts of users who violate copyright laws. Nonetheless, Napster is primarily used as a means for sharing illegally copied commercial music.

Indeed, several bands and organizations have sued Napster, most notably the Recording Industry Association of America (RIAA), which brought suit in December 1999. In the suit, the RIAA claimed that Napster creates a black market for illegal copies of digital music. It is seeking $100,000 for each song title that has been allegedly exchanged illegally.

Okay, so you've read all the copyright warnings and you still want to use Napster. First, go to Napster's download site (*www.napster.com*) and get the software. The program is described as a *beta* version, which means it's still in the testing phase. However, it's fully functional. The installation program is only 620KB in size, which is quite small by today's standards. Once you've downloaded the file, run it and the program will be installed. (A Macintosh platform Napster client will be available shortly. Until then, the Napster folks recommend Macster.)

As this book was going to press, Napster was involved in a life-or-death legal battle with the Recording Industry Association of America that could lead to the total shutdown of its Web site. Even if this comes to pass, Napster will not die. A copy of the Napster directory is running on the Open Source Napster Server, or OpenNap, at *opennap.sourceforge.net*. Napster fans can download one of the free clients, such as Napigator (*www.napigator.com*), and connect to an open-source Napster server.

*Napster looks
cute, but the
music industry
isn't laughing.*

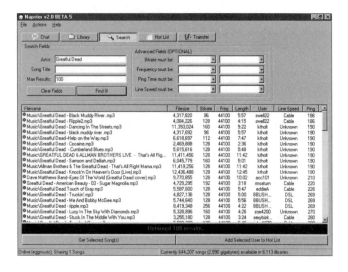

The first time you run Napster, you'll be asked to select your connection speed. ("I don't know" is one of the options.) You'll then
be prompted to choose a username and password. The username
is what other Napster users will see when you're connected. The
next screen asks for your real name, address, sex, and income.
Don't worry, you don't have to fill these in. Then you'll be asked
if Napster should scan your hard drive for MP3 files. If you agree,
these files can be made available for sharing with others, but you
don't have to do this. Finally, you can elect to use Napster's internal audio player, or you can use one you already have. You're also
prompted for the names of the folders that you'll be sharing.

After you've filled in this information, Napster will attempt to
connect to its server. Don't be surprised if this doesn't work the
first time. This is because of the popularity of the service. Just
keep trying and you'll eventually connect. Then, you can choose a
channel to join, such as the Alternative channel, Blues channel,
Comedy channel, etc. If you choose to join a channel, you can
chat with others in that channel. However, you don't have to join
a channel to search for songs.

To find songs, just click the Search button at the top of the
Napster screen. Type in the name of the artist and/or song title,
and you can see if it's available. If the song is found, a list of
members who have it will be listed, along with information about

their connection speeds. If more than one person is offering the file, choose the one with the highest connection speed. If the speeds are the same, choose the one with the smallest number in the Ping column. This column tells you how long it takes a packet of data to be sent to a computer and returned.

You may also find the same tune being offered at different *bitrates*, measured in kilobits per second or Kbps. A higher bitrate means higher fidelity but also a larger file size. 128Kbps is considered CD quality.

That's it! Napster is really easy to use, and you can quickly fill up your hard drive with MP3 files.

Gnutella

Although Napster has grabbed most of the headlines, it isn't the only way to share files over the Net. Other programs include iMesh, OnShare, and Gnutella, with new variations being developed every day. Many of these go beyond Napster and allow the sharing of any type of file.

Nullsoft, best known as the distributor of WinAmp, recently developed Gnutella. For a few days it was available for free from Nullsoft's Web site, but Nullsoft's owners, America Online, didn't see much value in the program. They probably didn't like the idea of people sharing files directly without connecting to any commercial Web site or service. The software was removed, but not before it had been downloaded thousands of times.

Gnutella is still freely available at *gnutella.wego.com*, which offers many flavors of the original product. The program is remarkably small and can be downloaded in practically no time, even with a slow connection.

After you've downloaded and installed the program, it may take a few minutes to figure out how it works. There's no help file or any other instructions to get you started. However, the Web site offers plenty of advice. The first thing you have to do is enter a network address, such as *gnet.dotcompost.com:8080*. Once again, the Web site can help. It always posts an address that is known to be working at the time.

Gnutella looks confusing at first, but it's actually easy to use.

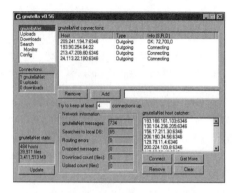

As soon as you enter the address, a remarkable thing happens. This single address leads to thousands of other interconnected addresses. It's reminiscent of the early days of the Internet, when computers connected to each other unaided by search engines and unlimited by portal sites. It's this sort of anarchy that made the Internet appealing in the first place. Of course, it's also what scares the corporate world.

To find a file, click on Search and type in your search words. You can also use partial words, or extensions such as .mp3. If you type .mp3, it may take a while for the results to come in because there are so many. MIDI files, images, and almost anything you can imagine can be found. Obviously, this is not a tool for children to use unsupervised.

If you want to share files of your own, click the Config menu and enter a directory name in the box labeled Path(s) to files. Just be sure that this directory contains only files you want to share. For example, entering just c:\ will make your entire hard drive available to strangers.

Wrapping It Up

Whew! That's a lot of information to cover in a short chapter. Now you know some of the secrets of savvy Net surfers. Usenet, IRC, and Napster and its successors all offer alternatives to the World Wide Web. Learning other programs and protocols will greatly increase your enjoyment. You don't have to become a computer geek, though. Just don't forget that the point of all this is to collect great music!

PART III

Ready to Rock

CHAPTER 10

The Lowdown on Downloading

I love Download Now buttons. They mean that goodies are within my reach, just waiting to be downloaded onto my hard drive to perform wonderful feats. But many people equate downloads with long wait times, or they're afraid that harmful files lurk behind every hyperlink. If you fear or loathe the act of downloading, this chapter will calm your fears and change your tune. Download now, I say!

Perhaps the most basic and essential task in acquiring e-music is downloading. If you don't know how to download, you can't get your hands on the huge bounty of MP3s out there. Perhaps more importantly, you can't get the e-music players and software programs that let you *play* that music.

Downloading can be a simple process, and you probably already have a grip on the basics, but there are some special downloading techniques that make managing your e-music easier. For instance, did you know that right-clicking a file (rather than the standard left-click) gives you many more download options? We'll give you all the tricks in this chapter, and we'll also share some safety tips so you can avoid downloading files that might corrupt your computer.

We'll also teach you the math behind downloading so you'll know how many games of solitaire you'll have to play while waiting for a 1GB file to download on a 56KB connection. You'll also learn how to cut down on your download wait time and resume broken downloads.

What You'll Learn in This Chapter:

- ▶ Downloading tips that will help you safely and easily acquire files
- ▶ How to determine how long a download will take
- ▶ How to reduce your download times

To *download* is to transfer a file from one computer to another. The Internet allows its users to download from a gigantic network of computers.

1-2-3 Download!

So...you've seen something on the Internet and you want it for yourself. You don't want to have to be online to use it, though. You want it at your fingertips, or at least in a handy folder on your home computer. Well, there's *one* way to nab it for good: download it.

Downloading a file means copying it off another computer and putting it on your own. It's simple—you simply click on a downloadable file and your Internet browser will do the rest, sometimes first asking you what to do with it or where to put it.

What's Downloadable, What's Not?

The Internet is teeming with files you can download. Popular programs like Napster and Gnutella serve as clearinghouses for downloadable files. But what about finding downloadable files on regular Web pages? How do you tell what's a download and what's not? Well, the answer differs from page to page.

A downloadable file on a Web page typically appears as a clickable hyperlink with the actual filename. For example, a link might be called rocksong.mp3 or installme.exe. On other pages, the hyperlink might indicate that the file can be downloaded with one click (Download Here or Click to Download). Sometimes, however, a Download Here hyperlink will just lead you to another page with the actual link to the download.

There's no hard and fast rule to how downloadable files are marked because the Internet has so many different users. However, there's one trick that may help you determine if a link is downloadable or not. Right-click on the link and select Properties from the menu that appears. On the Properties screen, look under Type. If it says Internet Document, the link takes you to another page. If it says Application or Media File, it's a downloadable file. Attentive Web page designers will always have Type filled in with helpful information. However, sometimes you'll find meaningless strings of letters and numbers on the Type line.

A page of links tells you that downloadable music is just a click away.

Safety First

Before you start downloading everything you see, perhaps a word of caution is in order. *You* are probably a good Netizen. *You* use the Internet to accomplish tasks, get cool stuff, read great sites, and learn new things. Unfortunately, not all Internet users have such noble intentions. Some people use the Net to wreak mindless havoc on others, maybe even you. For example, someone might email you with a file that's supposed to be really, really useful, but it actually might be a computer virus that can harm your computer. These ne'er-do-wells make up only a tiny part of the Net population, but running into just one of them (or, more to the point, one of their files) can really throw a giant monkey wrench into your computer fun.

The best way to avoid these guys is to protect yourself with an anti-virus program. There are many good protection programs available on the Internet, but the one I recommend is McAfee. This program will scan files for viruses before you open them. If a virus is found, McAfee will try to disinfect the file (or tell you it's best to get rid of it all together). You can get McAfee at *www.mcafee.com*. The site will tell you everything you need to know to install and use the program.

Get This:

Did you know that MP3s are currently the most commonly downloaded file type?

McAfee and other popular virus protection programs, such as
AVP and Symantec, all come with a small price tag—usually
about $20. The fee is more than worth it, given the recent boom
in computer viruses that have crippled entire computer networks.

*AVP puts out a
great line of virus
protection pro-
grams. Their site
will alert you to
common viruses
being spread on
the Internet.*

Do As They Say:

When you download
an application (such
as an e-music
player), the next
step is to install it.
Usually, the program
will ask you to close
everything else on
your computer
before you install
anything. You may
be tempted to
ignore this request,
but don't. You could
lose information
that you'll never get
back!

You can also protect yourself by only downloading from rep-
utable sites. Generally, sites that specialize in free, legal MP3s,
such as Rollingstone.com or emusic.com, can be trusted to deliver
safe, uncorrupted products. On the other hand, file exchange sites
like Napster and Gnutella contain many unknown variables. The
person you download files from *could* be a harmless college student in Ohio…or a bored computer hacker with ulterior motives
who lives next door. Although it's more likely that you'll
encounter the former, the latter does exist. It's a risk you
sometimes take.

Directing Your Downloads

Everything you'll learn about downloads in this chapter is completely pointless if you don't know where to find them once you
get them. Your computer is a wild and wooly place, full of nooks
and crannies, and downloaded files can become lost. A good way
to avoid this is to create a special folder just for downloads. This
way, you can pick up a slew of files from the Internet, always
knowing where they'll be when it's time to sort them out.

The folder I stick all my downloads into is rather unimaginatively called Downloads. You can name yours whatever you'd like. Just make sure you remember the folder's name and where it's located on your computer.

If you don't know how to create a folder, follow these steps:

Windows 95/98

1. Go to the desktop and right-click anywhere.

2. Select New from the options menu, and then select Folder.

3. A folder should appear on your desktop with its name, New Folder, highlighted. Type in a new name and press Enter.

▼ Try It Yourself

▲

Macintosh

1. In the Finder, go to the File menu and select New Folder.

2. An untitled folder should appear on your desktop. Type a new folder name over the default name.

3. Click anywhere else on the desktop to complete the task.

▼ Try It Yourself

▲

Once you've designated a folder for your downloads, here's how to make sure you direct all your downloads to the right place:

Internet Explorer

1. Left-click on a downloadable file.

2. On the File Download Screen, select Save This Program to Disk by clicking in the corresponding bubble.

3. The Save As window will appear. Navigate through the Save In: box at the top of the window to locate and select the folder you've designated for downloads.

4. Click the Save button to begin the download.

▼ Try It Yourself

▲

Netscape Navigator

1. Click on the Options Menu at the top of your browser and select General Preferences.

2. Select the Applications tab.

3. Downloads Directory: indicates where downloads are now being saved. Change folders by clicking on Browse and highlighting the appropriate folder.

▲ 4. Click Select to save changes.

Netscape Communicator

1. Click on the Edit Menu at the top of your browser and select Preferences.

2. Click on the arrow next to the Navigator option, and then select the Applications section.

3. Download Files To: indicates where downloads are now being saved. Change folders by clicking on the Choose button and highlighting the appropriate folder.

▲ 4. Click Select to save changes.

The One-Button Mac:

For years I've heard Apple users gripe that their computers are saddled with a one-button, limited-use mouse. But fear not, Mac users, because you can still unleash the power of the amazing PC right-click. While using Explorer or Netscape Navigator, simply hold down your mouse button and a pop-up menu will appear. Menus vary by program, just like on PCs, and some programs don't have a pop-up menu.

The Radical Right-Click

You've learned the basics of downloading. You know what's downloadable, how to safely grab it, and how to put it in the right spot. Now it's time to improve on this by changing the way you click.

If you aren't right-clicking your way through life, you're missing out on half the fun. You see, the left-click is your mouse's workhorse. It takes you where you want to go and selects the things you want to select. But the right mouse button gives you fast, at-your-fingertips options. And when it comes to downloading, you want things fast, right? *Right.*

When you want to download anything, anywhere, click with your right mouse button. A pop-up menu will appear, giving you a variety of helpful options. The options will depend on the program you're using.

If you're using your Internet browser, right-clicking on a down-loadable file will let you save it in any folder (use the Save Target As option in Internet Explorer), tell you more about the file (Properties), or save the download address to your Favorites or Bookmarks file. When you right-click on a link that's not a down-load, one very helpful option is Open Link in New Window. This opens the link in another browser window while leaving the origi-nal browser window where it is. This can be very handy if you're at a page with many links you want to visit. For example, say you're at emusic.com and you want to find free MP3s in the Blues section of the site, but you also want to know what they have to offer in their Jazz section. Just right-click the Blues link, select Open in New Window, right-click the Jazz link, and select Open. You'll have two browser windows full of download choices, and you can toggle between them.

Right-clicking using Internet Explorer.

Right-clicking in Napster is just as simple and helpful. If you right-click a song that comes up in your music search results win-dow, the pop-up menu lets you download it immediately or add the file's owner to your hotlist. (See more on Napster hotlists in Chapter 9, "Content Mining"). If you select a song to download, you're taken to Napster's File Transfer Page. If you right-click on a file on this page, you'll see more download options. Menu options include setting the priority of the download (moving one

download ahead of another), playing the song as it's downloading, canceling the download, or sending an instant message to the
file's owner.

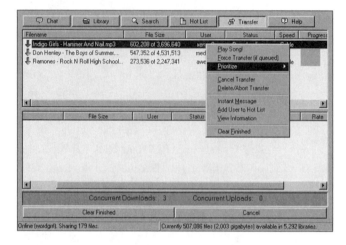

*Right-clicking on
Napster's File
Transfer Screen.*

Gnutella, FreeNet, and other programs have their own sets of
right-click options. In fact, so does the e-music player you're
using. Take a moment to right-click the next time you use these
programs. You may be able to do things faster or better just by
changing the way you click.

Time Table

It's always nice to know how long a download will take. That
way, you'll know when to check back on a particularly large
download, or you'll know not to start a download you won't have
time to finish.

Your download time depends on several factors, primarily the size
of the file and the speed of your Internet connection. If you're
downloading two or more files simultaneously, or if your computer is running other programs as you download, this will also
affect download times. The source you're downloading from also
affects download times. If you download from a busy Web site,
your download time probably will be slower. If you download
files from a program like Napster or Gnutella, download times
will be significantly affected by the Internet connection speed of
the files' owners.

Because of these variations, the following table is only a rough
estimate of download times for a typical MP3 file. When you're
using Napster or Gnutella, the slower internet connection of the
two (yours or the user you're downloading from) will determine
the rate of exchange.

Estimated Download Times with a 4-minute MP3 file (4MB)

Internet Connection Speed	Est. Download Time
T1	21 seconds
ISDN (128KB)	4 min. 30 sec.
ISDN (64KB)	8 min. 45 sec.
56KB	10 min.
33.6KB	16 min. 40 sec.
28.8KB	19 min. 30 sec.
14.4KB	39 min.

If download times are a big concern for you, you might want to
use a download calculator on the Web. Many sites provide them
free of charge, including versions that you can download to your
own computer. Enter any file size (in kilobytes, megabytes, or
gigabytes) and the calculator will estimate the download time
according to your connection speed. Use a download calculator
online at *www.gamex.net/downloads/dlcalc.shtml*, or download
one free of charge at *www.intel.com/home/club/
downloadcalculator2.htm*.

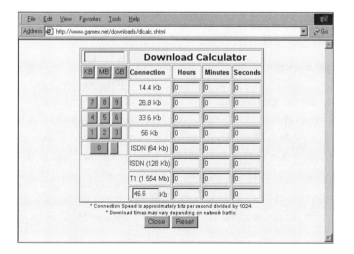

*Download calcula-
tors like this one
will approximate
your wait time for
downloads.*

Cutting Down Download Times

My mother always told me that patience is a virtue, which usually
only made me more impatient. If patience isn't your strong point
either, here are some pointers for cutting down on download
times:

- If you're getting a popular item from a popular site, avoid the
  crowds by downloading during off-peak hours. Early morning (before 9 a.m.) is usually a safe bet, and sometimes the
  site even tells you when traffic is slowest.

- Avoid downloading other files at the same time, or running
  large programs on your computer during the download.
  Every task you ask your computer to do slows it down, so
  just let it concentrate on that one important file.

- If you know a file will take more than a few hours to download, consider doing it overnight. Start the download before
  you go to bed, and then check back in the morning.

When Downloads Go Wrong

Sometimes a well-planned download can go bad. A file that has
been downloading for an hour can be rendered useless if the
download stops prematurely. Usually, these interrupted downloads
are caused by a broken Internet connection. Your Internet provider
decides you've been online long enough, or you get another call
on your phone line, and *boom*, your connection goes dead and
you've just wasted an hour. *But not necessarily.* There are ways to
resume your download from where you left off.

If you get back online immediately after you're booted off, sometimes Windows will resume the download for you. You don't have
to do anything except get back online, and Windows automatically does the rest of the work. Unfortunately, there's no way to
predict when Windows will do this for you and when it won't.
I've found that the faster I reconnect, the better the chance of
resuming from where I left off.

If a download is interrupted and Windows doesn't automatically
resume the transfer, you'll have to restart the download from

square one. There's no way to tell Windows to resume the download from where it left off, so the entire file needs to be downloaded from the beginning.

When you attempt to save the download with the same name you used in your failed download attempt, a warning screen will appear. It tells you that a file by that name already exists, and it asks if you want to replace the old file with the download you're about to begin. Since the partial file is non-operational, you *do* want to replace it. Click Yes and let the downloading begin—again.

Wrapping It Up

Now that you've read this chapter, downloading should be a piece of cake. While others complain of unexpectedly long download times and missing files, you'll know how to fetch things in the shortest time possible, and in the most orderly way. Let's recap what you've learned:

- How to download safely

- How to use your right mouse button to save time and increase your options

- How to calculate download times and shave seconds or minutes off your download time

CHAPTER 11

Easy Listening

Generation FAQ. That's what a friend of mine has dubbed Internet aficionados. He says that even more so than TV or music videos, the Web has taken away our collective attention span, and we now demand all our information served up as a bullet-point list or a Frequently Asked Questions (FAQ) page. He may be onto something. The most popular sites on the Web tend to have less text than a newspaper article. FAQs loom on every site. And have you noticed how many bullet-points fill *this* book alone? Maybe we *are* living in the era of fast, at-a-glance information. Maybe we have to be, seeing as how we encounter so much of it in just one venture onto the Internet.

In the spirit of Generation FAQ, this chapter summarizes all the essentials of e-music that are covered in more detail elsewhere in this book. You'll find quick lists about every e-music topic under the sun. When a quick fix isn't enough, follow the chapter references for more in-depth explanations and instructions.

Answers to the Five Most Frequently Asked Questions About E-Music

- **What's an MP3?**

  An MP3 is an audio file that has been highly compressed. It doesn't take up a lot of room on your computer, and it's easy to copy and download from the Internet. See more in Chapter 1, "What Is e-Music?"

- **Why all the fuss over MP3s?**

  They're so easy to duplicate and download that they're creating a music free-for-all and becoming a real headache to record companies. See more in Chapter 1.

- **Can I dive into digital music without breaking the law?**

  Yes! There are many free and legal digital music sources on the Internet. Read Chapter 9, "Content Mining," for more information.

- **Can my computer play digital music?**

  If you bought it within the last few years, your computer should be loaded and ready to go. If you're working with an older machine, you may need to add some new equipment. Find out more in Chapter 6, "Equipment Check."

- **Do I need special software to play digital music?**

  Yes, you need an MP3 player of some sort. See more in Chapter 7, "Choose Your Weapons Wisely—Software Matters."

The Ten Best Legal Music Sources on the Net

The following sites are the ten best places to find free, legal music on the Internet. The files at these sites have been posted by the artists and record companies that created them, who encourage you to download the files and have a listen. See more in Chapter 9.

- *www.MP3.com*

- *www.RollingStone.com*

- *www.emusic.com*

- *www.breakdown.musicpage.com*

- *www.traxinspace.com*

- *www.notype.com* (all independent artists)

- *www.amp3.com*

- *www.listeningroom.lycos.com/fan/TopDownloads.html*

- *www.free-mp3-downloads.com/mp3files.shtml*

- *www.vitaminic.co.uk/*

Traxinspace introduces new artists and hot picks every day.

The Four Best General Music Sources on the Net (Where You May Encounter Some Copyright Violations)

These sites will link you to programs that let you share music files with users worldwide. These programs are the most popular things going on the Internet today. In fact, Napster is the fastest growing program on the Internet to date. Unfortunately, not all the files you encounter on these programs are legal; many of them break copyright laws. Proceed at your own risk. Read more about it in Chapter 9.

- *www.napster.com*

- *www.gnutella.wego.com*

- *www.cutemx.com*

- *www.scour.net*

The Five Best e-Music Players

The following e-music players do a great job of handling your e-tunes. For more on choosing the right player for the job, see Chapter 2, "Layers of Players."

- The MusicMatch Jukebox (All-in-one player) at *www.musicmatch.com*

- The RealJukebox (All-in-one player) at *www.real.com*

- Winamp (Standalone MP3 player) at *www.winamp.com*

- Sonique (Standalone MP3 player) at *www.sonique.com*

- Audion (MP3 player for Macintosh computers) at *www.panic.com/ppack/audion*

The Gnutella site shows you how to share files with other MP3 owners.

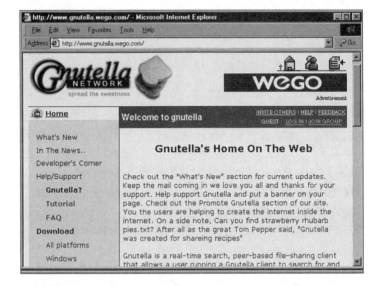

RealAudio gives you several players to choose from at real.com.

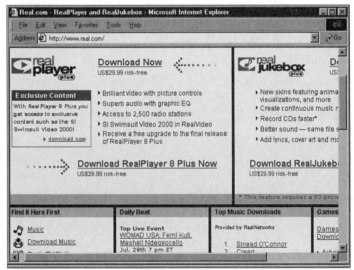

The Five Biggest Downloading Problems (and Their Solutions)

- *Problem:* My file gets cut off before it's finished downloading.

  Solution: See if the program you're using has a resume feature (Napster does). If not, start the download again. Sometimes Windows will automatically restart a broken download from the point where it stopped. Read more in Chapter 10, "The Lowdown on Downloading."

- *Problem:* I'm worried about breaking the law when downloading.

  Solution: Only download from sites where the files are guaranteed legal. See the list in this chapter, or find more in Chapter 9.

- *Problem:* Once it's downloaded, I can't find my MP3.

  Solution: Use the Find feature on the main Windows menu to locate the file. In the future, create a special folder just for downloads. See more in Chapter 10.

- *Problem:* The sound quality of my MP3 is bad.

  Solution: If you're using a file-sharing program such as Napster or Gnutella, make sure you select files with high-quality sound. Look for files that are quality-rated at 128Kbps per second or higher.

- *Problem:* My downloads are taking too long.

  Solution: The best solution is to get a faster Internet connection. If that's not an option, read the timesaving tips at the end of Chapter 10.

Pennywise:
All the players listed here are free downloads. However, for about the cost of a double album, you can upgrade these players and get more bells and whistles.

The Five Most Popular Portable Players

If you want to take your tunes with you, try one of these great gizmos. For more on portable tunes, read Part IV, "Ready to Walk."

- Diamond Rio Portable player (*www.RioPort.com*)

- Empeg Car Player (*www.empeg.com*)

- Impy3 Car Player (*www.impy3.com/impy3*)

- I-Jam Portable Player (*www.mp3ijam.com*)

- MPMan Portable Player (*www.eigerlabs.com*)

Take your tunes on the road with the products at empeg.com.

Top Five Search Engines for E-Music

Great Things to Come:

The players listed here store MP3s on flash memory cards, which are pricey. But at the time of this printing, Phillips has just announced a new player that lets you listen to MP3 files on a CD. If you have a CD burner, this is great news!

If you're looking for a specific track, artist, or musical genre, there are search engines specially designed to aid you in your e-music quest. Some of the best are listed here. Find out more about search engines in Chapter 8, "Users, Start Your Engines."

- *www.oth.net* (searches FTP sites)

- *www.altavista.com*

- *www.hotbot.com*

- *www.scour.net*

- *www.lycos.com*

Top Five Internet Radio Sites

When you want to have someone else order up your favorite tunes, turn to these great Internet radio stations:

- *www.live365.com*

- *www.broadcast.com*

- *www.netradio.com*

- *www.liveconcerts.com*

- *radio.altavista.com/altavista/default.htm*

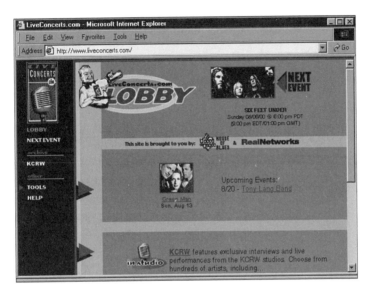

Skyrocketing concert prices got you down? Avoid the crowds and hit Liveconcerts.com, where there are new live acts every week.

Top Four Places to Follow the E-Music Revolution

The ins and outs of digital music are changing daily. Formats, applications, hardware, and even legal issues are being altered and reworked constantly. To keep up with the changes, check in with these Web sites. For more information, see Chapter 5, "What's Next?"

- *www.news.com*

- *www.wired.com/news/mp3*

- *music.zdnet.com/*

- *www.gmsv.com*

Top Four Programs for Artists

If you want to be the next digital music wunderkind, here are some programs to help you. Read more about it in Chapter 22, "Gather the Right Stuff."

- *www.cooledit.com*

- *www.soundforge.com*

- *www.fruityloops.com*

- *www.cakewalk.com*

Wrapping It Up

There you have it, fast answers to common e-music questions. In the spirit of these fast fact lists, here are the nine most important things you should take from this chapter:

- How to nab free and legal music at spots like *MP3.com* or *Rollingstone.com*.

- How to get to the most popular, but sometimes legally questionable, sites for music.

- Where to find an e-music player on the Internet.

- How to make downloads go smoothly.

- How to go portable.

- How to best search for e-music.

- How to tune into e-radio.

- How to tune into the future of e-music.

- And how to *be* the future of e-music by creating your own files on the best audio editing programs out there.

CHAPTER 12

Be a Jukebox Hero

How will you listen to music in the future? Chances are, you'll listen to it on an e-music jukebox on your computer. Jukeboxes are great because you don't have to be a computer geek to operate them. Yet they have enough features to satiate the geek in all of us—and the music aficionado, too.

Programs like MusicMatch Jukebox and RealJukebox make it easy to create the ultimate playlist or organize and reorganize your music at whim. And with jukeboxes, you can see the album art for the songs you play or read song lyrics or band information. Whereas the first wave of MP3 players simply let listeners *listen*, the jukebox generation lets music lovers immerse themselves in all aspects of the music, just as they can with LPs and CDs.

You've already learned how to find and install a jukebox in Chapter 7, "Choose Your Weapons Wisely—Software Matters." Now that you've got the goods, this chapter will show you how to rock the jukebox by using all the musical and aesthetic options it provides.

Why a Jukebox?

If you just want to play a tune, any old player will do. But if you want to really rock the house, you've got to get yourself an e-music jukebox. A jukebox gives you many more options than a standard, standalone MP3 player does.

Jukeboxes are the easy-bake oven of e-music: Put a few ingredients in, click some buttons, and watch something tasty come out. You can stick your CD collection in and make them come out as MP3s. Or put in an unorganized mass of songs and have them come out logically ordered.

What You'll Learn in This Chapter:

▶ What an e-music jukebox is and why you want one

▶ How to categorize and organize music in dynamic new ways with jukeboxes

▶ The quickest, easiest way to convert CDs to MP3s

▶ How you can use jukeboxes to add lyrics, cover art, and more to your e-music files

Jukeboxes are handy because they combine many software programs into one. Without a jukebox, you'd have to grab several programs to play, organize, and reformat your music. For instance, you could grab a standalone player like Winamp, combine it with an organization program like ShufflePlay, and use an encoder like AudioGrabber. You might choose this single-tool route if you require more specialized options than the broad-reaching jukeboxes. But for the average user, a jukebox should do the job. Plus, it's more convenient to learn and use just one program.

My Personal Favorite: The MusicMatch Jukebox

If you come over to my house and ask to hear some music, you're going to hear it on the MusicMatch Jukebox. I love this program! It makes my mammoth music collection manageable, and you don't have to be technically inclined to operate it. The buttons are laid out and marked well, and each one is extremely useful.

The MusicMatch Jukebox lets you rip and encode CDs, add cover art, lyrics, and artist information, label and organize your files to your heart's content, listen to music as you record it, link to online music sites and a CD database, and adjust the sound quality with an equalizer and normalizer.

This chapter tells you how to use these MusicMatch features. If you don't already have the MusicMatch Jukebox downloaded, installed, and ready to go, go back to Chapter 7 and follow the instructions. Then you'll be ready to see the following features in action.

Building a Library at the Speed of Light

Before you play around with your MP3s in the MusicMatch Jukebox, you've got to tell it where those MP3s are. Here's how:

Try It Yourself ▼

1. Open the Music Library by clicking on the button with the musical note in the lower-left corner of the player.

2. Click the Add button at the top of the Music Library. This brings up the Add Songs to Music Library window.

3. Follow the directions at the top of the window to add your files to the library.

Play That Funky Music

A list of your files should now appear in the Music Library. Want to give them a listen? It's easy. Just double-click on the file you want to hear. The file will then appear in the Playlist window in the upper-right corner of the screen. As it plays, the track information appears in the upper-left corner of the screen. The left window gives information on the current track; the right window holds the current playlist. To add more tracks to the list, just continue double-clicking the desired files from your music library. If you load a track and then decide you don't want to hear it, remove it from the playlist window by single-clicking on it and then pressing the Delete key on your keyboard. Make sure you highlight the track in your playlist and *not* in your music library, which would delete the track from your computer.

Use the Play, Pause, Stop, Next, and Previous buttons on the left side of the player to move through your playlist, just as you would with a regular CD player. This section of the player also contains the volume bar and the play bar. Adjust the volume by clicking on the volume button and moving it along the volume bar. Move the button on the play bar forward or backward to skip to a particular part of the song.

Playlist Options

It's easy to create a playlist using the MusicMatch Jukebox. Just use the buttons on top of the Playlist box in the upper-right corner of the player. Click Save to save a playlist, click Open to load a playlist you've already created, and click Clear to wipe the slate clean and create or open a new playlist. If you open a new playlist, your old list will be cleared from the playlist window automatically. For more on playlists, read "Playlists on the MusicMatch Jukebox" in Chapter 14, "Make Killer Playlists."

Organization

My favorite feature of the MusicMatch Jukebox is its organizational capabilities. The music I download off the Internet is never labeled quite right for my tastes, so I like being able to change things around and add more information to a file. I can enter information about the song, artist, album, track number, genre, and more. The more information I enter, the easier it is to find particular songs or build specialized playlists.

*Poorly labeled
songs that need
some changes.*

For instance, let's say I've downloaded some songs by The Refreshments off the Internet. When I got them off the Net, their labels are pretty spare. As you can see in the figure, they appear in my music library without an artist, album, or genre named, but just a title. Using only the original label information, my search options for this track are really limited. The only way I can find the track is alphabetically by title. But the tile label begins with "*The* Refreshments," so I have to remember not to look alphabetically by the actual title, but by the band name, and I have to look under the T's for "*The* Refreshments" and not the R's. My collection is huge, so if I had to remember all these little tricks, I'd be in big trouble.

Luckily, I can edit the track tag to make the file easy to find and use. To do this, I right-click on the track I want to edit, and I select Edit Track Tag from the pop-up menu.

*This pop-up menu
appears when you
right-click on a
track.*

This will bring up the Tag Song File window, where I can add all kinds of information about the track. My track starts out with virtually nothing entered. I can edit the information that's already there by highlighting it with my mouse and typing over it, and I can type in new information. Then I save it by clicking the OK button.

In the following figure, you can see the original track information contrasted with the new information I've entered. You don't have to make your file information as comprehensive as I've made mine, but in the following section I'll show you why you might want to.

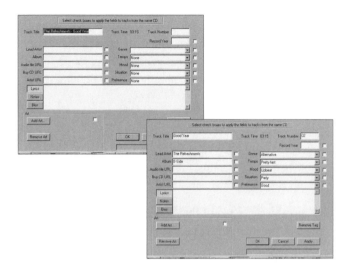

Before and after in the Tag Song File editing window.

Now that my file is correctly labeled with a lot of helpful information, I can do some impressive organizing and reorganizing. The track now shows the title, artist, and genre, all in their proper places. Now, when I organize my collection by any of those parameters, the song will show up in the correct spot.

In the following figure, you can see the file in a list of tracks formatted alphabetically by artist. But if I click the Genre column header at the top of the Music Library, the grouping quickly changes and the track sits nestled among other alternative favorites. This kind of grouping comes in handy when you're making playlists.

My Good Year track grouped first by artist, and then by genre.

Auto DJ

If you really want a shortcut to playlist-making, you've got to combine the tag-editing features with the Auto DJ feature on MusicMatch. Auto DJ asks you to enter musical criteria, and then it extracts just the right mix of music from your music library. Auto DJ will sort by album, artist, genre, tempo, mood, situation (party, background music, etc.), and musical preference (how much you like a tune).

Here's how to create a playlist using Auto DJ:

Try It Yourself ▼

1. Click the Auto DJ button, located on the row of Music Library buttons that sits above the library. This opens the Auto DJ Window.

2. In the box at the top of the screen, type in the length of the playlist you want to create.

3. Select at least one criterion, and as many as three, that you want Auto DJ to use when creating your playlist. Click on the criterion and a list of options will appear. Check the boxes for the options you want to include.

4. Click Preview to see the songs Auto DJ has selected. If you're satisfied, click Get Tracks. If you want to try again, adjust the criteria and click Preview again.

▲

The Auto DJ automatically puts its music mixes into the playlist window, so you can listen to the list right away or save it as a playlist. Note that if you haven't taken the time to label your music well, the Auto DJ isn't as effective. Without good labels, the Auto DJ doesn't know Chris Rock from alternative rock.

Rip It Good

As you can probably tell by now, organization is very important to me when it comes to my e-music. I can almost guarantee that it will also be important to you as your music collection grows and threatens to overtake your computer. I think the folks at MusicMatch are with me on the importance of organization. Every aspect of their jukebox makes labeling and categorization easy, including the CD ripping feature.

With some CD rippers, you're asked to enter an album title and artist, and then you're presented with a blur of nondescriptive track titles like "track 1" and "track 2." This leaves you with a pesky clean-up project; you have to go through the CD track by track and type in the information. Not so with MusicMatch. Not only can you convert a CD from your home collection to MP3s, but it labels each track. While you're online, MusicMatch taps into the world's largest CD Database (CDDB) and automatically labels your tracks with the correct information. Before it's even recorded and saved onto your hard drive, each track is tagged with the correct name, track number, album, artist, and genre.

MusicMatch gives you many recording options. You can change the quality of the recording, or even give songs a fade-in or fade-out time. You can look over your options and change them by clicking Options on the toolbar, selecting the Recorder sub-menu, and then selecting Settings. Most of the default settings should work fine for you, but I suggest making one adjustment. On the Recorder Settings screen, click the Songs Directory button. A screen appears that shows you where your recordings will be saved. The box labeled Directory for new songs should point MusicMatch to the folder where you store all your music files. If it doesn't have the right information, type it in, or browse through your directories for the right folder by clicking on the ... button.

Name that tune:
CDDB is massive, but it's not all-knowing! Occasionally, you'll stick in a CD and CDDB won't know which tracks it contains. When this happens, the recording program lists the tracks by number.

Are you ready to convert your CD collection to MP3s? Well, open MusicMatch, get your CDs, and begin:

1. Make sure you're connected to the Internet, and then insert the music CD of your choice into your CD-ROM drive.

2. Click the Rec button in the upper-left corner of the MusicMatch player. This opens the recorder, which automatically looks up track information on CDDB. A list of tracks on your CD should appear in the recorder.

3. Each track begins with a checkmark next to it, which indicates that it's slated to be copied and converted to MP3. If you want to prevent any particular track from being recorded, click on its checkmark to deselect it.

▼ **Try It Yourself**

4. Click the Start button on the recorder to begin the copying and conversion. The Recording Status box on the left side of the recorder will show you what percentage of the file is complete. When the process is finished, Recording Status will say "Adding Song to Library" and then "Ready."

Extras, Extras

Fatten up your collection:

Don't have enough of your own music? MusicMatch will help you. Click the Access Online Music button (the one with the globe icon) while you're online and MusicMatch will hook you up with free, legal MP3s.

One way to really juice up your jukebox is to use some of its extras that aren't fundamental to your listening experience. You know, the ones that are just for fun. In MusicMatch, these extras let you add art, lyrics, and artist information to your tracks.

The artwork you add appears in the box with the large MusicMatch Jukebox logo. You can add all sorts of art to this box. It can be actual album art, something you've created yourself, or something you associate with the band or the song. Just make sure it's a JPEG or bitmap file.

Once you have the art, here's how to add it to a track:

Try It Yourself ▼

1. Select the file you want to edit by clicking it once in your music library.

2. Right-click on the file and select Edit Track Tag from the pop-up menu.

3. Click the Add Art button in the bottom-left corner of the Tag Song File screen. A window will appear, showing your computer directories. Locate the art file you want to add and select it by double-clicking it, or highlight it and click the Open button.

4. The art should appear in the Art box. Check the empty box next to the art if you want to add it to the track. Click OK to update the track tag with the new art.

If you have several tracks that belong to the same album, the art you choose for one track will automatically be attached to the other tracks. You can change the artwork for subsequent tracks by selecting each one and repeating the preceding process with new artwork. When you do this, the rest of the album tracks maintain the initial artwork and the edited track shows the new artwork.

The Edit Track Tag screen that you use to add artwork is also where you add lyrics, notes, and artist biographies. Look for these fields above the Art box. Just click on the appropriate button and type the information in the large text box. You can add all the necessary information at once and then click OK to save it.

To see the information you've entered, play the song and do the following:

1. Click the Track Info button (the one with four straight horizontal lines) to the right of the Music Library button.

2. Click the Notes, Bios, and Lyrics buttons. The information should appear in the box directly below the buttons. If no information has been entered, the box will say <empty>.

▼ **Try It Yourself**

▲

The Track Info screen can be as informative as you like.

The RealJukebox Shines

Now that you've gone through these drills to master the MusicMatch Jukebox, you'll master the RealJukebox in no time. The buttons on this program are labeled and organized a little better than those on MusicMatch, and when you hover your mouse pointer over a button, a little text box pops up to explain the button's function.

Overall, I still prefer MusicMatch to the RealJukebox because it's easier to use and more streamlined. All those well-labeled buttons on the RealJukebox take up a lot of space, so the program is a huge screen hog. And it's a time-sapper as well. Almost any time a button is clicked, there's a delay of several seconds. It reminds me of surfing with a slow Internet connection, but it shouldn't be this slow because it doesn't have to travel through phone lines!

Plus, don't think you'll get the free player without a little corporate goodie or two. Look for rotating ads at the bottom of the player.

If you want to take RealJukebox for a spin, you need to download and install it as explained in Chapter 7. Then you'll be ready to explore the following features.

The Music Library

Options abound:

RealJukebox Version 2 promises to deliver better playlist features and a "hot new interface" (which looks like the hot *old* interface we've seen on Winamp for years). Check it out at Real.com.

Just like with MusicMatch, you have to populate your music library before you play around with any tracks. RealJukebox makes this extremely easy because it does all the searching for you. Just click on the File menu at the top of the player and select Import Wizard. Select the drives you want the wizard to search for music files. (I went with All Drives for a complete system check.) Then click the Start Search button, and the wizard will leap into action. Depending on the size and speed of your computer, the search could take a few minutes or a few seconds. After the wizard finds the music files, you'll get a report of how many files were found. Click Back if you want to do another search, and click Finish when you're satisfied. After you click Finish, all the tracks listed in the report will show up in your library.

Quick Play

The play options are pretty straightforward on the RealJukebox. The buttons at the top of the screen are just like those that you'd find on any CD player. Use them to play, pause, skip, or mute a song. You can also double-click on a song in your music library to play it.

Organization

The organizational options for this jukebox are superb. Right-click on a track and select Edit Track Info to add artist, album, track, and genre information. Then watch the categorization magic.

A whole row of buttons is dedicated to sorting through your music. Click All Tracks to see your whole collection, or click Genre or Artist/Album to see your collection broken down that way. When you click Artist/Album, you'll see a list of all the artists in your collection and the number of tracks you have for each one. When you click on an artist, you'll get a listing of their albums that you own and how many tracks you have off each album. Click on one of the albums to see or play the tracks.

My collection, broken down by artist.

If you've done a terrible job of labeling, you can click on the Search button and comb through your music collection for that one particular song. This is perfect if you never relabel downloads and you aren't sure if the track title will show up alphabetically by artist, song name, or album.

Playlists

As you'll learn in Chapter 14, there are many different ways to make a playlist in many different programs. The good news is that this jukebox easily lets you listen to playlists created in other players. The bad news is that it's harder to make playlists in this program than others.

If you've created playlists in other programs, you can get to them by clicking the Playlists button. All your playlists should appear. Double-click one to open and play it. If you want to create a new playlist, try this:

1. Click on New Playlist on the right side of the screen.

2. Follow the instructions that appear, but in the area labeled #2, make sure you choose Make an Empty Playlist.

3. Click OK to leave the screen. A window will appear that asks if you want to add tracks now. Click Yes.

▼ **Try It Yourself**

4. Your music collection will appear in a new screen. Click a track that you want to add to your playlist, and then click the Add Tracks button. Repeat this process until you're satisfied with the playlist. Then click Close.

Auto Playlists

Remember Auto DJ from MusicMatch? Well Auto Playlist is its counterpart in RealJukebox. When you click the New Auto Playlist button on the right side of the jukebox, a screen appears that gives you helpful, easy-to-follow instructions on how to make an Auto Playlist. You set the parameters for music type and mix length, and the RealJukebox comes up with a custom playlist built especially for you.

Recording Made Easy

Avoid those black holes:

Don't you hate it when you can't find your music? Make sure your recordings end up in the right folder by tweaking the recording preferences. Click the Tools menu, select Preferences, and then select the Music Files tab. Click the File Locations button to change the save destination of the tracks you record. Make sure you adjust both Recorded Music Files Location and Default Download Location to direct files to the folder where you save all your e-music files.

It's easy to copy files off an audio CD and turn them into MP3 files that you can listen to in your music library. Just stick a CD in your CD-ROM drive while you're online, and the tracks will appear in the Track window. If they don't appear, click the CD button on the left side of the screen. Like MusicMatch, RealJukebox gets the track names and information from CDDB and automatically attaches them to the files.

Select the tracks you want to record by clicking them. Then click the red Record button at the top of RealJukebox (next to the Play button) to begin recording. The first time you try to record a CD, a window might appear asking you to first test your CD-ROM drive to improve the quality of recordings. This test isn't required, but it's highly recommended.

Easy Additions

Although the RealJukebox lets you add lyrics and art, it's not as easy to see the items as it is with MusicMatch. Like MusicMatch, you add the items by right-clicking on a track and selecting Edit Track Info. There's a whole set of items you can adjust and edit here, including photos, art, and information about specific types of music such as classical or jazz. These screens are some of the slowest-moving in RealJukebox, and they made me question whether aesthetic add-ons are really worth it...especially when the information you enter gets lost on the huge, button-heavy RealJukebox screen. To see the information, you have to click on View Track Info. A half-screen will appear with artist information. There are several different ways to display this artist information. Some require you to be online, others don't. To change your view, click on the small Info icon at the top of the new half-screen and select a choice from the menu that appears.

A better extra that this jukebox gives you is the visualization feature, which automatically pops up on the right side of the screen when you play a song. There are all sorts of visualizations included in the program. One has a soulful sheep keeping time with the music you play, and another is a manic display of lights and colors that shrink and explode to the tempo of your tunes.

If a visualization doesn't appear on your jukebox when you fire it up, click on the View menu and select Visualizations. Right-click on the visualizations box to change the effect.

Other Jukeboxes

You've learned about the features of two of the most popular jukeboxes on the Net today. But as music junkies switch from simple standalone players to the popular all-in-one players, you can bet there will be a boom in jukebox options. There are a few other choices emerging right now, including the Desktop Jukebox (*www.llerrah.com/dj/*) and The Shuffler (*www.illustrate.org/*).

Once you've tried your hand at MusicMatch or the RealJukebox, using new players will be easy because most of the buttons and functions will operate in similar ways. (Note how the Auto DJ and Auto Playlist functions duplicate each other.) As new jukeboxes emerge, you can also expect new, improved versions of old favorites from MusicMatch and RealNetworks, with a few new tricks that even an old dog can learn.

The Skinny on Skins:

At Real.com, you can change the look of your RealJukebox by downloading *skins*. Although these skins can make your Jukebox look high-tech or downright prehistoric (a dinosaur skin is available), they don't alter any of the RealJukebox functions and features.

Wrapping It Up

Are you ready to really get down with your music? Not just *listen* to it, but make it multidimensional with visuals or music mixes that follow just the right theme or tempo? Sure you're ready! You've got your jukebox loaded, and you know how to make it rock with these great tricks:

- You can organize your music collection to a T.

- You can quickly create playlists or order the jukebox to make them according to your parameters.

- You know how to add art to your e-music tracks, or lyrics, or band bios...or even a dancing sheep!

CHAPTER 13

Get Your Collection in Order

The Internet has made obtaining music simple, fast, and painless. (And this book has helped too, I hope.) However, if your ever-growing digital music collection isn't well-organized, finding and listening to your favorite tunes can turn into a laborious, tedious, and altogether tiresome task.

It can happen before you know it. You download a song here, a song there, shoving them into any folder that's handy at the time. Maybe you stick a few in Downloads and then decide to put others in the Temporary Files folder. Then you create a special folder for a special artist, but a few weeks later you forget where it is and you have to create another one.

It's best to avoid these problems immediately by keeping things organized from the start. This chapter will show you how. We'll also take organization to the next level, teaching you how to properly label and group your music with database or jukebox software. And if your hard drive is a little overloaded and needs a good spring cleaning, we'll help you move your music files onto disks or an Internet storage site.

What You'll Learn in This Chapter:

► Basic organization tips for downloading and saving music files

► How to use ID3 tags to enhance file organization

► How software like ShufflePlay can help you manage your files

► Organization options for jukebox collections

► How to neatly store your files when you can't keep them on your computer

One File, One Purpose

Imagine you have a gigantic CD collection, but no CD racks. Instead, your CDs sit in small piles all over your house. Some are in the corner of the living room, some are on your bedside table, some are on your office floor, and a few dozen are randomly scattered between books, papers, couch cushions and office supplies. (Wait... this is *my* house!) If you ever need one specific album by one specific artist, you're in for a chore. This is what happens to computer users who don't preplan the storage and organization of music files.

An *ID3 tag* is an identification tag for MP3s. These data tags can contain information about the song title, artist, and genre of music.

This leads us to the first simple step to organizing your e-music collection: Keep it together. Create one central folder and keep all the e-music on your computer there. If you haven't already done this, do it now. It's a simple step that will save you a lot of effort and time. Create the folder in a directory that's easy to find and remember. If you listen to or download e-music frequently, make sure the folder can be reached in just one or two clicks. Don't tuck it away in a folder within a folder within a folder. My e-music is stored in a file called Audio on my desktop. The only things stored in my e-music folder are audio files and playlists. When I look for a particular song, there's no question where I'll find it. If only my house was that organized!

Group Now, Group Often

My main folder, Audio, contains many subfolders, which further decreases my search time for songs. My subfolders are grouped by artist, but grouping by genre works well, too. No matter how you break songs into subgroups, try to follow this one rule: Create your filing system as you acquire songs. If you postpone organizing them, it becomes a larger, harder task. Immediate organization also saves you time in making and using playlists, which have to be reformatted each time any of their songs are moved. Moving files around a lot will waste a good deal of time. (You'll learn how to create playlists in the next chapter.)

Labeling Your Files

Even if you've set aside one folder to hold all your e-music, you'll still have a hard time finding your favorite song if it isn't labeled properly. When a file is saved to your computer, it has a filename and an ID3 tag tacked onto it by its previous owner/ creator. The filename is what you see when you open a file. The ID3 tag can contain many different kinds of information which will be discussed later on. Most notably, it provides the information that scrolls along the play window on most MP3 players.

Often, filenames and ID3 tags are written haphazardly, with the artist, song name, track number, or album all denoted in the Song Name entry box (or nowhere at all). A Public Enemy track I recently downloaded was named PE8_r4. I don't know what kind of organization system the original file owner used, but that file-name didn't indicate to me that this was actually a song called "Bring the Noise."

Filenames

An unclear filename should be changed immediately after you download the file. There are many ways to do this, but perhaps the best is to go into a program like Windows Explorer, right-click on the file, and select Rename. Then simply enter a more appropriate filename, followed by the file extension of the original file (.mp3, .ra, .wav, and so forth), and press Enter. Adding the correct file extension is imperative! Your computer won't know how to read the file unless it contains a period followed by the correct extension.

Remember, if you're going to change an unclear filename, do it as soon as you get the file. Otherwise, playlists or jukeboxes that are programmed to look for the old filename will have to be redirected to the new one.

ID3 Tags

Filenames are essential to your e-music collection. After all, every file has one. On the other hand, ID3 tags are just nice extras. You don't need them, you don't have to alter them, and you don't have to really sink your teeth into them. But if you're big on e-music, you'll probably want to.

An ID3 tag doesn't alter a file's name or location; it just lets you store more information about the file. The more information you enter about each of your files, the more ways you can categorize and organize your music. If you create ID3 tags that contain the artist, song title, album, year published, and musical genre, you can use a database program or jukebox to rapidly reorganize your e-music collection by any of those categories with just one click. This means you can instantly see a grouping of all your reggae music and, in the next millisecond, change the ordering to show all your music from 1988.

Let's look at how to change ID3 tags in the music database program ShufflePlay and the MusicMatch Jukebox.

A *file extension* is the segment of a file label that indicates the file type. The file extension is separated from the filename by a period (.). E-music file extensions include .mp3, .ra, and .wav.

For the Serious Collector: ShufflePlay

Are you an e-music maverick? Do you download at least twice a week? Do your music files outnumber all your other computer files combined? If you answered yes to any of these, or if you *hope* to answer yes one day, you should consider getting some special software to help you organize your collection.

ShufflePlay is an excellent software program that will help sort, group, label, and relabel your music collection. It functions as a music database, as well as a playlist editor and file management system. You can download it at *www.pinoyware.com/shuffleplay/ index.shtml*. It costs $10 to register it, but you can try it out for a few weeks free of charge and see if it's for you.

ShufflePlay's site lets you download the latest version of the product for a free trial period.

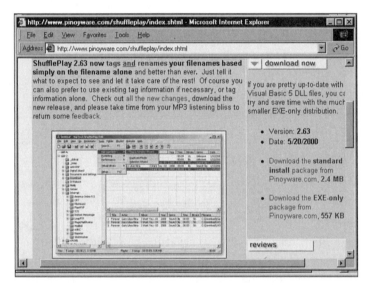

If you've used a file management system like Microsoft Windows Explorer, or if you've ever managed files on a Macintosh, operating ShufflePlay should come naturally. The systems are all similar; you just click through your computer drives and folders in the top-left corner of the screen, and their contents appear in the top-right corner of the screen. Double-clicking on a folder or file will move it into your music database, which fills the bottom half of the screen.

I use Shuffleplay as a music database where I can modify ID3 tags and search for songs in my music library by many different criteria. Using the Properties window in Shuffleplay, I can easily change or modify the ID3 tags on all my music files. I like to do this with every song I download so that all my files contain the same information, categorized in the same way. ShufflePlay's Properties window has many different fields to fill in, but I typically stick to the artist, song title, album, year, and genre fields. All the tag adjusting is easy to do, and once you do it in Shuffleplay, the change shows up wherever you use the file.

Once you download, install, and open ShufflePlay, here's how to adjust your ID3 tags:

1. Right-click on one of your music files in your music library.

2. Select Properties from the menu that appears.

3. Adjust any or all of the fields (artist, song, genre, track number, etc.) and click OK to finish.

Once my music is labeled, I can see my collection broken down by genre, artist, or the other parameters I've entered with just one click. Remember when I told you about using subfolders to make things easier to find? I said you could subdivide by artist or genre. But if you fill out ID3 tags and use a database like ShufflePlay, you don't need subfolders because one large folder can be arranged and rearranged to your liking. Do this by clicking on the index heading of your choice. For instance, click on the Artist heading to alphabetically list your collection by artist. Quickly change things around by clicking the Genre heading, which alphabetizes by music type, and so on.

An added bonus that ShufflePlay offers is called the Duplicate Finder. It looks for songs that have similar titles and then asks if you'd like to delete any of them. If you're acquiring new music rapidly, duplicate songs can be a big waste of space. Sometimes you forget you already have a song, or sometimes a song fails to download properly, and you neglect to delete the partial file before getting a new, complete version. ShufflePlay will let you easily clear the decks of all those extra copies.

▼ **Try It Yourself**

▲

What's Up with Read-Onlys?

When you try to change an ID3 tag, sometimes you get a message that the file is read-only and can't be adjusted. This can be remedied easily. Open your music folder in Windows Explorer, or a similar program, and right-click on the file in question. Select Properties from the menu and a window full of information appears. At the bottom of the window, under Attributes, the box next to Read-only is probably checked. Uncheck it by clicking inside the box, and then click OK. Voilà! Your ID3 tag is now adjustable!

The bottom section of ShufflePlay shows the music I've placed in my music database, while the top sections are used to explore my computer and add new files.

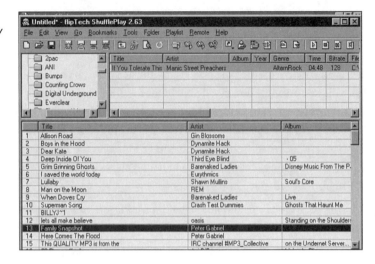

Shortcut or Disaster?

ShufflePlay has an interesting feature called Rename Wizard, which attempts to sort out and relabel all your ID3 tags so all your files have the correct artist, track, and title information. This would be an invaluable, time-saving feature if it was error-proof, but it's not. In fact, it can really mix up a set of tags that started out perfectly fine. Luckily, Rename Wizard has a preview option, so you can tell if the renaming does more harm than good before any permanent damage is done.

ShufflePlay has many other features not discussed here. For more information, go to the program's help menu, or take the tour at their Web site.

Organizing with Jukeboxes

If you've chosen a jukebox to serve as your MP3 player, you can use many of its tools to not only organize your music collection, but to really make it sizzle. Jukeboxes let you adjust ID3 tags just as you would in ShufflePlay, but they also let you add lyrics, art, artist bios, and other interesting stuff.

Like ShufflePlay, jukeboxes allow you to organize and reorganize your music collection according to each parameter you enter in the ID3 tag. With one click, you can organize your songs alphabetically by artist, and in the next click, you can organize them by genre. Let's edit some ID3 tags on the most popular jukebox out there, MusicMatch Jukebox. If you use another jukebox, you'll have to tweak the process a bit, but all the jukeboxes function similarly. If you don't yet have the MusicMatch Jukebox, read Chapter 7 for download and installation information and Chapter 12 for more on jukeboxes.

1. Bring up your Music Library by clicking the musical note icon in the top-left corner of the MusicMatch player.

2. Right-click on one of your music files in the bottom half of your screen and select Edit Track Tag from the menu.

3. Adjust any or all of the fields (artist, song, genre, track number, mood, situation, etc.) and click OK to finish.

▼ Try It Yourself

▲

On the MusicMatch Edit Track Tag page, you'll also find buttons that allow you to insert album art, lyrics, and other extras. If the album art or lyrics are somewhere else on your computer, this is a great way to bring all elements of your music collection together into one nicely organized place. For more on using these features, read Chapter 12, "Be a Jukebox Hero."

When You Can't Store Songs on Your Computer

Is your hard drive low on space? If you fret over downloading Meatloaf-length rock anthems, it's time to consider new storage solutions for your e-music collection. There are a few different directions you can take, depending on your equipment. You can store your music on zip disks or floppy disks, burn them to CDs, or store them on the Internet. Let's go over the options, discuss what you'll need to get started, and see which option fits you best.

Too many files, too little space? If this is your concern, it's time to consider some storage options.

Storing on Zip Disks and Floppy Disks

If you have a zip drive or floppy disk drive, you can opt to save e-music to disk automatically. It's as easy as downloading to your computer. When you go to download, select the appropriate disk drive as the download destination. Zip disks will hold approximately 90+ minutes of MP3 music. Floppy disks aren't large enough to handle an MP3 file, but they can store real audio files. To play songs saved on a disk, it has to be in the drive. You can make playlists that contain songs on a disk, but again, the disk has to be in the drive. If you decide to move the songs to your computer, you can copy them quickly and easily by using the copy and paste features in programs like Windows Explorer.

Storing Music on CDs

You can store a lot more music on a CD than you can on a zip or floppy disk, but you need some extra equipment to pull it off. Not only do you need a CD-ROM drive, but you also need a CD writer (or *burner*) and a program that writes MP3s to CD. If you've got the goods, this is an excellent storage solution. CDs can hold as much as 300+ minutes of music in MP3 format, or 74 minutes in WAV format (which you can use on a regular CD player). In Chapter 21, "Born to Burn (Make Your Own CDs)," you'll learn everything you need to know.

Storing Music on the Web

Imagine businesses offering online storage lockers for e-music, free of charge. Besides the fear that they'd run away with your goods, it seems like a nice offer. Well, some e-businesses are doing just that, offering sizeable chunks of free storage space on their Web sites. Several sites are specifically devoted to storing e-music. Many of them compliment their storage space with links to free downloads or music-related sites.

The benefits of storing e-music files on the Web go beyond simply saving disk space on your home computer. With your music on the Web, you can get to it virtually anywhere. Stuck with the out-of-town relatives for Thanksgiving? You can make Aunt Edna's computer rock to "Sweet Child of Mine" just by visiting your personal online vault of e-music. And you never have to

worry about losing or damaging any kind of disk. You just have to
ponder over the people behind the Web site. Will they ruin or
destroy your files? Will they go snooping around and turn you
over to Lars Ulrich of Metallica? Let's take a look at your e-
storage options and see what some sites say about these and other
issues.

MySpace.com

This site gives you 25MB of storage space to start out with, but if
you complete a survey, they'll up it to 300MB. Remember, 1MB
equals about 1 minute of MP3 music, so you can't store your
Alice Cooper box set here. What you can do is upload your music
files quickly; MySpace.com lets you upload several files simultaneously. You can also share files with friends, and you're allotted
more storage space when you refer them to the site.

Are your files safe with this site? The owners say yes. They
promise to keep their collective nose out of your files, and they
say they have a stringent backup procedure, so files are never lost
or irretrievable. You can sign up for free storage space at
www.myspace.com. They'll ask for your email address, but no
other personal information.

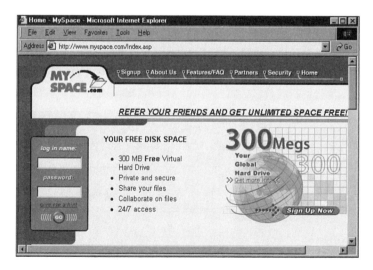

There are many ways to increase your storage space at Myspace.com.

Myplay.com

This site gives you a whopping 3 gigabytes of free storage space. You could store as much as 3,072??? minutes of music (or approximately 50 albums)! Plus, the site has partnered with music sites like Rollingstone.com and emusic.com to provide you with quick links to free MP3s. And the music you download from the partner sites doesn't count against your 3GB storage limit.

The storage space is called your *locker*, and it's easy to sign up for one. They ask for very little personal information; just your email address and a user name. Uploading and listening to your files is easy—all the buttons are clearly marked, and the instructions are clearly written and easy to follow. But a word to the wise: Store your music here, but don't expect to listen to it on the site. Unless you have a lightning-fast Internet connection, trying to listen to streaming files directly from your locker is unbearably frustrating. The site claims it does some prebuffering, but each time I tried to listen with my 56KB connection, the files played, then paused, then played, then paused…

A peek into my mostly empty locker.

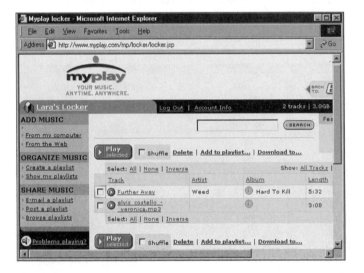

Flynote

This site offers you 1GB of free storage space, plus it allots you an additional 900MB to store your own music in its Public Music Library. The library is a key feature of the site; it's filled with thousands of free and legal mp3s by relatively unknown artists.

The Flynote Site has a lot to offer music lovers.

Flynote is still a beta product (it's still being tested) as of this writing, and there are definitely some bugs to be worked out. The streaming audio feature is slow and clunky, making it nearly impossible to listen to your audio collection on the site. Even more bothersome, the link to the company's privacy statement takes you to a blank page that simply says "Privacy Statement." It's hard to say how safe your files are on this beta site, but future editions will merit a close look because Flynote has a lot of potential.

Wrapping It Up

Organizing your music certainly isn't the most fun you could be having with it, but it makes the e-music experience more enjoy-able in the long run. A little forethought in organizing your collec-tion will save a lot of time, and possibly a lot of anguish. After all, what's worse than needing to hear that one song that has that one line by that one guy? (You know the one, it came out about '91, '92. Sort of a hip-hop thing?) The eternal search for that one song should come a little easier now that you've read this chapter.

Here's what you've learned:

- Some essential folder and filename tips

- How to use ID3 tags, teamed with ShufflePlay or music Jukeboxes, to really get organized

- How to store and organize your files without eating up hard drive space

CHAPTER 14

Make Killer Playlists

Remember the mix tape, that carefully crafted collection of songs you made to match a certain mood, or to capture the fervor of a particularly potent romantic relationship? I have an assortment of them in a bottom dresser drawer. Some of them are terrible recordings of songs I tried to grab off the radio, and others are pretty good groupings of songs I recorded off my CD collection. (If only record companies put together compilations as well as I did.)

If you've ever made or been given a mix tape, you're going to love playlists. Just like a mix tape, a playlist is any combination of songs you want to group. Unlike a mix tape, which has to fit on a cassette, a playlist can be as long as you want. Once you've read this chapter, you'll find playlists a lot easier to create than their time-consuming forefathers.

My Collection Runneth Over!

Once you start collecting e-music, you'll find that you just can't stop. It's not enough to have ten of your favorite songs; it's not even enough to have the complete collections from ten of your favorite artists. You'll want more, more, more! And the wonderful thing is that you can have it! You can build a collection that's bigger than your hard drive (using tools and methods discussed in Chapter 13, "Get Your Collection in Order"). The only problem is that once your collection reaches a certain threshold, selecting songs to play from it becomes a bit of a chore. Even worse, a lot of your collection can go unplayed because you forget exactly what you've acquired along the way.

But it doesn't have to be that way. You can create and save playlists so you'll have an easy shortcut to all your favorite tunes. Playlists are simple to make, no matter what type of player you're using.

What You'll Learn in This Chapter:

▶ How and why playlists make e-music more enjoyable

▶ How to create your own playlists using jukebox software

▶ How to create playlists with Winamp, the MusicMatch Jukebox, and Napster

▶ How to trade playlists with friends

A Map to Your Music

Move It!

Not only does a playlist tell your computer what song to play, but where to find that song on your computer. If you move a song to a different folder, your playlist looks for it at the old location, doesn't find it, and gives up. To avoid this problem, remember to modify your playlists when you move files around. Better yet, come up with a solid organization system from the start.

A playlist is a small computer file that instructs your music player to fetch certain songs. The playlist file doesn't contain the actual songs; it's just a map to those songs. Because of this, you don't have to worry about a playlist taking up a lot of memory or hard drive space. If you created and named 1,000 different playlists, all pointing to the same three songs, you wouldn't have to store 3,000 space-intensive songs on your computer. You'd just have to store the three songs and the 1,000 small *pointer* (playlist) files.

Creating Playlists on Popular Players

This chapter will show you how to create and listen to a playlist using Winamp, MusicMatch Jukebox, and the Napster list-making software. These programs are the most popular of their kind when it comes to standalone players, all-in-one jukeboxes, and MP3 acquisition sites. If you use a player that isn't listed here, follow along with the instructions that most closely match your player (Sonique is similar to Winamp, RealJukebox is similar to MusicMatch, and so on). Most players follow the same basic parameters for creating playlists, so this section should still aid you.

Playlists on Winamp

Before you begin, you must have the Winamp player and two or more MP3 files on your hard drive. If you don't have these items yet and need help, see Chapters 7, "Choose Your Weapons Wisely—Software Matters," and 9, "Content Mining."

Try It Yourself ▼

1. Open Winamp and click on the PL button in the lower-right corner.

2. Click the ADD button in the lower-left corner of the Winamp Playlist window. The button will turn into three buttons: ADD URL (add an Internet address), ADD DIR (add a directory), and ADD FILE (add a music file).

3. Click on the ADD FILE button. The Add file(s) to playlist window will appear. Use this window to locate and open the folder that holds your MP3 files. Double-click the file you want to add to your playlist.

4. The file you've selected should now appear on the Winamp Playlist window. Repeat steps 2 and 3 to add more files to your playlist.

5. Once you've added all the files to your playlist, it's time to save it. Click on the LIST OPTS button in the bottom-right corner of the Winamp Playlist window. Three buttons appear; click the SAVE LIST button. This opens the Save playlist window. In the Save in: box at the top of the window, make sure you note the directory and folder that the playlist will be saved to. In the File name: box, type playlist1. In the Save as type: box, make sure the file type is M3U Playlist. Then click the Save button.

Congratulations! You've successfully completed your first playlist. Now let's go over how to fetch a playlist you've created.

The Winamp Playlist window should still be stocked with all the files you've just chosen. In order to start from zero, you need to clear out all those songs by clicking the LIST OPTS button and then the NEW LIST button. Is the Winamp Playlist empty? Great. Now let's work on getting those files back.

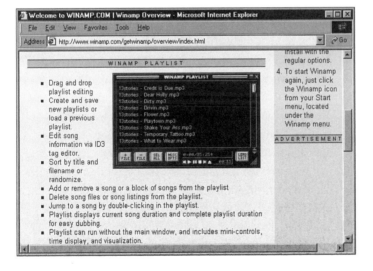

Quick Tip:

If you have a lot of MP3 files to add to a playlist and they're all sitting in the same folder, hold down the Ctrl key, click on each one, and then click the Save button. All of them will be added to the playlist at once, saving you a lot of time!

The Winamp site explains some of the player's special playlist features.

Shake Things Up A Bit:

Do you want to rearrange the order of your playlist? Maybe move song number three before song number two? Simply left-click on the song and drag it up or down to the spot you want it in the list. Once the song is in the right place, let go of the left mouse button.

1. Click on the LIST OPTS button and select the LOAD LIST option.

2. This brings up the Load Playlist window. Find the file Playlist1.m3u and double-click on it (or you can highlight it and then click the Open button).

3. Your playlist should appear in the Winamp Playlist box, ready to play.

▲

Playlists on the MusicMatch Jukebox

There are a few more steps to making playlists with the MusicMatch Jukebox than with standalone players like Winamp. To begin the process, you must have the latest version of MusicMatch Jukebox and at least two MP3 files on your computer.

1. Open MusicMatch Jukebox and click the button with the musical note on the left side of the box. This is the Music Library button.

2. Your Music Library appears. If it's filled with the files you want to add to your playlist, skip to step 4. If your Music Library is empty or doesn't contain the files you want in your playlist, follow step 3.

3. To the right of the words "Music Library", there's a button marked Add. When you click this button, a large window appears where you can locate music files on your computer and add them to your Music Library. Look through your directories on the left side of the window. As you do, your available e-music files appear on the right side of the window. If you store all your e-music files in one folder, bring up that folder on the left and all the files appear on the right. Click Select All. All the files are highlighted, indicating that they will be added to your Music Library. Click the OK button when you're finished adding files.

4. It's time to select the files you want in your playlist. To do this, double-click on the appropriate files in your music library, or click-and-drag them up to the Playlist window in the upper-right corner.

▲

5. Once the Playlist Window contains all the files that make up your desired playlist, click on the button above the window labeled Save. This brings up the Save window. Type Playlist2 in the Playlist Name box at the bottom of the screen, and then click the Save button.

You've done it! You've created a shortcut to a list of some of your favorite music files. Now you just have to learn how to bring up the list for future use. Before you do this, clear the playlist window of all your songs by clicking the Clear button next to the Save button you used earlier.

1. Click on the Open button above the Playlist window.

▼ Try It Yourself

2. A new window appears with several choices. Along the left side of the screen, there are several buttons. Select the Playlist button and all your saved Playlists will appear on the right side of the screen.

3. Double-click on Playlist2, or click on it once and then click on the Play button. The first song on your playlist should start playing automatically.

Using Playlists in Napster

Napster (version 2.0, Beta 6) has its own playlist editor, which makes it simple to play files while searching for or downloading music. To try it out, you need the latest version of Napster, an MP3 player such as Winamp or Sonique, and a few MP3 files in your Napster Music Library. (See Chapter 9 for more on Napster's Music Library.)

1. Open Napster. If you're not connected to the Internet when you open Napster, it will alert you that you can't connect to a Napster server. You don't need to be on a Napster server to use the playlist, so just click the OK button.

▼ Try It Yourself

2. Click on the Library tab at the top of the screen. This takes you to a list of MP3 files you currently share with other Napster users. The Playlist editor is located in the bottom-right corner of the screen.

3. Click on a file you want to add to the playlist, and then click the Add button on the playlist editor. Repeat this process until your playlist is complete.

4. To save your playlist, click Save on the playlist editor. The save screen will appear. Enter Playlist3 in the File Name box, and select M3U as the file type.

The best way to listen to this list is to open it using a player that handles M3U files, such as Winamp. Click the LIST OPT button, choose the LOAD LIST option, and then look through your files for Playlist3.M3U. Please note that unless you changed the directory on the Save window of the Napster Playlist Editor, the playlist was automatically saved to the Napster folder on your computer.

Other Programs

Save Some Time:

If you keep all your playlists and MP3 files in the same folder, you'll save yourself laborious searches through all your computer files. If your music collection is a little too big for one folder, divide it into several subfolders grouped by artist, genre, or era.

Now you know how to create a playlist using three different programs. With this knowledge and just a bit of tweaking, no program or playlist editor should be hard to master. Just get acquainted with the program's playlist editor buttons and always note where you save your MP3s and playlists, and you've got it made.

Swapping Playlists

One of the best things about the mix tapes I made in high school was sharing them with friends. I'd create the perfect, not-to-be-topped driving mix, stick it in the cassette player in my friend Michelle's Dodge Dart, and count the seconds until she asked for her own copy. Then it was just a matter of dubbing my tape onto her blank tape, using the very advanced high-speed dubbing feature on my Magnavox stereo. In about 40 minutes, she had a copy of my well-crafted work.

Not surprisingly, you can share playlists just like mix tapes, but it can be a bit more complex than using your dual-tape deck.

For some music lovers, it's not enough to share a playlist with friends. They have to share it with the world by posting it on their Web sites.

You could email a playlist to a friend just as you would a document or a graphics file. However, a playlist is only a map to the music. If your friend doesn't have the same music files you do, labeled the same way and in the same directory, the playlist will be useless.

In order to swap a playlist, you must include all the music files associated with that playlist. Since even the most compact music files are still rather large, emailing them all or putting them on a floppy disk isn't a viable option. If you and your friend both have zip drives, you can save the playlists and files on zip disks and then exchange them.

But if your friend lives across the world and exchanging physical items is difficult or bothersome, there are some online options to consider. You could upload your music and playlist to an online storage site such as Myspace.com or Myplace.com (see Storing Music on the Web in Chapter 13). From there, your friends could easily download the files just as they would from a music site like MP3.com. You could also coordinate an exchange on a file-sharing service such as Gnutella or Napster, or you could put the files on your own Web site.

Storage sites make it easy to share music with friends.

Wrapping It Up

Now you're ready to make playlists at will. Group your favorite polkas, make a "He Loves Me Not" playlist of angry-girl anthems, or create a special mix for that special someone. Let's look at all the things you've learned about playlists:

- It's a roadmap to music on your computer, not an actual collection of tunes.

- You can make and use one with Winamp, the MusicMatch Jukebox, and Napster.

- You can win friends and influence people by swapping or sharing playlists.

CHAPTER 15

Your PC Wants to Be Your Stereo—So Let It

By now, you probably have an e-music player on your computer, and you might be wondering why you'd ever need to worry about bringing your home stereo into the e-music mix. The answer is simple: Your home stereo speakers will deliver a better sound quality, and they're easy to set up. This chapter will further explain the benefits of using your home stereo to listen to e-music. Then it will guide you through several methods of linking your computer and stereo.

Your Old Friend, the Stereo

Remember that home stereo you never used to turn off? Remember how you deliberated for months over which set of speakers to buy? You carefully set them up, determined to get the perfect, room-enveloping, crackle-free, rattle-your-bones, blow-your-mind sound. But now, with all your favorite music stored on your computer, you can hardly remember the last time you reached for the stereo remote. It doesn't have to be that way. In fact, it really *shouldn't* be that way.

Computers Don't Cut It

The thing is, your computer wasn't meant to replace your stereo. It can do the job, but it won't excel the way a good stereo system will. Standard computer speakers (the kind that come with your computer system) are functional, but they lack the depth of sound that stereo speakers provide. After all, just a few years back, computer speakers only had to perform the simplest of tasks, such as sounding off error messages or simple computer game music.

What You'll Learn in This Chapter:

- Why you should set up your stereo to play your e-music files

- How you can easily link your stereo to your computer with just one wire

- How to link your computer to your stereo, even if they're rooms apart

- How to adjust your stereo and computer to give optimum sound performance

Another option:
If you decide against linking your stereo and computer, you might want to consider upgrading your computer speakers. Most e-music listeners complain of tinny, substandard sound from built-in speakers.

You could always buy better speakers for your computer, but why not transfer your music duties to the home appliance already built for it: your home stereo? It's easy and cheap.

Are You Good to Go?

Before you link up your systems, you need to make sure that your computer is up to the task. Basically, all your computer needs is a sound card. You can assume that you have a sound card if you've ever heard any audio files come out of your computer (or even the Windows startup music), or if you've bought your system in the last two years. If you're unsure, read Chapter 6, "Equipment Check," to find out more about system hardware.

Wireless versus Wired

There are two ways to link your PC and home stereo: with a wireless signal or with a cable. Wireless is ideal if your computer is stationed several rooms away from your stereo. However, a cable is far less expensive than a wireless device, and some cables reach as far as 300 feet.

Wiring It Up

The only equipment you need for this project is a measuring tape and a cable. Measure the distance between your stereo and PC. This will determine what length of cable you buy. Make sure you buy a few extra feet cable so you can run it along the floor or ceiling. Then it's time to go to the local electronics store. Ask for a cable that has a 1/8-inch mini headphone jack on one end and two dual RCA plugs on the other end.

In my experience:
If you don't see *exactly* what you need immediately, be sure to ask a store employee. This equipment is common, so he'll be able to fill your order easily.

It's all downhill from here; you'll be listening to your Barry Manilow MP3s in surround sound any moment now. Next, go to your stereo and insert the RCA jacks into the back of your receiver. The best place to insert them is the auxiliary input, sometimes called the *phono* input.

Finally, plug the headphone jack into your computer's line output. You should find this on the back of your computer, marked Line Out. (You can also put the headphone jack into the speaker output, but the signal won't be as clean.)

Now you should be wired and ready to go. Turn on your stereo, start up an MP3, and skip to "Sound Advice" later in this chapter to further optimize the sound coming out of your stereo speakers.

Not leaving the house anytime soon? Order your cables online at www. radioshack.com.

Wireless Options

Several products are designed to connect your computer and stereo without wires. Two of the best are the Netplay Radio and MP3Anywhere.

The Netplay Radio costs about $190 and allows you to use the FM radio band on your stereo to broadcast audio files from your PC. With this product, you can also stream an Internet radio station into your backyard boom box or listen to your MP3 collection on radio headphones as you work out in your home gym.

Because Netplay sends out a powerful radio signal, your Walkman, boom box, and home stereo could all be broadcasting the same output at once. You can download the software for Netplay Radio at *www.netplayradio.com*. However, physical components for the system have to be shipped (so much for instant gratification). The installation instructions are easy to follow, though.

New product alert:

Sonicbox (*www.sonicbox. com*) plans to release a wireless product that rivals the options listed here, but the device isn't available yet at the time of this printing.

Choose one of the thousands of commercial-free radio stations listed at Radio365.com, and add it to your radio dial using Netplay.

Now hear this:

Want to share your music with the neighborhood? If you live in an apartment, you might be able to. Because Netplay Radio sends an FM signal that travels over 100 feet, your neighbors can tune to the same station.

MP3Anywhere works a little different than Netplay. Instead of a radio signal, it sends a signal from a wireless sender at your PC to a wireless receiver at the stereo of your choice. You can order it for under $50 at *www.x10.com*, and it comes with a $20 gift certificate for other products. You'd be wise to put that $20 toward a video remote extender kit, which costs $39.95 at the site. This will let you use the universal remote included with MP3Anywhere up to 100 feet away from the sending device, so you can skip, pause, play, or stop an MP3 while standing in front of your stereo.

MP3Anywhere comes with its own set of software for playing and organizing your digital music, but you can also opt to use your own digital audio player (such as Winamp). The MP3Anywhere takes about a week to ship out and includes in-depth instructions, as well as a phone number for 24-hour technical support.

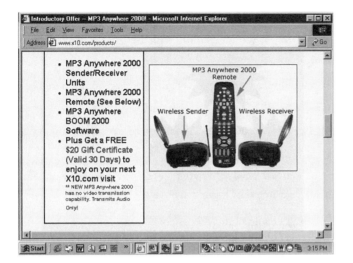

Get a closer look at the MP3Anywhere device and universal remote at www.x10.com/products.

Sound Advice

Now that your PC and stereo are linked, it's time for a little tweaking and fine-tuning. Even the perfect sound settings for music on your computer won't be ideal for a full-bodied home stereo. Adjust the sound on your computer by double-clicking the speaker icon in the lower-right corner of your screen. If you single-click the icon, only one volume bar appears; you must double-click to make the Volume Control window appear. Try turning down the volume levels for CD-Audio, Line-In, and Microphone. This should cut down interference. Now turn the volume up on your stereo and expect a cleaner-sounding "Copacabana."

Help! I Can't Hear Anything!

Here are a few troubleshooting tips:

- Are the volume levels on your PC high enough? Find out by double-clicking the speaker icon and adjusting the Volume Control and Wave levels.

- Is the cable properly connected to the PC? Try the output in another jack, such as Speaker Out.

- Is your stereo in Auxiliary Mode?

- Are you sure you have a sound card? Read Chapter 6 to make sure.

Wrapping It Up

Now that your stereo is jamming with that special playlist you
created:

- Your computer speakers have no business taking over the
  duties of your sacred stereo.

- If you have a sound card, you only need one a cable to connect it to your stereo and CD player.

- You can wirelessly link your stereo and your PC with a mini-
  mal investment of money and time.

- Cutting down on interference between computer audio
  devices by reducing the volume levels will improve the
  sound.

PART IV

Ready to Walk

CHAPTER 16

Take a Walk with Your PMP (Personal Media Player)

Recently I was standing in my local electronics superstore—you know, those places that sell everything from computers to DVD players to TV sets. All around me were gadgets and widgets of every kind, walls of video monitors, and equipment with unreadable manuals translated from Japanese. I think there was even a digital toaster—apparently it plays the radio while it toasts your bread, and it has 37 presets based on your mood.

Besides being assaulted by Muzak (a synthesizer-only version of a Madonna song), I was surrounded on every side by credit card-carrying consumers eagerly buying all sorts of new and exciting gadgets. (Batteries not included.)

The problem was, my own credit card was beginning to twitch. You see, I'd found my way to the portable electronics department. After some eager searching, there they were…the portable MP3 players. The Diamond Rio, the RCA Lyra, the MPMan 20.

Now, there's cool gear, and then there's *really* cool gear. The MP3 portables fall into the second category, without a doubt.

As I stood there, trying to keep my credit card in my wallet but watching my hand pull it out and hand it to the nice salesclerk, one thought was very clear:

I want my MP3.

Then Again, I Might Have Been in a Museum

But when I stopped to think about it, that portable electronics department gave me a different perspective on MP3 players. I

What You'll Learn in This Chapter:

▶ Why today's portable music players are so far ahead of earlier players

▶ The best of the new personal media players

▶ Where personal players are heading

took a look around and saw that portable music players weren't invented in the late '90s.

Goodness no. The MP3 portables are the newest generation, but looking around the store, I saw their many ancestors. There was the portable CD player, whose era reached dazzling heights with the majestic CD Walkman. Going further back, there was the portable cassette player—not too impressive by today's standards, but useful in its day. Going all the way back, I saw the portable transistor radio, which enabled dudes and dudettes to go to the beach and still hear rock 'n' roll. Truly a cool idea.

But today's players—the MP3 portables—have them all beat. Yes, MP3 players might be just the latest generation in portable enter-tainment, but this generation is a quantum leap forward. The rea-son is the selection and availability of content. Users of '90s-style portable CD players might have had 10 racks of new CDs at the local music store. But the MP3 portable user can choose from offerings provided by thousands and thousands of Web sites on the ever-expanding Internet.

And the music is free. Amazing, isn't it? Simply log on to the Internet, surf to one the many sites stocked with downloadable MP3 files, and click on a song you like. It downloads to your hard drive, you download it to your portable player, and you can run around town with your personal playlist at your fingertips. No wonder this has gotten popular.

Minidisc: A Format That's New Again

If you go to your local electronics superstore to shop for an MP3 portable, you'll see units that were once an endangered species: minidisc players. Introduced several years back, minidisc players never gained the mass user base of traditional CD players. These diminutive disc players might have disappeared altogether if not for a recent breath of life.

You used to have to record music onto a minidisc in real-time. This meant it took a half-hour or more to transfer your favorite playlist onto a minidisc. But no more. Like MP3 portables that use flash memory for storage, you can now drag and drop MP3 files onto a minidisc hooked up to your PC. So the newer minidiscs are just as fast and easy to use as the leading flash memory units. And blank minidiscs retail for about $1.50 a piece—a fraction of the cost of a flash memory card. So take a look at the newer minidisc units before you decide which MP3 portable to buy.

One Explosion Creates Another

The massive surge of music downloading has caused a corresponding surge in the development of MP3 portables. In the late
'90s, there was a grand total of one portable MP3 player on the
American market with any name recognition: the Diamond Rio.
The recording industry, justifiably concerned about copyright
issues created by these new players, tried to stop the Rio with
legal action. That attempt at a legal blockade failed, and the
floodgates were opened.

Now the category once dominated by the Rio is rapidly filling up
with portable players. There are multi-functional MP3 players
that contain radios as well. There are players that read CD-ROMs
filled with MP3s. There are players that contain removable hard
drives, and there are players that fit into your car cassette player.
There are wristwatch models, and there are players that use their
own proprietary formats. Sanyo has announced plans for a cell
phone that plays MP3s. And there's a mobile MP3 player by
Casio that also takes photos.

In addition, we still have all the old formats, and they keep on
selling: portable CD players, cassette/CD player/radios, mini
discs, and portable cassette players made for the jogging crowd.
Heck, they still sell portable transistor radios. (Is someone out
there still buying little portable radios? Hello?)

In fact, there are so many portable players out there that this book
can't cover every last one of them. To fully cover this exploding
field would take a book all its own. Instead, this book is going to
concentrate on the newer players that make it easy to take music
from your PC out to play with you.

This chapter will do a roundup of some of these players, looking
at the ones that offer the most promise. (And fun!) The next chapter will look at getting your music into and out of these devices.
And the third chapter in this section will take at look at flash
memory cards, which provide the storage for these compact
portables.

Memory

Most MP3 portables have onboard storage—little memory chips that hold 16 to 64MB (or more) of memory. This onboard storage medium is referred to as *flash memory*. 64MB of flash memory holds about an hour of MP3 music if the files were ripped at 128 kbps (the default setting for MP3). Other players have no onboard memory and rely entirely on removable flash cards (called different names by different companies), which will hold more memory as the technology develops. Still other manufacturers are betting on the small removable hard drive model, which is rapidly developing as this book goes to press. This model will hold quite a bit more music and will be able to play higher-quality sound.

Another format you'll encounter is a player that reads CD-ROMs filled with MP3s. The advantage to this method is that you can fit many more songs in MP3 format on a CD-ROM than will fit on an audio CD. But of course, the player must have a special decoder that can read MP3 files.

Our Roundup of Portable Players

How can a music fan keep up with this rapidly developing new technology? It's much like buying a new PC—you can bet that as soon as you make a purchase, a faster, better unit will show up. Still, it helps to look at what's out there so you'll know where to begin when you're ready to take the plunge. So, here are today's top personal media players.

Diamond Rio 500

The Diamond Rio is a top-selling unit, and it had very little competition until the recent flood of MP3 portables hit the market. To maintain its status as King of the Portables, Rio will need to move in the direction of the rest of the industry and make its MP3 player multi-functional by including a radio or a complete personal organizer.

But hey, if you're looking for a straightforward MP3 player, the Rio is a good one. It's known for its ease of use, and its USB connection makes transferring music to it from your PC efficient and fast. For you book-on-tape fans, the Rio supports Audible.com's narrated text format. And its software works well with

RealJukebox and MusicMatch. It's available in translucent blue or purple, or in the traditional shiny gray.

> Storage: 64MB, expandable to 96MB
>
> Price: $279
>
> Web site: *http://www.riohome.com*
>
> Computer connection: USB port

The Diamond Rio.

Nomad

Manufactured by Creative Labs, known for making great sound cards, the Nomad is a top contender. In mid-2000, Creative plans to introduce the Nomad Jukebox, a portable with a hard drive. At 6GB (yes, that's *gigabytes*), the Jukebox will have enough capacity for almost any mobile music fan.

The Nomad has a sleek magnesium case, which increases its coolness factor exponentially. And it has an FM tuner so you can listen to the radio when you get bored with your MP3 collection. The Nomad also has a tiny voice recorder, so you can look like a Russian double agent while recording a memo about what to pick up at the grocery store.

> Storage: 64MB
>
> Price: $249
>
> Web site: *http://www.nomadworld.com*
>
> Computer connection: Parallel port

The Nomad.

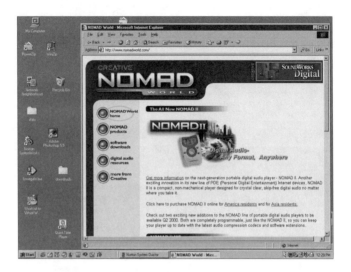

Sony VAIO Music Clip

Sony's entry into the portable market is conveniently small, about
the size and shape of a fat pen. In addition to storing MP3s and
WAVs, it supports Sony's proprietary ATRAC3 format. (Does
Sony really think we *need* another format?) It's got a wide variety
of playback modes, including repeat and random play. All in all,
the Music Clip is a quality product that's going to be around for
awhile.

Storage: 64MB	
Price: $299	
Web site: *http://www.ita.sel.sony.com/products/vmc*	
Computer connection: USB	

MPMan F20

Eiger Labs' introductory model of MPMan received lukewarm
reviews, but the improved F20 gives you a good player at an even
better price. If you're willing to do without frills to save money,
the F20 is a prime choice. It comes in deep black for those book-
on-tape straight-arrow types, but the cobalt blue model will with-
stand style scrutiny from the purple-hair crowd. And there's now
an F30 model, which has more features.

Storage: 32MB

Price: $199

Web site: *http://www.mpman.com*

Computer connection: Parallel Port

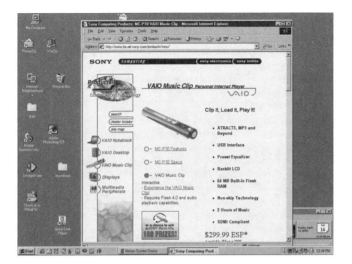

The Sony VAIO Music Clip.

The MPMan.

Frontier Labs Nex

This light and tiny player is determined to be the fashion plate of the MP3 portables. It comes with a dazzling array of removable "skins" in black, silver, red, blue, AlienSkin, ElectricRed, and Zebra Nexskins. Cool, huh? Hey, it worked for the Imac, maybe it will work for Frontier Labs. Not a bad price, and it can be expanded with a memory card.

Storage: 64MB, expandable to 96MB

Price: $239

Web site: *http://www.frontierlabs.com*

Computer connection: Parallel port

The Frontier Labs Nex.

I-Jam MP3 Player

The I-Jam player is a top contender. Its price is about as low as you can go, and it includes an FM radio. No, it doesn't have the memory capability that some other players have, but it has a pretty snazzy color choice: LA Orange, Lemon Drop, or Purple Haze. If I was going to buy a portable, I'd consider this unit.

Storage: 32MB

Price: $199

Web site: *http://www.ijamworld.com*

Computer connection: Parallel port

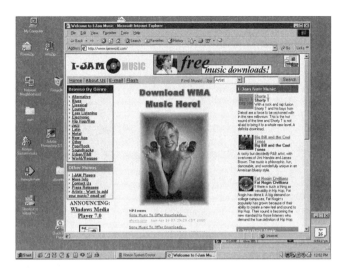

The I-Jam Player.

When You're Ready to Shop

Head to your local electronics store to take a close look at the MP3 portable players. But before you buy, take the time to shop online and find the best prices. Start your comparison shopping at some of these Web sites:

Supreme Video and Electronics
http://www.supremevideo.net

Mobshop
http://www.mobshop.com

800.com Electronics and More
http://www.800.com

Computers4Sure
http://www.computers4sure.com

WorldSpy
http://www.worldspy.com

More Audio Video
http://www.moreaudiovideo.com

TurboPrice
http://www.turboprice.com

Pontis SP503

This player, originally called the Mplayer3, is slightly larger than some of the others. The nicest feature of the Pontis is its cross-platform compatibility: whether you run Mac, Linux, or any type of Windows, the Pontis can sing in your language. Its memory is limited, but its price is nice. Plus, it's got a matte-black finish that gives it an elegant look.

Storage: 8-16MB

Price: $199

Web site: *http://www.pontis.de/*

Computer connection: Serial port

The Pontis SP503.

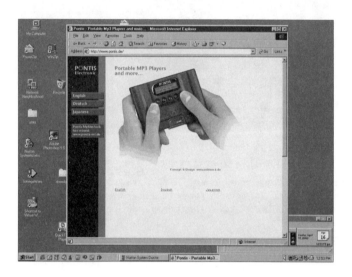

i2Go eGo Car

No, I don't totally understand this unit's awkward name either, but it's one hot player. The i2Go is great in both form and function: It's got a handy hip clip, windshield and visor mounts, a cassette adapter for car use, and an external speaker (some players just have headphone jacks). The LCD display gets brighter in daylight and is backlit at night. And the i2Go reads your email to you and lets you reply by recording in your own voice. The memory is expandable to a category-crushing 680MB. A great choice.

Storage: 64MB, expandable to 680MB

Price: $269

Web site: *http://www.i2go.com*

Computer connection: USB

The i2Go eGo Car.

RFC jazPiper

Yes, it's an MP3 player, but in keeping with the direction the industry is going, it's also more. If you decide to compose a letter in the park, you can use the Piper's voice recorder. And if you meet someone interesting while you're there, the Piper lets you store up to 250 phone numbers. No, the memory isn't huge, but the price is one of the best in the industry.

Storage: 32MB	
Price: $189	
Web site: *http://www.jazpiper.nl*	
Computer connection: Parallel port	

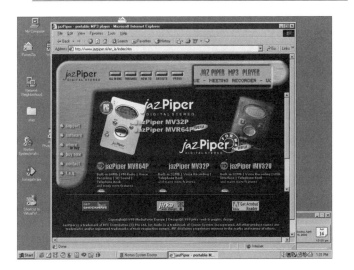

The RFC jazPiper.

Lyra

RCA's offering in the MP3 portable market is designed around format flexibility, so you can download various software plug-ins to read a wide variety of formats. It will play RealNetworks G2 files as well as MP3s. And this platform flexibility will allow it to keep up with ever-changing music formats. If you expand to 64MB of memory, you also get the car kit.

Storage: 32MB, expandable to 64MB
Price: $199
Web site: *http://www.lyrazone.com*
Computer connection: Parallel port

The RCA Lyra.

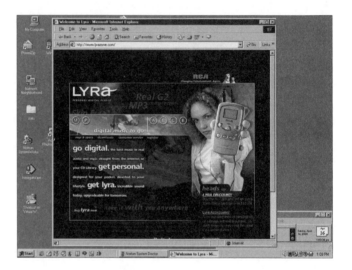

RaveMP

Manufactured by Sensory Science, this compact MP3 player also records voice memos and can store 64,000 phone numbers. (Does anyone have that many phone numbers?) As a nice touch, the ear-buds it comes with are made by esteemed audio manufacturer Sennheiser.

Storage: 64MB, expandable to 96MB
Price: $209
Web site: *http://www.ravemp.com/ravehome.html*
Computer connection: Parallel port

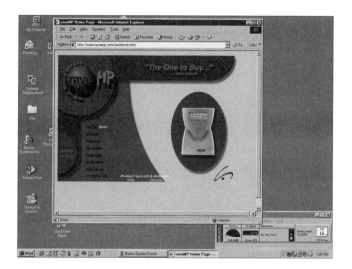

The RaveMP.

Audiovox MP1000

Audiovox's cheapest model, the MP1000, is a good entry-level player. You can spend more for an Audiovox—the 64MB version goes for $239, and the top-of-the-line MP3000 (with USB or parallel port connection) retails for $279. But this basic unit wins honorable mention for its rock-bottom price and perfectly adequate features, including record and playback capability, PC compatibility, and storage space for a half-hour of high-quality MP3s.

Storage: 32MB

Price: $179

Web site: *http://www.audiovox.com*

Computer connection: Parallel port

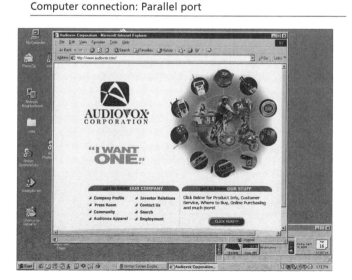

Audiovox.com.

Samsung Yepp64

Considering that the Yepp64 is offered by the electronics giant Samsung, it could be more of a standout unit than it is. It has many of the typical features, such as voice recording and a telephone number organizer. It's a perfectly good MP3 player, but it's priced near the top and has little to set it apart. Its choice of colors is—yawn—teal, blue, or silver.

Storage: 64MB

Price: $279

Web site: *http://www.samsungyepp.com/yepp64.html*

Computer connection: Parallel port

The Samsung Yepp64.

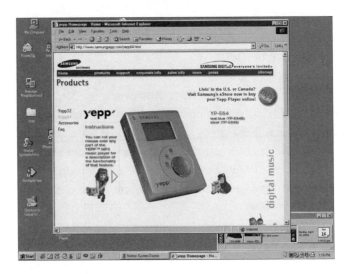

Unitech Rome

This portable from Unitech Electronics has an exceptionally inventive design: It's identical in size and shape to an audio cassette. So when you're on foot, you can use the earbuds, and when you're in the car, you can pop the Rome into your cassette player to pump MP3 tunes through your car speakers.

Storage: 32MB, expandable to 64MB

Price: $279

Web site: *http://www.mp-3.co.kr/*

Computer connection: Parallel port

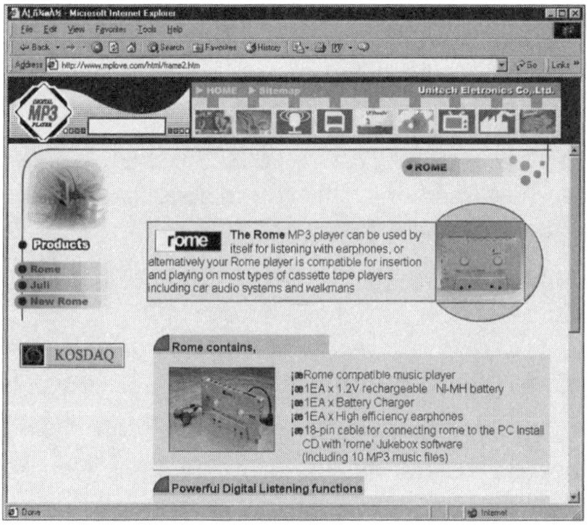

The Rome.

Casio's Casiopeia E-105

This entry is an odd fit in the MP3 player category, but it's an example of where the industry is heading. The Casiopeia is designed for the Windows CE Palmtop, which wasn't originally intended as a music player. As such, the sound quality is lower than most MP3 players—but then, this unit is a complete personal organizer as well. As a further example of where things are headed, Casio is also coming out with a wristwatch MP3 player with 32MB of memory that will retail for around $250. Windows CE owners can find a broad array of MP3 player software at *http://www.utopiasoft.com*.

Storage: 32MB

Price: $599

Web site: *http://www.casio.com*

Computer connection: Docking cradle connected to serial port

The Future of MP3 Portables

If you're a gadget nut, you'll find a lot to be excited about in the next few years. From its humble beginnings with the Rio, the personal media player will continue to change and grow, getting ever more sophisticated—and popular. Here are a few developments to watch for:

- **Portable hard drives**   As mentioned, most of today's popular players use flash memory cards. The compact size of flash
  memory makes it perfect for portables, but expect hard drive
  technology to continue its exponential slope upward and
  replace flash memory. This will increase storage enormously.
  Nomad's Jukebox ($599) is an example, and look for another
  such unit called Personal Jukebox from Remote Solutions
  ($799).

- **The Data Player Portable**   As home CD writers become
  more prevalent, more manufacturers will introduce players
  that decode CD-ROMs. You'll simply dump your MP3 files
  onto a CD-ROM from your desktop computer, pop the CD-
  ROM into a player that can decode MP3 files, and off
  you'll go.

- **Convergence**   MP3 players will become incorporated into a
  wide variety of entertainment platforms. Expect portable and
  home-based MP3 players to converge with CD, DVD, radio,
  and cassette players.

Wrapping It Up

Okay, you're on your mountain bike, traveling about 57 miles an
hour, downhill through the middle of a huge forest. But as you
dodge right, left, right, avoiding major collisions, you're still listening to the latest release from the Insane Tree Huggers—thanks
to your personal media player. Let's stop the bike for a second—
whoa, watch out for that tree—and look at what you've learned in
this chapter:

- You learned that today's media players have a major advantage over earlier players—the enormous choice of music
  offered by the Net.

- You surveyed many of today's best personal media players,
  learning about the features of each one.

- You took a look into the not-too-distant future, when many
  players will be able to handle many formats—CD, DVD,
  and MP3.

CHAPTER 17

Managing Your PMP

So, you've taken the plunge. You went out and purchased a shiny new portable media player. You've ripped open the package, which is about eight times bigger than the unit itself, and there it is. Cool.

After you get over that initial feeling—"Why did I spend $200 on something this small?"—you'll probably have a number of powerful emotions.

You'll want to take it on a long bike ride, you'll want to bring it to work, and you'll want to show it to friends. You won't want to go anywhere without it. You'll look forward to never having to leave your music at home.

But there's a problem. This bright and shiny new player is totally silent. Right out of the box, there isn't a bit of music on it. It's the neatest little thing in the world, but at the moment it's making as much music as the Great Wall of China.

You look at your computer—that's where all your music files are, neatly arranged in playlists you spent weeks creating. You look at your MP3 portable—this is where you want all your music files to be. You'd like to arrange a meeting between your computer and your portable, a meeting in which all those great tunes were transferred from one to the other. But where to begin?

What You'll Learn in This Chapter:

- ► How to load your personal media player with songs
- ► How to use MusicMatch Jukebox to coordinate your at-home listening with your on-the-go listening
- ► Hints for general care and feeding of your portable
- ► The need for compatibility in your digital music center

WearableGear. com is full of links about portable music players. You'll also find information about everything from new gadgets for mobile workers to articles about underwater keyboards. And don't miss the section on Beepware.

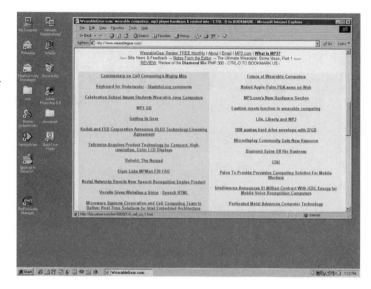

The Road to Rio

Where to begin depends on what player you've chosen. In today's wide open market, with new players introduced every month, it could be one of a dozen or more. You might have a Mini-Disc, which is turning out to be a popular choice, or you might have a Nomad II, a sleek portable with a radio built in. Heck, you might have an old-fashioned portable CD player, and if you've got a CD writer with your PC, you can always create fresh mix discs. There are all sorts of choices—some say too many—for today's music fan on the run.

It's beyond the scope of this book to look at every one, so we will take a look at the unit that started it all, which continues to be a major player in the player market: the Diamond Rio.

More specifically, the Rio 500, which can be found at *www. riohome.com*. This most recent player by Diamond has taken the leap forward into Mac compatibility. And, it interfaces well with MusicMatch Jukebox, the MP3/CD-R software that comes with this book. In addition, many of the techniques used by the Rio are common to many players.

The Diamond Rio 500 continues to be a leading MP3 player. This newest Rio is compatible with Mac as well as Windows.

Industry analysts expect future MP3 portable players to play only copyright-protected files. As this trend develops, you'll see hybrid players that can play both copyright-protected and illegal files.

All Right, Let's Rip Open the Package!

I'm happy to report that the single AA battery needed to run the Rio 500 is included, so there's no need to delay gratification. Put that battery in, and you'll see the pretty blue light momentarily light up, informing you that you have 64MB (megabytes) of memory (that's about an hour of MP3s).

Use the USB connecting cable to connect the player with your computer. After the player is connected, turn it on—it needs to be "awake" for you to install its software.

Now put the Rio Installation CD into your CD-ROM drive. It will launch automatically. If not, open My Computer and double-click on your CD-ROM drive icon. When the Installation disc opens, double-click on the Setup.exe file.

When you've finished with installation, you'll see the RioPort Audio Manager. Click on the Devices button, and the Manager will look for your Rio. After the Manager software recognizes the Rio, it will automatically download the operating software to the player.

At this point, you're finished with set up. It was easy, huh? I have to give the Rio's designers credit for making the process simple and efficient. It's almost the easiest computer install I've ever done.

The Diamond Rio has a reputation for being user-friendly.

By the way, the printed manual that comes with the Rio—all two pages of it—leaves something to be desired. However, click on the Help button, and you'll find extensive guidance on all sorts of Rio topics.

The RioPort Manager

As soon as I saw the RioPort Manager all fired up and ready to go, I clicked on Playlist. I knew I hadn't imported any songs yet, but I could hardly wait. The RioPort gave me the response seen in the following figure.

If you try to play music before you've loaded any, you'll get the dreaded Database Is Empty dialog.

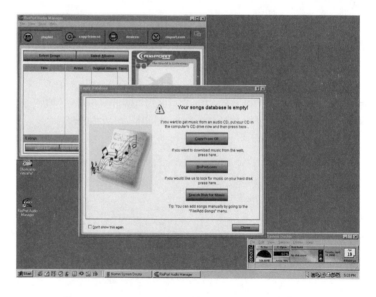

You need to add songs to the Manager's playlist before you can load your Rio. The Manager gives you three options to fill the playlist. You can copy music from a CD, connect to the Web and download files, or browse your hard drive for files. So the Manager integrates the three main methods of acquiring music for your portable in one easy-to-navigate tool.

The Four Modes of the RioPort Manager

Look across the top of the Manager software and you'll see the
four different ways the Rio can be used, each of which helps you
manage your personal media player.

Playlist

Click on Playlist to see the songs in your playlist. All the songs in
this list can either be listened to or copied to your Rio. If you've
got audio files on your hard drive that you'd like to get into your
playlist, the Manager gives you two choices:

- **Click on File, Search Hard Disks for Songs**—This scans
  your entire hard drive for audio files, creating a list of every
  audio file you have. You might even find files you forgot
  you had.

- **Click on File, Add Song**—This method enables you to
  browse through your hard drive, adding songs from whatever
  folders you choose.

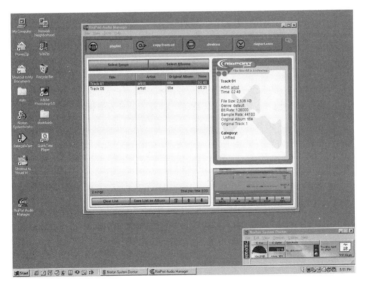

*You'll want to fill
up the RioPort
Manager's playlist
so that you can
copy those songs
to your portable.*

Copy From CD

Click on the Copy from CD button, and—if you have a disc in
your drive—you'll see all the CD's tracks and lengths. If you're
connected to the Internet, the online database CDDB will auto-

matically supply the artist and song title. (That is, if the information is in the CDDB's database. If not, you can type in the song information yourself.)

To select which songs you'd like to copy from the CD, put a check mark in that song's Tag box, or click Tag All. Notice that when you make a selection, the Manager lets you know how much computer space is required to copy that track onto your hard drive.

The RioPort Audio Manager makes it easy to turn tracks from CDs into MP3s.

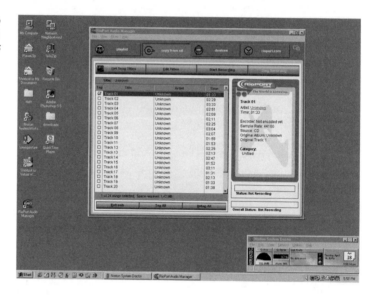

Because you can copy music from a CD in either WAV or MP3 format, you want to make sure that you're copying in MP3 format—this compressed format takes up only one-tenth of the memory.

The exception to this is if you plan to burn a CD. In that case, you want to keep the music in CD quality WAV format. But realize that if you want to copy an entire CD this way, you will need hundreds of megabytes of free space on your hard drive. To copy songs from CD in WAV format, click on View and choose Options, Read CD. In the Record File As dialog box, choose WAV. (The default is MP3.)

Devices

When you're ready to copy songs from your hard drive to the Rio, click on Devices. The Copy to Portable bar becomes visible. To copy songs to your Rio, put a check mark in the Tag box, and click Copy to Portable. Notice how much faster the music transfers than if you were dubbing music to a tape. Typically, copying a five minute song to your portable takes much less than a minute.

Rioport.com

In my opinion this button is misnamed. Clicking here takes you to the Manager's built-in mini-browser, allowing you to access any site on the Internet. And yes, the default Web site is Rioport.com (where you'll find plenty of offers to buy music) .

Use the Rioport.com Web portal to surf to some of the most popular MP3 file swapping sites, like Napster (*http://www.napster.com*) or CuteMX (*http://www.cutemx.com*).

But you can click on the Rioport.com button and type in *any* Web address. So use this built-in browser to access, for example, MP3.com, to surf over to MP3Central.com, or visit MTV.com—it's a big world out there. That said, Rioport.com is a great feature that enables an easy and efficient transfer of MP3s from the Web to your Rio.

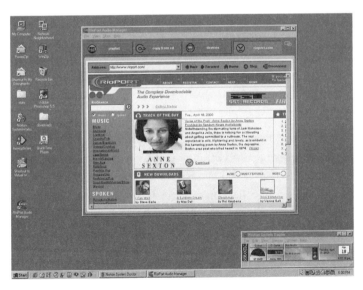

The Manager's Rioport.com feature is a mini browser. Use it to help download MP3 files from anywhere on the Web.

Managing Playlists on Your Portable

Say that you're about to go skydiving, and you're taking your Rio with you, but you want all new songs in your Rio's playlist. The group of songs that powered you through your marathon mountain bike ride won't work at 5,000 feet.

Make sure that your Rio is connected to your PC, and click on Devices. You'll see all the songs currently on your Rio in the song list on the right. Any changes you make in this playlist will change the playlist on the Rio.

Click on the RioPort Manager's Devices button, and the Copy to Portable bar becomes functional.

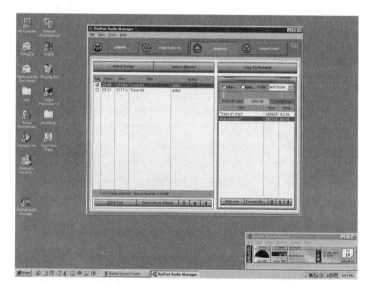

The Manager provides you with a number of ways to change and rearrange your Rio's playlist.

- Use the Internal and External buttons to switch the view between your Rio's built-in memory and any extra memory cards you have. You might have several memory cards, each with its own collection of songs (the "I'm happy" collection, the "I'm mellow" collection, and so on). Use the Refresh button when you put a new memory card in so that the Manager displays the current playlist.

- To move a highlighted song up in the playlist, click on the Up arrow. Use the Down arrow to move it later in the list.

- Click on the trashcan icon to remove a selected song from the list.

- If you want to wipe a memory card clean and add all new songs, click on the Format Media button (shortened to Format Me… on the button's face).

Some MP3 fans are fanatical about creating playlists. I know one frequent downloader who has over 85 different playlists.

The MusicMatch Jukebox Connection: PC to Portable

MusicMatch Jukebox has become one of the leading programs for today's PC music enthusiast—it seems to turn up everywhere audio files are used. This popular program is included on the CD-ROM that comes with this book. It's useful for copying music from CDs, organizing and playing MP3s, and writing CDs. It will also help you record old records and tapes onto your computer, although there's better software for this (see Chapter 20, "Teach Old Dogs New Tricks (Analog to Digital)").

MusicMatch can communicate with your Rio—its Copy To Portable feature allows you to copy a MusicMatch playlist onto your portable. And, this MusicMatch feature works with other leading portables: RCA's Lyra, Creative's Nomad, and Memcorp's SoulMate.

To use the MusicMatch's Copy to Portable feature, you have to download a plug in from the MusicMatch Web site. Before you groan, "No, not another plug-in," rest assured of two key facts—first, it's free, and second, all you have to do is click on the Web link, wait a few moments, and you're up and running. Downloading this plug-in adds an important choice to the MusicMatch Options menu: Send to Device.

To copy your MusicMatch playlist to your Rio, click on Options, and choose Send to Device, Download Playlist to Rio. You'll see the Download to Rio dialog box, with the songs in your MusicMatch playlist on the left and the Rio's destination folders on the right.

Go to the Plug-in section of the MusicMatch Web site to download the Send to Device plug-in.

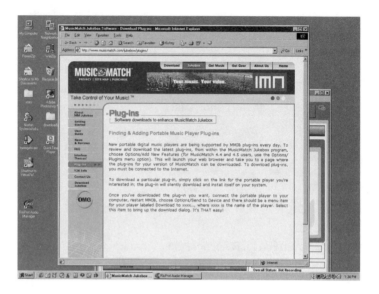

Notice the small box in the upper left, Bitrate Limit. This truly handy feature lets you convert the bitrate of your MP3s as you copy them to your portable. The default bitrate setting for MP3s is 128Kbps. This is considered a CD quality MP3. But if you make the setting smaller—which decreases the sound quality— you can fit more songs on your portable. So you can choose to limit your bitrate setting to 128, 96, 64, or 32Kbps. You'll be able to squeeze twice as many songs on your portable at 64Kbps as 128 (about two hours on a 64MB flash memory card). Again, though, the music won't sound as good at this lower setting.

> If you want to know how good an MP3 can sound, try saving it at 320Kbps. Be aware, though, that this will make the file size larger than the default 128Kbps setting.

The nice thing about this feature is that the MP3s on your hard drive are unaffected. Only the files you copy to your portable are at the lower setting.

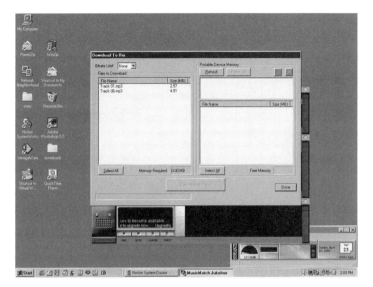

*The MusicMatch
Download to Rio
dialog box lets
you change the
bitrate of your
MP3s as you copy
them to your
portable.*

Equalization Controls

Just about all portables offer some form of control over equalization, also called EQ. To equalize music is to turn up or down its high or low end to create a better sound. Equalization, at its most sophisticated, allows enormous controls over a song's sound quality.

Like many of the portables, the Rio simplifies EQ by offering preset options for Classic, Jazz and Rock, and Custom. (What, there's a preset for Classical but none for Urban or Hip Hop? Do the designers at Diamond think the MP3 crowd is downloading Mozart's 40th?)

To access the Rio 500's EQ controls, press the Multi button on the side of the unit. The Multi button is, as the name suggests, multifunctional, and you can either rotate it or press it. Impressive, huh?

> If you want to use the EQ controls to make a song sound brighter, turn up the 1KHz to 3KHz range.

Press Multi and you'll get a choice between EQ or Backlight.
Rotate the button to highlight EQ, and press again. Rotate the button to highlight your desired preset, or choose Custom. Pressing
Custom gives independent control over Treble and Bass, each on
a scale of 1 to 10. If you're looking for that missing Hip Hop setting, turn up the bass to about 6, and leave the treble alone. Those
bass lines will be thumpin'.

A Note About Batteries:

Here's an unlikely scenario: Say that you aren't going to use your
portable for several days or even weeks—I know, you plan on listening
every day, but say that you give it a rest. In this case, it's a good idea to
take the batteries out of your unit. Leaving them in the unit can cause a
slow drain of battery power, even when the unit isn't making music.
And in the worst case scenario, batteries left in for months can leak battery acid, causing your portable music player to be as silent as the Grand
Canyon. Quite disappointing.

By the way, if you're going to burn through a lot of batteries, it's
cheaper to buy rechargeable batteries. Yes, I know they're more expensive at first, but if you're going to be a serious portable user (and I know
you are), it's less money out of your pocket over a long term. Also,
rechargeables are better for this planet we live on—you know, reduce,
reuse, recycle.

*If you want to
shop for gear for
your portable—or
a new unit—
MySimon.com is a
good place to
start.*

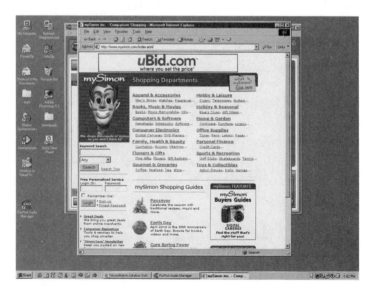

And Then There's That Pesky Cable

When you get home from the store with your new portable and tear open all the excess packaging, you'll see something you want to take very good care of: the connecting cable.

Hang on to this cable.

The many brands of portables require different types of connecting cables, but many are hard to find separate from a new unit. They are much harder to find than many of the connectors that are necessary for home electronics. In fact I called some big electronic suppliers looking for a portable MP3 player connecting cable, and was told, "Nope, we don't have 'em."

Perhaps by the time you read this, the industry will have caught on. But for the moment, hang on to your cable. If you lose it, it might require a lot of effort to find a new one.

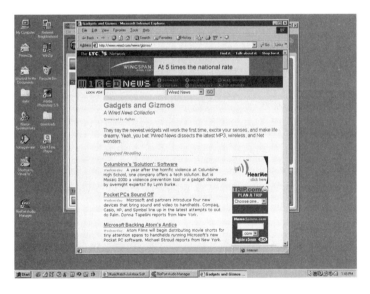

One of the best places to keep up with the ever changing world of portable music players is the Gizmos and Gadgets section of Wired.com. Visit the site at http://www.wired.com/news/gizmos.

Putting It All Together: The Future

Notice that as we looked at managing your portable, we saw that these handy music players are clearly not standalone devices. In this chapter alone, we saw two different pieces of software that can communicate with your portable. There's also the hard drive connection: Being able to dump your files stored on your PC quickly and easily makes these portables much more popular. Of course, your PC has a CD-ROM drive, which connects your portable to the library of music on CD.

So your portable is the latest link in an even more connected digital music universe. The stereo system used to be the focal point of the music fans world; it's rapidly shifting to the PC, if it isn't already there.

What all this interconnection means for the portable user is that compatibility is key. As you continue using your portable, consider upgrading, or buying a new unit—or your first unit—think in terms of connectivity. Will this new player/upgrade/software communicate with the rest of my system?

The RCA Lyra, for example, is designed to handle new software updates, so it's positioned to handle unforeseen technological developments. The Pontis SP503 is compatible with not only the Windows operating system but also Mac and Linux. The i2go has an expandable memory to 680MB—this gives it some staying power. I'm not necessarily recommending any of these units, but these are the types of features to look for as you acquire more gear, or purchase add-ons to your existing portable.

The bottom line is that things will change rapidly. As they do, you should manage your portable with an eye toward maintaining a long-lived connection with everything in your overall system.

Wrapping It Up

You're getting ready to go out—maybe a long hike, maybe mountain climbing—and you're copying songs from your hard drive to your portable. You've gotten to the point in which you can't go anywhere without your music. That's understandable. Before you hit the road, we will look at what was covered in this chapter.

- We looked at how to copy a playlist from a hard drive to a Diamond Rio.

- We used MusicMatch Jukebox to make our favorite at-home music our favorite on-the-go music.

- I talked about how helpful it is to hang on to that connecting cable that comes with your portable, and I also discussed battery usage.

- I talked about how interconnected all the aspects of the PC-music collection have become and how key it is to keep this interconnection in mind as you continue to use your portable.

CHAPTER 18

PMP Power with Memory Cards

As manufacturers have rushed to market with personal media players, all manner of portable storage media has developed— SmartMedia, CompactFlash, memory stick, multimedia card, microdrive, minidisk, and portable hard drive. Yes, many of the newer devices use SmartMedia, but that's really only the beginning. As you can see from the list, the choices are plentiful. And they are only becoming more so.

It would have been nice if the manufacturers developed a single standard, perhaps an inexpensive card, useable in all players, that could be switched and swapped easily. Yes, that would have been nice, but it isn't so.

The fundamental problem, of course, is caused by the smallness of the portable players. How do you store dozens of CD quality song files on something that fits in the palm of your hand? Your PC has a hard drive, but hey, do you really want to carry a PC on a camping trip? Do you want to take your PC to the beach?

So manufacturers have been forced to find storage technology that is small and lightweight, has no moving parts (less likely to skip when jogging), and can be powered by a small battery. And these storage devices, like a hard drive, need to be able to store information even when the power is turned off.

What You'll Learn in This Chapter:

▶ How memory cards for personal media players have evolved

▶ What some of the challenges are for manufacturers in developing memory storage for players

• What the various choices are for memory choices

▶ Some future possibilities for portable memory storage

*The Personal
Computer
Memory Card
International
Association
(PCMCIA) is a
compendium of
resources about
the growing field
of memory cards.
Visit them at
http://www.
pcmcia.org.*

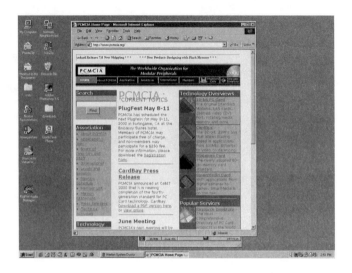

Let's take a look at what they've come up with so far.

SmartMedia

SmartMedia, which is used by the Diamond Rio, is the leader of the pack for portable MP3 players. These small removable storage cards are used by quite a few of the original MP3 players. Originally designed as storage for other portable digital devices (like cameras) SmartMedia cards are simply constructed and very simple to use. Unlike CompactFlash, they have no onboard circuitry.

You can find SmartMedia cards in sizes ranging from 8 to 64MB (megabyte). The 64MB card is enough space to store about one hour of music if your MP3s are at the default setting of 128kbps. You can squeeze your songs down to 80kbps to fit about 40 percent more on a card, although this gives your music a "portable cassette" sound.

Some SmartMedia users collect a number of storage cards and use them like a portable album collection—one card for each part of their music collection. That way they can put a new card in whenever they leave the house, or take a few with them on an extended trip.

If you're ready to shop for SmartMedia cards, visit the Digital Camera Center at *www.digital-camera-center.com*. There you'll find a wide array of these storage cards.

However, this quickly gets expensive. A 64MB card can cost— hang on to your hat—about $100. This expense is one of the major criticisms of this type of storage media. Either this cost will come down (likely), or there will be an industry move away from SmartMedia.

This expense, too, is why many SmartMedia users have only one extra card, and continually add and replace songs to that card. (Fortunately many of the portables have built-in memory, so you don't need any extra cards if you're strapped for cash.) This refor-matting is a bit of a hassle, but that's life in this transition period of portable players.

By the way, you might be thinking, "I've got some flash cards for my camera, I'll just use them." Be aware that the Rio, for exam-ple, uses proprietary formatting so that once you use a memory card in the Rio, you must reformat it again to use it in your camera.

CompactFlash

Introduced in 1994, CompactFlash (*www.compactflash.org*) is used by some of the newer MP3 portables, notably the RCA Lyra. It's also used in many of the newer digital cameras.

CF cards are available in two sizes, Type I and Type II. Type II, the thicker of the two, has a greater storage capacity, holding up to 160MB. Type I, most commonly used for MP3 portables, holds up to 128MB. Interestingly, you can use a Type I card in a Type II slot, but you can't fit a Type II card in a Type I slot. A call to my local electronics store informed me that a 32MB Type II Card goes for $90, and a 16MB Type I retails for around $55. So CompactFlash, like SmartMedia, is quite pricey.

The Compact Flash Association is a non-profit group dedicated to maintaining the CF format.

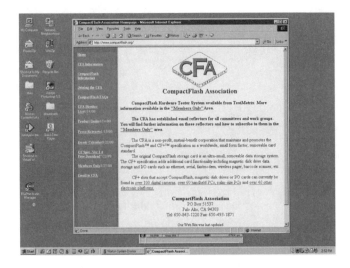

But the nice feature of CF cards is that they can be used like little removable hard drives. MP3 files can be copied to or removed from CF cards without special software. Because they contain the necessary controller circuitry, any portable player designed to use CF cards can use any brand. There are no problems with proprietary formatting with these handy storage cards.

Check out the Simpletech Web site (at *www.simpletech.com/ flash/intro.htm*)—there's a lot to read there.

The Flash section of the Simpletech Web site provides plenty of background about flash storage.

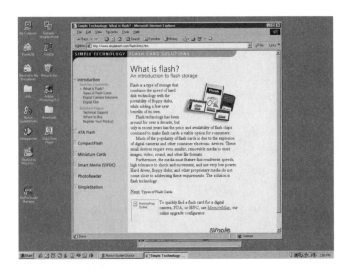

The MiniDisc

You might be wondering, why include the minidisc? Didn't these mini-CDs disappear a few years ago? The answer is yes, it wasn't a favored format for a while, but it's back in style and bigger than ever, actually.

Walk into your local electronics store and the salesperson might tell you that the minidisc, by Sony and other companies, is a cheaper alternative than portables using flash memory. You can buy a blank minidisc that holds an album's worth of songs for only $1.50. Compare that with a 64MB SmartMedia for about $100, and you can see why the minidisc is hot.

Because of the MiniDisc's new found compatibility with the MP3 format, expect it to remain a popular selling item.

Until recently, there was a drawback to the minidisc format. Music was stored on them as audio tracks, similar to the way it would be on a standard CD. This meant copying music onto a minidisc was like making a dub onto a cassette tape—slow and time-consuming. And if you wanted to change the order of the songs, you'd have to copy all the songs over again.

However, Sony has recently introduced a minidisc player that allows the same style drag-and-drop file transfer as many flash memory MP3 portables. It comes with a USB 1/8-inch mini-plug connecting cable, allowing you all the flexibility and speed of, say, the Rio. Take a look at *http://www.sel.sony.com/SEL/ consumer/md/prods_portables.html*.

This development promises to make big waves in the portable MP3 world. With minidisc storage only a fraction of the cost of flash memory, and now with the its expanded capabilities, expect minidiscs to sell well.

*Expect the
portable minidiscs
by Sony to be top
sellers.*

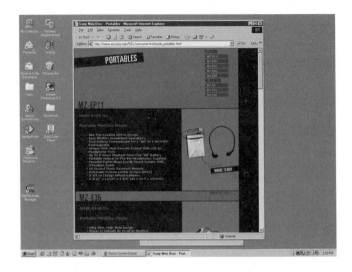

Memory Stick

Introduced by Sony in 1998, the Memory Stick holds 4 to 64MB
of flash memory, with larger capacities out soon. The attractive
feature of these gum-stick sized storage units is that they are compatible with a large array of (Sony) devices. So you can easily
dump your MP3 or other music files from PC to laptop to
portable music player. By summer of 2000, Sony plans on having
28 Memory Stick compatible devices, from digital camcorders to
voice recorders and—of course—portable audio players.

> While the Memory Stick can be an expensive option, the fact that it's mar-
> keted by Sony means that it may gain an extensive user base.

But you'll pay for this high-end interoperability. A 64MB
Memory Stick retails in the neighborhood of $200. Some predict
that this same 64MB will fall to $5 within five years. And that's
clearly necessary if Memory Sticks are to be universally popular,
regardless of their universal connectivity.

The easiest way to find out about it on the Web is to go the Sony
Web site (Sony.com) and type Memory Stick in the search box.

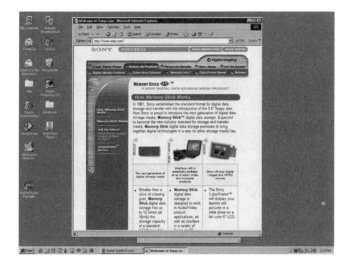

The advantage of the Memory Stick is that it will transfer files to and from many devices, including music players.

Secure Digital Card

SD Cards are in many ways similar to Memory Sticks. Jointly introduced by Panasonic, Toshiba, and San Disk, SD Cards are also compatible with a wide array of digital devices. Expect to see SD cards in everything from cellular phones to MP3 portables.

As the name suggest, SD cards support copyright protection for artists as detailed by the Secure Digital Music Initiative (SDMI). (The Memory Stick also supports SDMI.) Many industry watchers are hoping this copyright protection will greatly facilitate Web-based sales of music and video.

Similar to the Memory Stick, SD Cards are expensive, in the $200 range for 64MB. Considering the similarities between these two storage systems, it looks as if there will be head-to-head competition between them. However, if files from one are transferable to the other—entirely possible—they might both gain a significant user base. Read the press release of this new format at *http://www.panasonic.com/MECA/press_releases/ sdmedia_99.08.25.html.*

*The copyright
protection that's
afforded SD Cards
might facilitate
the distribution of
major label audio
and video.*

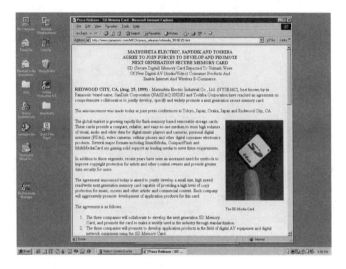

Portable Hard Drives...

Music players incorporating fully portable hard drives have been slow to come to market for a variety of reasons. They require more power than the typical flash memory portable does—you can't power a hard drive with an AA battery. And, it isn't yet possible to offer a mini hard drive player at a price that competes with, say, the Rio.

But the advantages are obvious. Nomad expects to introduce the Jukebox in summer of 2000, with a 6GB hard drive that will hold about 150 CDs of music. This fanny pack sized player will have a USB port for easy transfer from your home hard drive, and will retail for $599. The South Korean manufacturer Hango (which does business in the U.S. as Remote Solutions) offers its Personal Jukebox for $799. The Jukebox's 2-inch, 4GB hard drive holds about 81 hours of music.

> At one time it would have taken a device the size of your refrigerator to store 4GB. Now it can fit into your hand.

IBM's entry into this growing market is the Microdrive (*www.ibm.com/storage/microdrive*). This tiny portable hard drive is about the size of a large coin, and holds a whopping (for a portable) 340MB, or about six times the built-in capacity of the Rio 500. I've read that Diamond Multimedia expects to introduce a Rio that uses a Microdrive, but I haven't seen any sign of it. The Microdrive, with a PC Card adapter for a standard PC slot, retails in the neighborhood of $499.

As you can see, the portable hard drives are pricey, but have a storage capacity that dwarfs flash memory. And, a portable equipped with a hard drive could be a mini workstation, allowing you to change song order, even edit songs, as you would on your home PC. As hard drive prices fall, which is inevitable, expect to see more portable MP3 players with mini (and not so mini) hard drives.

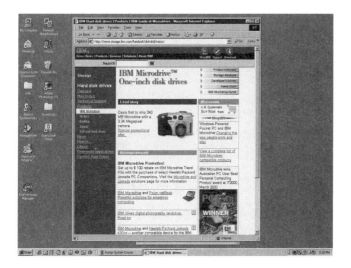

Yes, the IBM Microdrive is small—but it holds a lot: 340MB.

...and Beyond

Similar to the Web in its earliest days, memory for MP3 portables is in a period of rapid—some might say chaotic—development. There are many contenders: flash memory, the minidisk, the Memory Stick, Secure Cards, and portable hard drives. It's far from clear which memory storage system will be the winner. It isn't even clear which will exist: an environment with a single standard or many competing standards.

If a winner is to emerge, it will be the system that combines ease of use (perhaps the more important criteria) with low cost, high storage capacity, and plenty of extra features. Long term, my guess is that the portable hard drives will beat the competition. They will have computing power that, for example, minidisks don't have. And they will eventually become cheap, small, and travel-ready enough to become an extremely popular choice.

> If advances in portable storage continue, one day you'll be able to carry your entire music collection with you at all times.

The other issue looming large for portable manufacturers is the issue of copyright security. With current negotiations taking place for the development of SDMI (Secure Digital Music Initiative), hardware manufacturers are being asked to develop portables that can only store or play secure files. The questions this raises for portables are numerous and thorny. Should the portable even be able to load nonsecure (possibly illegal) files into its memory? What about the portables already on the market that can play illegally copied music? How can portables that can only accept secure files hope to compete with portables whose memory accepts all files?

One choice that might gain great acceptance develops the MP3 portable's potential in a completely different direction. But the winner for storage system might be wireless. In other words, you could use your wireless MP3 portable to access a large database of music from servers distributed throughout the country. So a portable's storage method becomes secondary.

In a sense, this is a return to the radio model, but with a quantum leap. A wireless portable dedicated to playing MP3 (or other music format) is a quantum leap over radio because you can shuffle and play the songs as you like. User choice would be first and foremost. And it's user choice, after all, that has been a central force in the creation of the MP3 revolution.

At this moment in time, in fact for the next couple of years, it looks as if the keyword for portables will be transition. Don't expect to see a clear solution to the memory question too soon.

Instead, expect to see new portable devices, with new combinations of storage and capability, introduced on a regular basis. The only thing you can be sure of is as soon as you buy an MP3 portable, a better and cheaper one will be on the market in about 90 days.

If you're thinking of taking the plunge into the ever-changing world of MP3 portables, take a look at *http://www.mp3shopping.com/english/mp3players.htm.*

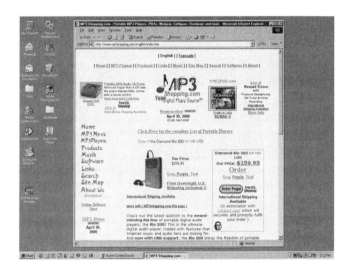

Check out the new product announcements at MP3Shopping.com.

Wrapping It Up

So, you're thinking about buying a portable, and you're considering all your options. You want to buy one with a memory storage system that will last longer than the life of a fruit fly. Should you buy one with flash memory, or should you go with Sony's Memory Stick? What about choosing the portable hard drive model?

If you're like me, as you realize there's a blizzard of choices, a feeling of confusion sets in. That's understandable—portables are going through a rapid period of transition in which it's difficult to know what memory storage system will become the leader. But let's put that confusion aside for a moment, and look at what you learned in this chapter.

- I discussed some of the difficulties facing manufacturers in developing memory storage for portable MP3 players.

- We looked at how memory storage for personal media players is evolving and changing.

- We went through the various choices for portable music player memory.

- We took a look at some future possibilities for portable memory storage, knowing that still more methods are being developed.

PART V

Make Your Own

CHAPTER 19

Let 'Er Rip! Make CDs into MP3s

I'm Guessing You've Heard...

In case you've been stuck on a desert island, totally cut off from the Web's biggest developments, MP3 has become wildly popular in the last few years. At one point, "MP3" was a more popular term on search engines than "sex." Now *that's* popular.

As noted previously, MP3.com is the epicenter of the MP3 universe. But there are thousands of sites that provide MP3 music files. Enter "MP3" into any search engine and you'll find MP3s of every conceivable style of music, as well as reams of information and opinion about MP3 software and hardware.

Of course, MP3 mania wouldn't be possible if it was difficult to create these files. In fact, creating and playing MP3s is only slightly more difficult than playing CDs.

Let's take a look at what you'll need to get started.

> To the audio purist, the MP3 version of a song doesn't sound as good as it did on CD. Compressing the music to one-tenth of its original size takes away a certain sparkle. But who cares about being a purist when you've got tunes playing? Heck, this is rock 'n' roll, this is funk, this is hip-hop—who cares about a few missing megabytes?

MP3 or Bust: Software and Hardware

To be an active member of the MP3 revolution, you need two things: a computer with an internal CD-ROM drive and software that rips and encodes MP3s.

What You'll Learn in This Chapter

- How to make an MP3 from a CD
- How to make an MP3 from a WAV file or other audio file
- How to make a WAV file from a CD
- Some special techniques to make your MP3s sound better
- MP3 jargon like *ripper, encoder,* and *bitrate*
- How skins can be used to personalize your MP3 software

Visit mtv.com and enter "MP3" in the search box. You'll find dozens of up-to-date links about MP3.

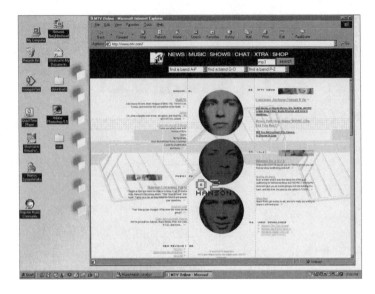

A *ripper* takes the audio from the CD and creates a separate audio file, usually a WAV. An *encoder* converts this WAV into an MP3. Until recently, MP3 fans needed two different pieces of software for these two processes. But today's modern encoders do both at the same time. In one step, an encoder rips the audio from the CD and encodes it into an MP3. These days, when someone refers to an MP3 encoder, they're usually referring to software that both rips and encodes. An MP3 encoder is doing a lot of work. It's performing a type of compression known as *lossy* compression. As the name suggests, the original file loses data in its journey from CD to MP3. What's amazing about the MP3 compression scheme is that these compressed files sound almost as good as CDs. They don't have the rich bottom end or the bright high end, but they sound surprisingly good. This is impressive, considering how much smaller an MP3 file is than a CD audio file.

> The smart folks who are responsible for this major step forward in music compression, Motion Picture Experts Group (MPEG), can be found on the Web at *http://www.mpeg.org*. MPEG developed the standards that led to this compression technology. The full name for MP3 is Motion Picture Experts Group 1, Layer 3.

Winamp is one of the original MP3 programs, and it's still one of the most popular. It's a player only—you can't rip MP3s with it.

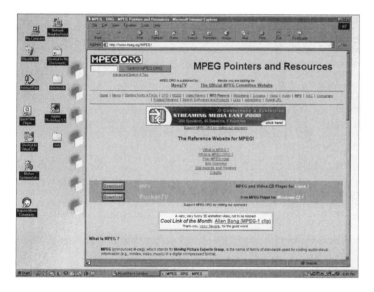

At mpeg.org, be prepared for some long technical explanations. These people get excited about compression!

One Encoder, Please

Before we take a look at some of the most popular encoders, let's look at some facts about encoders:

- Some MP3 players are just that—players. You can't rip MP3s with them. It's a good idea to get a multipurpose program that not only plays but rips and encodes in one step.

- Some encoders are much more than encoders—they're complete music organization systems. Called *jukeboxes*, they turn your music collection into an easily accessed database, allowing you to organize hundreds of songs for quick recall. The best encoders also include equalization so you can turn up the high or low end.

- Not all encoders encode equally. Think about how tough the encoder's job is—it has to squeeze a 10MB file into 1MB and still produce a pleasant-sounding audio file. Some encoders make better-sounding MP3s than others, although much of this is a matter of opinion. When you become an MP3 expert, you can make statements like, "I really like the bottom end produced by the so-and-so encoder."

- Some encoders will let you encode *on-the-fly*. That is, you can play the song off the CD and encode while listening. Although this is very convenient, it's not the best way to encode MP3s. You'll get a better-sounding MP3 if you don't play the CD while you're encoding. This lets the software take its time.

- Most encoders let you choose the bitrate before encoding. You can choose from 96Kbps, 128Kbps, 320Kbps, or some other number. *Kbps* stands for *kilobits per second*. Setting a higher bitrate creates a higher-quality MP3, but it also creates a larger file—not good if you don't want people to wait for download. At the very low bitrates, your file is small but your music sounds like it's coming over the telephone. A good default setting is 128Kbps, which is close to CD quality.

- Depending on the speed of your CD-ROM and your computer, your encoder may be able to work faster than real-time. If you have a newer computer, you may be able to copy a five-minute song in less than a minute.

- Many encoders are available in both free and "pro" versions. Typically, the free version can't record a CD-quality MP3, or it will only perform a limited number of encodes. This is changing, though, and you shouldn't be surprised to see more companies offering high-quality, all-in-one ripper/encoders for free. We'll see.

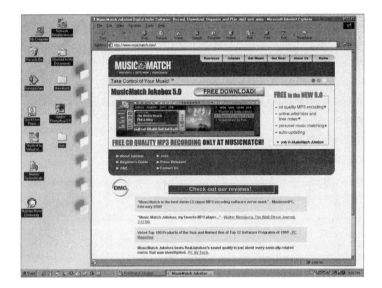

Musicmatch.com offers its high-quality MP3 program for free. You can buy the retail version for $29.99.

The Encoders Honor Roll

Before you go hunting for MP3 software on the Web, you should realize that new programs come out at a rapid rate. It's relatively easy for a knowledgeable programmer to write an MP3 application. At this rate, soon there will be more programs than Britney Spears has screaming teenage fans.

So the following is a list of some of the top encoders—but don't stop your hunt for the best encoder with this group.

MusicMatch (included on this book's CD-ROM— *http://www.musicmatch.com*

MusicMatch has taken the unusual step of offering its CD-quality encoder for free. (Most companies consider this to be the "pro" version and charge for it.) MusicMatch has the distinct advantage of being heavily recommended by MP3.com, so it's one of the most popular MP3 programs. And it's a good one. It's much more than an encoder and player—it's a complete jukebox that helps you turn your music collection into an easily sorted and accessed database. As if that weren't enough, it also supports CD burning.

Xing Audio Catalyst—*http://www.xingtech.com*

Xingtech offers both Mac and Windows versions—which is rare in the Windows-centric world of MP3, unfortunately. And this program is packed with capabilities. You can set start and stop points for recording, and you can *normalize* your music files, which helps keep all songs at the same volume. Audio Catalyst can record from 32 to 320Kbps. (If you can actually hear something recorded at 32Kbps, I'm impressed.) Xingtech offers a free trial version that's much less capable than the retail version, which goes for $29.95

RealJukebox—*http://www.real.com*

This multipurpose encoder/player is brought to you by the people who developed RealAudio, which is still the Web's dominant streaming media player. A useful feature of RealJukebox is that it can play many different audio formats—not just MP3s. Also, RealJukebox will create RealAudio files from CD, which is even more useful as streaming audio becomes more popular. And it organizes your music collection into a readily accessed jukebox. The demo is free, and the retail version is $29.99.

Real.com is well worth a visit. Home to RealJukebox, this highly popular site is full of resources about streaming audio.

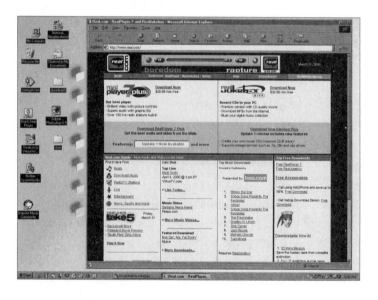

RioPort Audio Manager—*http://www.rioport.com*

The makers of the Diamond Rio portable MP3 player offer this player/encoder for Mac or Windows. It's easy to use, it lets you load MP3s onto the Diamond Rio, and it supports encoding rates from 64 to 256Kbps. It comes free with the Diamond Rio, and it retails for $9.95 if you buy it separately.

Visiosonic—*http://www.pcdj.com*

The most interesting feature of this player/encoder for Windows is that you can play two MP3s at once and cross-fade between them like a club DJ. The PCDJ Mixmaster version is $29.99, and the basic version (which can't encode) is free.

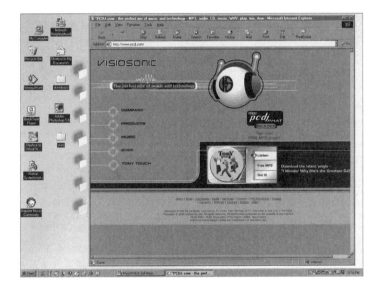

The pcdj.com site is where you'll find Visiosonic, the MP3 player for today's modern mixmaster.

Before Blastoff: Your CD-ROM Drive

Okay, there's good news and bad news.

First, the bad news—not all CD-ROM drives can rip audio. If your CD-ROM drive doesn't support Digital Audio Extraction (DAE), an MP3 program can't read data directly from the drive.

The good news—almost all CD-ROM drives *do* support DAE. Yours probably does too. And even if it doesn't, there's still a way to encode MP3s with it. The CD-ROM drive will route the sound through your sound card, converting it to analog before encoding it as MP3. (The MusicMatch MP3 program does this automatically.) This will slightly decrease your MP3's sound quality, but it's not too bad.

Your CD-ROM drive's speed will have a big impact on the encoding process. A fast drive can dramatically speed up encoding, especially if you're encoding a big batch of songs. If you get really serious about encoding but you have an older CD-ROM drive, you might consider buying a faster external unit.

Bottom line: If you have a CD-ROM drive, you most likely have what you need.

> As of this writing, it's estimated that 14 million Americans have downloaded music from the Internet.

Rippin' a WAV with MusicMatch Jukebox

Now the excitement begins—that is, if you've installed the free MusicMatch MP3 software that's included in this book's CD-ROM. After installation, simply double-click the MusicMatch icon on your desktop.

The first time you run MusicMatch, make sure there's an audio CD in your CD-ROM drive. The program will perform a short test on your drive the first time it boots up.

After the test, right-click on the top bar of the Recorder window and choose Recorder, Quality, WAV Format. Right-click again, choose Recorder, Source, and specify your CD drive as the recording source.

Let the ripping begin!. Notice the Recorder bar on the MusicMatch Jukebox—you can click here or on Options to make your recording selections.

Recorder bar

At this point, make sure your computer is connected to the Internet. If it is, MusicMatch will automatically connect to an online database called CDDB. The CDDB Web site sends back song information about the CD in your drive: album name, artist,

and song title. It adds a tag with this information to your MP3.
Pretty nifty, huh?

However, CDDB can only add tags if the CD's information is in
its database. If the CD that you're encoding from is your band's
first demo, CDDB won't be able to add the tags. However, you
can still type in the information yourself. Go ahead and do
this now.

Select individual tracks to rip by checking the box next to the
track name. Click Record and—voilà!—you're now ripping.

Be aware that your song may not play perfectly if you're
encoding while listening. If your song is starting and stopping,
it means your computer is so busy encoding that it can't play the
CD properly. Don't worry, the WAV file will play back properly
when you're finished encoding. After you've finished your first
rip, locate where MusicMatch put the WAV file on your hard
drive. Right-click the top Recorder bar and select Recorder,
Settings to bring up the Options dialog box. Click on the
Recorder tab, and then click Songs Directory. Browse through the
files to locate the WAV you just ripped. See it? You're ready to
continue.

The Ear Test

Are any of your friends audiophiles? Here's a quick and easy test to see
who has the most discriminating ears. Play a song off a CD, and then
play the MP3 of the song. Play both versions through your computer's
speakers. Can your friends tell which is which? The test becomes more
difficult if you're playing the music at medium to low volume. Set up
several CD and MP3 versions back to back to make it a comprehensive
ear exam.

Or, to Make Your Life Easier...

You can take this WAV you just ripped and encode it into an
MP3. That's been standard procedure since the dawn of the MP3
era (in other words, since the mid '90s). However, with
MusicMatch and many newer encoders, MP3 creation doesn't
have to be a two-step procedure. MusicMatch can encode from
your CD directly to MP3.

So let's look at one-step encoding. Remember, if this is the first time you've booted up MusicMatch, it will perform a test on your CD-ROM drive. Make sure you have a CD in the drive.

First, choose your encoding options. Click Options and choose Recorder, Settings. You'll have a choice of bitrate, ranging from 8Kbps to 320Kbps. This choice will determine how good your MP3s will sound—the higher the Kbps, the better.

The MusicMatch Settings box lets you choose the bitrate, as well as many other recording options.

Default bitrate setting

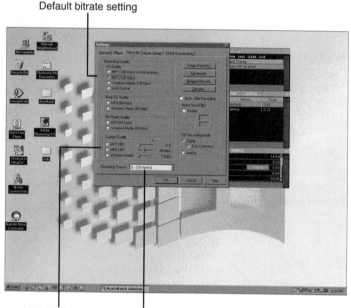

Variable bitrate   Recording Source

As noted elsewhere, Kbps is a measurement of data rate. If you're not sure which rate to choose, select 128Kbps—that's the default MP3 setting. Choose 96Kbps if you need your files to be smaller, but be aware that this will lessen the sound quality. If you love this song and want it to sound its absolute best, choose 320Kbps. Just be aware that the file size will be very large.

You'll see a choice called VBR, which stands for *variable bitrate*. You can set this between 1% (lowest quality) and 100% (the very best). VBR allows the software to allocate more memory if required. For example, if a section of a song has a lot of rapid volume changes or many instruments creating a complex texture, VBR will allocate more memory for these passages so that they still sound good after being compressed. This is why VBR files tend to be larger (although if the music requires less memory, VBR files can be smaller). Not all players will play VBR MP3s.

Or, you can compress your files using CBR, or *constant bitrate*. This is the default choice, and most MP3s are compressed with it. This lets you choose your own bitrate, from 8 to 320Kbps. Again, 128Kbps is the best choice, and it's a preset near the top of the dialog box. CBR is helpful if you need to make small files and you're willing to go down to 70 to 80Kbps. If sound quality isn't critical or your file is voice only, this is okay. (By the way, if you have nothing better to do, chose 8Kbps. This is what computer audio sounded like in the early '90s. Pretty awful.)

As when you ripped a WAV, choose your CD-ROM drive as the recording source. In Recording mode, select Digital—this tells MusicMatch that it will be encoding information directly off the CD. Put a check in the Error Correction box—this tells the software not to add any noises created by a misreading of the CD data. Error correction makes encoding take longer, but your MP3s will sound better.

Next, click the Record button on the Player window to open the Record window. You'll see a list with the album and the artist on the left and the song titles on the right. If the song titles aren't there, make sure you're connected to the Internet and click Refresh. MusicMatch will access the CDDB Web site for the names. Remember, if CDDB doesn't have the information in its online database, you can type in your own information. Do this now.

You can enter
song, artist, and
album informa-
tion in the
MusicMatch
Record window.

Artist

Album title   Song title

Put a check next to each track you want to encode as an MP3. Or, if you want to encode the entire batch of songs, check All. (Make sure you have enough disk space for all those files.)

Click on Record to begin encoding. Congratulations! You're now encoding an MP3, the music format that has changed the music industry forever.

To play the MP3 you just encoded, double-click on it in the music library. Enjoy!

But What About That WAV You Ripped?

You might ask, "If I can rip and encode in one step, why would I want to first rip a WAV and then encode it?"

Good question—and there are a couple of good answers. First, you might want to edit your music. Maybe it's a recording of your first piano recital, and you want to edit out that section where you completely forgot what notes to play (highly recommended). Or maybe the music isn't on CD in the first place—perhaps a friend sent you a WAV. Either way, you're in luck because MP3 software is designed to encode WAV files.

In MusicMatch, click on Options and choose File, Convert. Select WAV as the source data type. (Many encoders allow you to encode from a variety of audio file types. Just make sure you choose the right file type before encoding.) Browse through your hard drive until you find the WAV you want, and then click on it so that it's highlighted. Again, you'll need to choose a bitrate. Remember, 128Kbps is the most common and is considered CD-quality. Choose a destination folder for the encoded MP3, click Record, and let your computer do the encoding. Congratulations! You're now a member of the MP3 revolution.

Source Directory　　Destination Directory

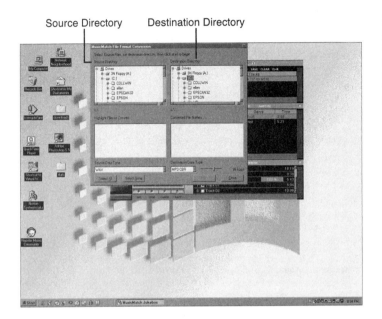

Select the WAV you want to convert in the MusicMatch File Format Conversion window.

Your MP3s Can Sound Better Than Your Friends'

Although making MP3s is pretty straightforward, there are a few insider's tips that can give your files an extra edge. If nothing else, the following tips should provide you with some obscure technical jargon. Not only will your music sound better, but you'll be able to use terms your friends don't understand. Cool!

- **Encoding Speed**　Some encoders let you choose the speed of the encoding process. The slower encoding speed is worth waiting for—it will take a few minutes longer, but your music will always sound better. And it's vastly preferable to choose the slower speed if you want the files you encode at lower bitrates (less than 128Kbps) to sound good.

- **Stereo Mode**　Your encoder may give you a choice called *joint stereo*. Some aspects of a stereo recording are duplicated on both the right and left side. The joint stereo encoding method takes advantage of this duplication to make smaller size files. However, this lessens the richness of the stereo image, so it's better to choose normal stereo mode.

- **Filtering**   Sometimes called frequency reduction, filtering cuts off all of the high-end frequencies—anything above 10KHz to 12KHz. Yes, it does make the file size smaller, but c'mon, we music fans want our bright high end. I don't recommend using filtering.

- **Error Correction**   If your encoding program offers error correction, use it. Encoding will take longer, but you'll have fewer problems with unwanted noises in your songs.

Skins are a rapidly growing Internet phenomenon. It seems as if there are more options to personalize your music software all the time, and there are many sites that can help you.

Start your search at *http://www.winamp.com*. There you'll find thousands of wild skins. Also take a look though the selection at *http://skins.sonique. com*. And you'll find many of the latest styles at *http://www.mp3.com/skins*.

To find skins for instant messengers as well as audio players, visit *http://www.dezina.com*. The SkinKing at *http://www.skinking.com* offers interfaces for ICQ Plus, Winamp, and others. And don't miss *http://www. skinz.org* for additional skins and desktop decorations. Go wild!

Skins—When You're Ready to Be In with the In-Crowd

There are casual MP3 fans, and then there are the real MP3 aficionados. To figure out which camp you're in, ask yourself this question: "Does my MP3 player have its own skin?"

If you answer "Yes," breathe a sigh of relief. You're a true member of the MP3 revolution. If your answer is "What's a skin?", we need to talk.

A *skin* is a personalized interface for your MP3 player. You can give your MP3 player its own look, from bright Day-Glo green to wild psychedelic to Space Invader chic. You can pick out what you want, mix and match, and give your player a look that reflects your distinct personality. (That is, if you *have* a distinct personality. If you don't, hey, just copy someone else's.)

MP3 programs are among the few software applications that let you personalize them in this way. For example, Microsoft Word is going to look the way that the good folks at Microsoft designed it to look, and that's that. But the MP3 crowd has a distinctly individualistic slant, is Net-savvy and comfortable with technology, and isn't inclined to follow the corporate cookie-cutter approach.

So explore making your own skin. Be aware that not all players support skins, but some players have thousands of skins designed for them. The venerable Winamp player has been around since the beginning and has the most skins. There are also quite a few available for Sonique. Skin developers are turning out new skins all the time.

Now, how about a leopard skin pattern done in bright yellow and purple...

Wrapping It Up

As you sit listening to your recently encoded MP3, probably blaring at full-blast (yeah!), let's look at the information you ripped and encoded in this chapter:

- You learned why this new compression scheme called MP3 has caused such excitement among music fans—it makes music easy and fast to upload and download.

- You went step by step through the process of making a song on CD into a WAV and then an MP3, including the best settings to use.

- You learned about the encoding options for MP3 encoding. The higher an MP3's bitrate, the better it sounds—but larger bitrates create larger files. The default MP3 bitrate is 128Kbps. VBR stands for variable bitrate, an advanced MP3 compression scheme that not all players can play.

- You learned about MusicMatch Jukebox, an all-in-one MP3 ripper/encoder that's included on this book's CD-ROM.

- You explored the world of skins, the personalized interface for your MP3 players. Skins give your player a distinctly individual look.

CHAPTER 20

Teach Old Dogs New Tricks (Analog to Digital)

So, you've got a pile of old cassette tapes, some old records (it's okay, vinyl albums *used* to be cool), and maybe even an ancient 8-track cassette. Hey, don't laugh, someday they'll be collector's items! You want to keep listening to the music on these old relics, but you wish it were more convenient. If the music was on CD, you could go from track to track without having to rewind. If the songs were MP3s, you could organize them into playlists that you could hear at the click of a mouse. If those old tunes were WAV files, you could edit them and cut out the stuff you didn't want—like that 20-minute guitar solo you've never liked.

Well, there's hope. You can turn all that old music into MP3s, CDs, or WAV files. But first you have to gather up all those tapes and records and *digitize* them.

There are a lot of great audio resources at Webmonkey. Visit the audio section of the site at *http://hotwired.lycos.com/webmonkey/audio_mp3/*.

Digitize Them?

Although digitizing audio sounds high-tech, it's not very complicated. When you digitize audio, you turn previously recorded sound—tapes and records—into computer files. The music that once lived on a vinyl album will live happily on your computer's hard drive. And once it's there, you can do all sorts of fun things with it.

Digital audio is drastically different than analog audio (records and tapes). Analog recording adds a layer of hiss to audio, and when you copy from tape to tape, you add still more hiss. Digital sound is completely free of this unwanted hiss.

What You'll Learn in This Chapter

- ▶ How to turn your tapes and records into digital sound files
- ▶ What equipment you'll need for digitizing
- ▶ How to use various software options
- ▶ How to improve the sound quality of your files using the Normalize and Equalize options
- ▶ What file formats to use to make your file sizes smaller

Webmonkey,
which is part of
hotwired.com, has
an excellent arti-
cle about digitiz-
ing tapes and
records.

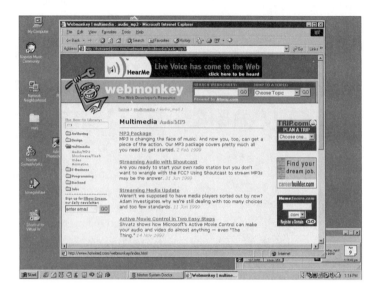

When you digitize your analog sound, you'll still have the hiss,
but you don't add more. Digitizing creates a crystal-clear audio
"snapshot" of the sound. (This also means it faithfully reproduces
the flaws of the original recording.)

Homerecording.
com is dedicated
to helping the
home audio
enthusiast.

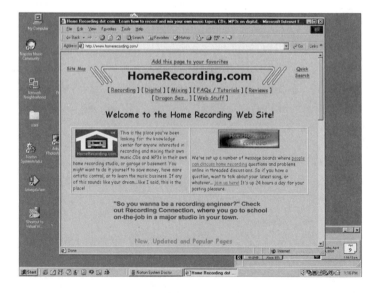

Digital sound can be manipulated in ways that analog sound can't
touch. You can raise the volume on a track, or a section of a track,

with a couple of mouse clicks. You can slow it down, speed it up, warp it, add all sorts of reverb and effects, and change pitch without changing tempo. You can archive music so you don't lose it when the analog tape rots away. And although you can't remove all the analog hiss and pops from your old tapes, digital software can minimize them.

Perhaps best of all, you can turn computer sound files into CDs and MP3s, you can put them up on the Web, and you can email them to friends.

Alright, let's get digitizing!

> **Getting the Gear:**
> Online stores that sell audio hardware and software are popping up all the time, so it's worth the time to shop around.

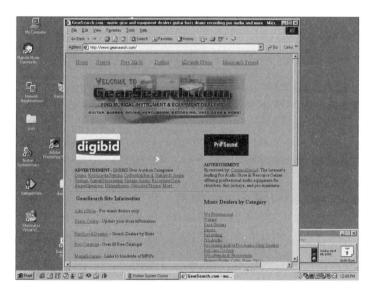

When you're ready to start digitizing, Gearsearch.com is a good place to begin your online hunt for the needed gear.

What You'll Need

Although digitizing audio is far from complicated, it does require some basic gear. One of the frustrations of this simple process is getting midway through and realizing you don't have what you need. So before you begin, you're going to need the following:

- **Plenty of disk space**   If your hard drive is almost out of space, you'll need to clear it off. Audio files eat up a *lot* of room—one minute of CD-quality audio eats up 10 megabytes.

- **Sound card**   Most PCs come with them. Unless you're planning on doing a lot of high-end recording, your PC's built-in card should be fine.

- **Audio recording software**   There are several inexpensive options, and some that are not so inexpensive. I'll discuss some choices later in this chapter.

- **Playback deck**   This is the unit you'll use to play that cassette tape, vinyl album, minidisc, or DAT (digital audio tape). To function as a playback deck, a unit must have a *line out jack* into which you can insert a connecting cable to send a signal out to your computer.

- **Connecting cables**   These connect your tape deck (or turntable, 8-track player, and so on) to your computer. Getting the right cables is one of life's little difficulties. I'll go through some possibilities later in the chapter.

- **A microphone**   You'll only need a mic if you want to record your voice or other natural sound. Again, many PCs come with a built-in mic, which is fine for casual use. If you want to take a step up, you can buy one at the local electronics store for about $50.

Tips for Buying a Microphone:

Even a low-end mic will give you significantly better sound than your computer's built-in mic, so it's worth the expense. Inexpensive mics come in two categories, the low end and the *really* low end.

I was pleasantly surprised to find a microphone for $9.99 at my local electronics store. I didn't try it out, but it seemed to have the basics. This ultra-cheap model came with a three-foot cord and a mini-plug jack to connect it to a computer. Like most cheap microphones, it won't record the high end. (This one stopped at 10Khz, and human hearing goes up to 20Khz.) And it's only capable of omnidirectional recording, which mean it picks up sound in a complete circle around itself.

If you're willing to spend $30 to $60, you can get a mic that will record in a *cardiod* pattern, which means it focuses on what's directly in front of it. This makes recordings quieter and cleaner. In addition, these slightly more expensive mics will record up to 15Khz, so you capture more of the high end that gives a recording its brightness.

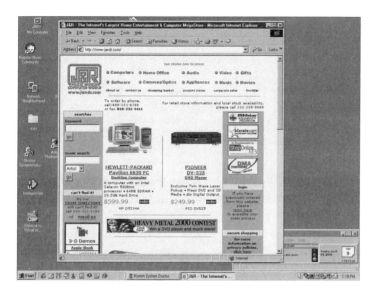

When you're shopping for equipment online, J and R is well worth a visit. This megastore's inventory is immense.

Cables: A Pain in the, Ah, Neck

If I had a dime for every minute I've spent searching for the right cables for a task, I'd be featured on *Lifestyles of the Rich and Famous*. The difficulty here is that connectors come in many different sizes—$\frac{1}{4}$-inch, miniplug, RCA, TT, XLR—and every cable has a male and female version.

What size cable will *you* need? Take a look at the back of your sound card and the back (or top) of your playback deck. What sizes are the input and output connections? The size is rarely labeled, unfortunately, but there are a few common guidelines.

Most sound cards require a $\frac{1}{8}$-inch plug, commonly called a *miniplug*—the same size as the headphones for a portable CD player or one of the less expensive cassette players. So if you're digitizing audio from one of these smaller units, you'll need a cable that has a miniplug on both ends, sometimes called a *miniplug to miniplug*.

Some cassette and CD players have two RCA outputs, one for the left side of the stereo image and one for the right side. In this case, you'll need a cable with two RCA plugs on one end and a miniplug on the other, called a *stereo RCA to miniplug*.

In most other cases, some variation of these two cables will get you connected. It's helpful to own a few *adapters*, which are small input/output connectors that can change an RCA plug to a miniplug, for example.

If your playback deck is something more exotic, like a reel-to-reel tape machine or a DAT deck, you may need adapters that change a quarter-inch plug to a miniplug, or an XLR plug to an RCA plug.

If you're digitizing from a turntable, you'll need a device called an *external preamp* to boost the turntable's output volume. You can pick one up for about $35. Without this boost, the turntable's output will hardly register on your sound card. If you don't want to spend the $35, you can connect the turntable's output to an amplifier and then connect the amp's output to your sound card. (Careful—start with very low volume. You could damage your sound card by sending an excessive signal.)

You can find all of this connecting gear at your local electronics store. The people who work there get a lot of questions about adapters and cables, so no question is too basic to ask.

Shareware Wonders:

The Shareware Music Machine is a treasure trove of inexpensive audio shareware. Surf to *http://www.hitsquad.com/smm/*.

When you're ready to start digitizing, the Shareware Music Machine is a good place to look for software.

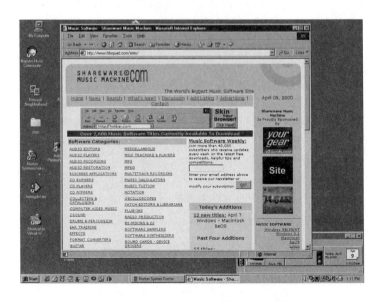

Audio Recording Software

Audio software has risen to an amazing level in the last 10 years
or so. Today's top audio applications can do nearly anything
you'd ever want to do to sound. Visit your local movie theater and
listen to the spaceships whoosh, the ocean liners break up, and
the orchestras swell. Although creating this cutting-edge sound
requires highly skilled sound designers (with "Titanic" budgets),
the latest advances in audio software give these designers the
tools they need.

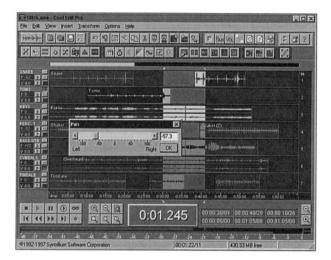

*Today's audio
software gives
sound designers
the flexibility they
need to create
stunning sound-
tracks.*

Even desktop audio software can do things that would have been
unthinkable just a few years back. For under $500, you can pur-
chase an audio recording program that not only records and edits,
but plays dozens of tracks simultaneously, adds effects like
reverb, chorus, and delay, and runs in sync with a video deck.
Pretty hot stuff! Especially for under $500. This much capability
used to cost thousands. It's this improvement in inexpensive audio
recording software that has enabled so many music enthusiasts to
build great home studios.

*The capabilities
offered by today's
desktop audio
software used to
cost thousands of
dollars.*

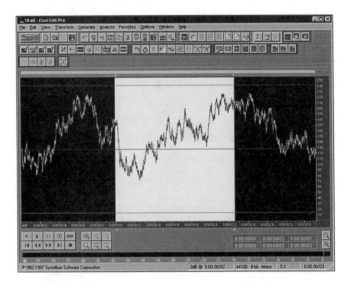

Of course, for your purposes, it's certainly not necessary to spend $500 on software. Some perfectly adequate programs are shareware, and many computers come with a basic audio program already installed. Most of these are fine for basic digitizing. Let's take a look at some simple and inexpensive solutions.

Digitizing with MusicMatch Jukebox

MusicMatch, one of the software programs included on the CD that came with this book, can be used for basic audio digitizing.

However, MusicMatch can't edit sound files. Yes, you can record a CD with audio you've digitized with MusicMatch, and it's great for making MP3s. But if you're digitizing audio from records or tapes, you're probably going to want to trim the silence before each song and optimize your files (more on this later). Because of this, it's best to use recording software that's designed for editing.

Okay, I've given my warning, but suppose you're not a purist. You want to digitize some audio, and you want to do it right now. (So you get in a hurry like me, huh?) Yes, MusicMatch might leave a couple of seconds of silence before each song, but hey—the software is right in your hands, you don't have to hunt the Web for it, and you don't have to pay anything extra for it.

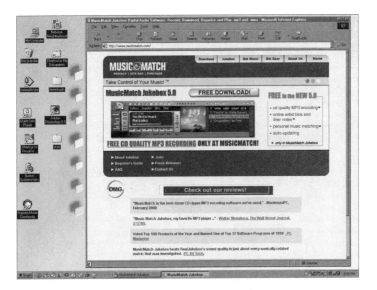

MusicMatch Jukebox is included on the CD that comes with this book.

Let's take a look at digitizing an audio cassette with MusicMatch.

The first time you boot up MusicMatch, make sure there's an audio CD in your CD-ROM drive. The program will perform a short test on your drive the first time it runs. Even if you're not recording from an internal drive, MusicMatch seems to want to complete this test.

After the test, right-click on the top bar of the Recorder window and select Recording, Settings from the pop-up menu. In the Options dialog box, click the WAV option under Format.

Keep the Options window open. Click Song Directory to bring up a dialog box that lets you select the destination folder for the WAV.

You'll see some other options. Choose 44.1 for the sample rate and 16-bit for the bit depth. This is CD-quality audio. Unless you're really low on hard drive space, it's always best to record at the highest quality. Click OK when you're done with the dialog box.

Right-click again on the Recorder bar and choose Recorder, Source, Line In. This lets the software know that signal is coming from an external analog source. If you're recording from a microphone, choose Mic In.

*Use the
MusicMatch
Settings window
to choose the des-
tination folder for
the WAV you're
recording.*

(By the way, if you're recording with a microphone, you may want to turn down your computer's speakers to avoid feedback.)

You'll want to name your songs before recording. Type in the album, artist, and song title in the track information box. Remember what you're calling each cut—it will come in handy when you want to find it later.

Use the connecting cables discussed in the previous section to send signal from your tape deck to your computer. It's a good thing you got all those cables together ahead of time. (You *did* get the cables, didn't you?)

Important: Before you begin to record, make sure the volume on your tape deck is turned down to a safe level. High volume could produce a distorted recording—or even damage your sound card.

Click the MusicMatch Record button and start your tape deck. (Don't click Record until your tape deck is cued up and you're ready to push Play.) When the song is done, click Stop and also stop your tape deck. MusicMatch takes a moment (or longer) to write the file to your hard drive. Repeat this naming and record-ing procedure for each of the songs you're digitizing.

Remember, if you're recording at CD-quality sound (recom-mended), each minute of music can eat up 10MB of memory. Do you have enough disk space?

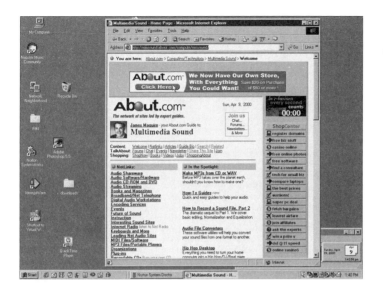

The Multimedia Sound site at About.com (run by yours truly) is a good resource for home project musicians, and it also includes information and opinions on many other audio topics.

Digitizing with Audio Recording Software

There are so many good audio recording programs on the market today that I hesitate to recommend one over the rest. Suffice it to say that with a few hundred dollars and a fast computer, you can lay the foundation for a workable home recording studio.

That said, a few music applications have come close to becoming industry leaders.

For Windows, Cool Edit Pro is a program you'll find on the hard drives of many home studios. It's loaded with sound design capabilities and allows you to mix down 64 separate tracks. (To put that in perspective, the Beatles recorded much of their early music with only four tracks.) You can take a look at Cool Edit at *http://www.syntrillium.com.*

Sound Forge by Sonic Foundry is another versatile and powerful audio program for Windows. It includes dozens of high-quality audio effects and processing tools to help you fine-tune your sound. It can handle many different audio file types and can con-vert dozens of files at a time from one format to another. Visit Sonic Foundry at *http://www.sonicfoundry.com.*

Cool Edit Pro is packed with options that used to cost thousands of dollars. And there's a new plug-in called ClickFix 2000 that eliminates clicks and pops.

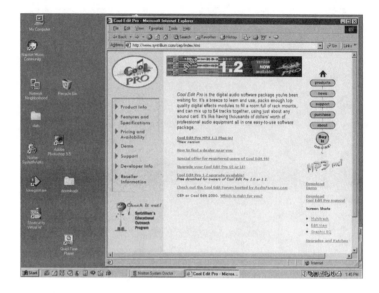

For Macintosh, Pro Tools is the top sound design program. This program is scaleable—the basic version is quite useful for the home user, while many top recording studios use the high-end version. You'll see mention of Pro Tools in the credits of many major motion pictures. Explore Pro Tools at *http://www.digidesign.com.*

Pro Tools by Digidesign has become extremely popular in the last few years.

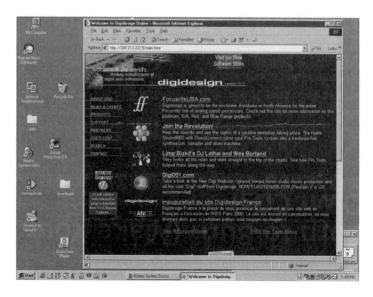

Another cutting-edge Mac audio program is Bias Deck, which is geared toward the home user and is loaded with capabilities. This program was a pioneer in desktop recording and is still found in many good home studios. Explore the Bias Deck site at *http://www.bias-inc.com.*

No matter what audio software you choose, there are many procedures that are common to all of them. Let's take a step-by-step look at digitizing audio that will pertain to you no matter what audio program you choose. Much of this will be familiar if you've used MusicMatch—the difference will come when you edit and optimize your newly digitized audio files.

Dust off that old tape and stop playing Frisbee with that ancient vinyl album. When you're ready to digitize those well-loved favorites, you'll need to do the following:

- Use your connecting cables to connect the output of your playback deck with the input of your computer. ("Let's see, now where did I put those cables?")

- *Important*: Be careful with the input level. Sending in too much level can distort your audio or even damage your sound card. If this is the first time you're sending audio into your sound card, turn the volume down on your audio player and perform a test. Adjust the input level, using the volume control on your playback deck, until even the loudest parts of your music can be recorded without distortion.

- Select an input mode: Line In if you're digitizing from a tape deck, Mic In if you're using a microphone. (If you're recording with a mic, turn down your computer's speakers.)

- Select a sample rate and bit depth. Again, it's always best to record at CD quality, 44.1KHz, 16-bit stereo and then reduce your file size later if need be.

- Give your music file a name and select a destination folder on your hard drive. (And don't forget where it is!)

- Select a file type and a proper file extension. File types include WAV, AIF, SND—there are more than a dozen possibilities. WAV is the most common, and virtually any sound

program can read it. After you select the file type, it's important to give your file the right extension, which is the tag
on the end of the filename (for example, *soundfile.wav* or
soundfile.aif). Without this extension, your computer can't
play your sound file.

- Virtually all audio recording software provides a graphic display of the sound file. This is a small area that represents the
length and volume of your sound with plenty of squiggly
lines. However, you won't see this while recording—your
computer can't create this graphic display until the sound file
is written to the hard drive.

- Click Record on your audio software and push Play on your
tape deck. Let the excitement begin—you are now digitizing!
As soon as you're done recording, click Save—this would be
a terrible time to lose everything you've just digitized.

*The Audio
Engineering
Society site has
plenty of links to
sites with advice
on handling digi-
tal audio.*

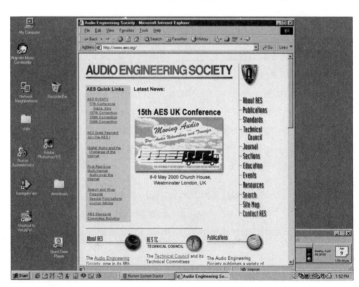

Optimizing Your Files

One of the terrible truths about digitizing audio is that creating an
audio file from your 1957 Blind Lemon Jefferson album won't
make it sound like a spiffy high-tech MP3 file. The music is still
going to sound hissy and crackly. If anything, the computer reproduces these flaws more clearly than your old tape deck or

turntable. However, there are a few important things you can do
to make your audio files sound their best.

*The graphic dis-
play of a sound
file makes editing
much easier.*

Look at the illustration with the jagged lines. No, this isn't a picture of the Italian Alps. It's the graphic display of your sound file.
As you might guess, the peaks and valleys represent high and low
volumes.

First, let's trim the sound. On the far left, notice that the display
starts with a short flat line. This represents silence—you want to
edit this out. Eliminating unnecessary noise or silence reduces the
file size. In addition, this will make your music start as soon as
you click Play.

Select this small flat line. All audio editing software allows you to
select a small section without affecting the rest of the file. After
you've selected it, click Delete. The silence is gone.

While you're trimming your sound, go ahead and trim any other
unwanted sections. Maybe there's a pause between songs that's
too long. Perhaps you recorded someone giving a speech who
coughed between paragraphs—select these coughs and delete
them. Anything you can do to make the file size smaller—and
eliminate unwanted sounds—should be done at this time.

Normalize

This is a simple but important function. Select your entire file and
browse through your editing software's editing choices. Choose
Normalize. (I've yet to come across decent editing software that
doesn't offer this choice.) Normalize boosts a file to its maximum. The software will find the sound's *ceiling* (the level above
which it begins to distort) and raise it to this exact level.

If you have many files, choose Normalize for all of them. This
will help even out the differences in volume between various
songs you've digitized. Normalize is the digitizer's best friend.

Equalization

Equalization—it's a rather big word, isn't it? I remember a vague feeling of dread the first time I came across it—what complicated theorems would I need to understand? Fortunately, though, learning basic equalization isn't too hard, and equalized audio sounds far superior to non-equalized audio.

First, the basics. *Equalizing* a sound means increasing or decreasing its low, middle, or high range. The human range of hearing runs from about 20Hz (Hertz) at the low end to about 20,000Hz at the high end (but it cuts off at about 15,000Hz for people raised on loud rock music, which is great for causing hearing impairment).

By turning up or down various frequencies of a sound file, you can greatly improve its quality.

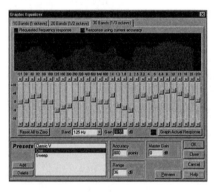

The trick to equalizing your files is to figure out which frequency you should turn up, and how much, to make your audio sound better.

Search through your audio software's effects menu and find the equalizer. Then try the following, listening to the sound after each adjustment to see if you like it:

- If the music sounds thin, add some richness and bottom end by turning up the 250 to 500Hz range.

- If you want your music to sound crisper, project more, and have more presence, turn up the midrange in the 1,000 to 3,000Hz area (often called *1k to 3k*).

- If that old tape is sounding dull, give it a brighter quality by turning up the high end in the 5k to 8k range. In addition, you might try turning down the low end. Decreasing the 250 to 500Hz range makes audio sound brighter.

- One of the most common complaints about turning old records and tapes into computer files is, "There's a lot of hiss—I want to get rid of it." This is a tough one. To decrease the hiss, turn down the 6k to 8k range quite a bit. However, if you turn this range down too much, your music will sound dull. So you have to try a few settings and decide which is the best balance.

How much should you turn up or down a given range? It's good to experiment, but try 3 to 5dB to start. (dB stands for *decibel*, a measurement of volume.)

Ultimately, equalizing a sound means trying a setting and then listening to see if you like it, and experts disagree on what sounds good. So if turning up the bottom end makes the music sound more pleasant to you, go for it. It's *your* music, and it has to sound good to *you*. But be forewarned that you can spend a few minutes, a few hours, or a few days equalizing your sound. There's no perfect equalization, just an improvement over the original sound.

The Final Frontier: Saving Your File

When you've done everything you can to optimize your audio files—trimmed, normalized and equalized them—you're ready to save them.

Hopefully, you recorded your music at CD quality. If so, one minute of sound eats up about 10MB of hard drive space. This means that if you digitize an entire album, the resulting audio files might take up 500MB of your hard drive.

Even though the files can take up a lot of space, save copies at the original high resolution. Transfer these originals onto an external hard drive if need be, but keep a copy of them. You never know when computer formats will change, and you'll want to transfer the originals to a file format that hasn't been invented yet. (A new format seems to come along every 18 months.)

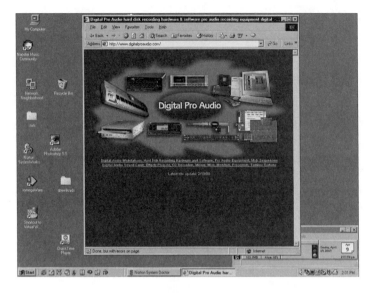

But you may want to save your music files as smaller files. Perhaps you want to upload a file to a Web site or email it to a friend. If you need smaller files that eat up less memory, save copies of your files in the following formats:

- Saving your stereo file as a mono file cuts the file size in half. That 10MB file becomes a 5MB file. (I know, I know— you'd rather have stereo file. But sometimes you have to compromise.)

- Saving a 44.1KHz file as a 22KHz file cuts your file size in half again.

- Saving a 16-bit file as an 8-bit file cuts your file size in half again. But this is a bad trade-off—anything you can do to retain 16-bit is worth doing.

- You can save your file as an MP3 file, which shrinks file size by about 90%. (See Chapter 19, "Let 'Er Rip! Make CDs into MP3s.")

- If you want to post your files on the Web but don't want to make them MP3s, a good default setting is 22KHz, 16-bit, mono. This produces a small file, but it still sounds reasonably good.

Wrapping It Up

So now you're sitting by the computer, listening to those new sound files. Turn them down—just for a second—and look at what you learned in this chapter:

- You looked at the various gear needed for digitizing—connecting cables, adapters, and an external preamp for that turntable.

- You looked at some of the advances in audio software—specifically, how some of these programs can be used for digitizing.

- You went step-by-step through the digitizing process.

- You worked on making your music files sound better by using the Normalize and Equalize options.

- You stored our sound files in the best possible format, considering file size and sound quality issues.

CHAPTER 21

Born to Burn (Make Your Own CDs)

It wasn't that long ago that having a CD of your own music was a very big deal. Friends who were in bands might have cassettes of their demos, but it took serious money to burn CDs. Having your music on CD seemed to make it more important, more worthy of a listen.

And making CDs was a complicated process. It usually entailed sending your master tape off to an obscure, faraway pressing plant, where there were probably big, complicated pressing machines run by lab technicians in white lab coats. It was only at these special pressing plants that something as high-tech as a CD could be created.

Yes, there was some sort of magical dividing line. Anyone could put their music on cassette, but if you had it on CD—wow, you might be on your way to something big.

But CDs Are Still Pretty Cool

Even today, CDs are a great medium for music. First, they're digital. They have that crisp, clear digital sound that we've all gotten used to—no vinyl pops, no tape hiss. And you can access any track with no rewinding or fast-forwarding. CDs are small, easily portable, and pretty well indestructible. Put that favorite song on repeat and just let it play. (Please, don't try this with a turntable.)

What You'll Learn in This Chapter:

▶ The digital audio technology of compact discs

▶ What to look for when you're setting up your home CD writer: hardware, software, and recordable media

▶ How a CD is created, step-by-step

▶ Important principles to keep in mind when you're making your own CDs

Manufacturing CDs is less costly for record companies, so they don't have to sell as many copies to make a profit. This means that labels can afford to sign artists who reach a smaller audience than would have been profitable in the vinyl era, which has led to an explosion in the quantity and diversity of recording artists.

Because of all this, CDs and CD players are just about everywhere. You'll find players not only in living rooms but in cars, gyms, schools, jogging trails—most people don't leave home without them.

CD-Info.com includes links to everything from directories of vendors to technical FAQs. Surf on over to *www.cd-info.com*.

CD-Info.com is a great source of information about burning CDs.

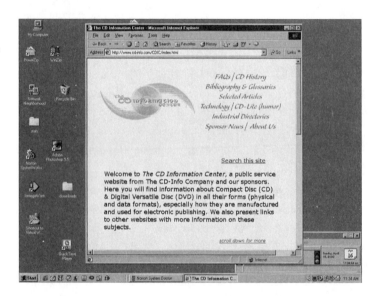

It's no surprise that CD technology has found its way to the home computer. Not only is it easy to burn a CD with your desktop CD writer, but it's relatively inexpensive. Virtually anyone who has music stored as digital audio files—MP3s, WAVs, and other file formats—can put them on CD for easy and portable listening.

The CD-R Technical Directory goes through hundreds of terms alphabetically, explaining CD terminology in an easy-to-understand style. Visit it at *www.eciusa.com/cdr/techdic.htm*.

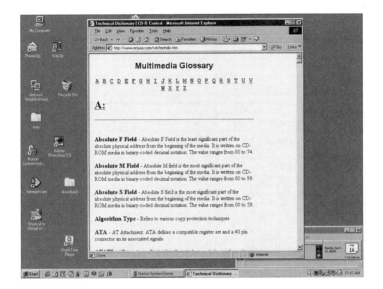

The CD-R Technical Dictionary site is an ambitious effort.

The Hidden Secrets of CDs

I have to admit to being pretty amazed by CD technology. I could go on and on about the complexities of this process. I'll spare you that, but let's do a quick overview before you learn the nuts and bolts of how to burn a CD.

Digital sound, like all computer-based information, is stored on your computer as a series of ones and zeroes. Each WAV file on your hard drive contains thousands and thousands of ones and zeroes that instruct your computer about that file's volume, pitch, and length.

This same pattern of ones and zeroes is found on a CD. If you looked at a compact disc at the microscopic level, you'd see a series of microscopic marks known as *pits* (tiny depressions) and *lands* (small raised areas). Your CD player focuses a small but extremely sensitive laser beam on the zillions of pits and lands that are embedded in the CD's surface, interpreting them as ones and zeroes.

To make a CD at home, you need a blank CD-R (recordable CD) whose surface contains a pregrooved spiral. This pregrooved track guides the laser as it burns the pattern of pits and lands on the CD's surface. So the term "burn a CD" is pretty accurate.

The CD-R Primer is part of a site called It's a DAT, DAT, DAT, DAT World!, which covers digital audio recording. Visit it at *http://www.digitalexperience.com/cdrprimer.html.*

The CD-R Primer does a good job of explaining CD writing.

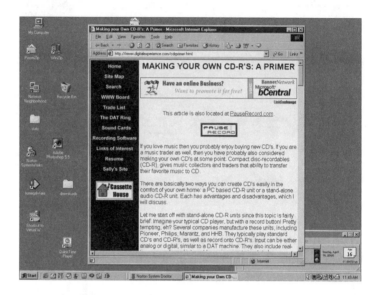

What Color Is Your Book?

A compact disc can hold more than one type of information. There are CD-ROMs that contain video and multimedia files, and there are CDs that hold data instead of music. Each of these CD formats uses a different standard that defines how it stores and retrieves information. Like many aspects of digital audio in this time of transition, there's a good bit of confusion about formats. There are more standards than we need, and many will fade into obscurity. But there are three standards you should be aware of:

- **Red Book**   This standard is used by the typical music CD. It's designed for storing and playing audio only. A Red Book standard CD can hold no more than 74 minutes of music.

- **Yellow Book**   When you buy a prerecorded CD-ROM, you're buying a Yellow Book standard CD. Yellow Book is designed to hold a variety of multimedia files and can hold up to 650 megabytes of data.

- **Orange Book**   This is similar to Yellow Book, but it defines CD-R and CD-RW. The CD-RW (CD-rewritable) format allows you to write over a CD repeatedly.

In short, Red Book is the music CD standard, and Yellow Book and Orange Book are data CD standards. To add some confusion, you can store music on a data CD, but it's stored as compressed audio files (typically in MP3 format) and you'll need a decoder to play it back. A regular CD player can't play music files from a data CD.

Visit *www.digido.com* for all your technical questions. There's enough there to satisfy even the most ardent tech-head.

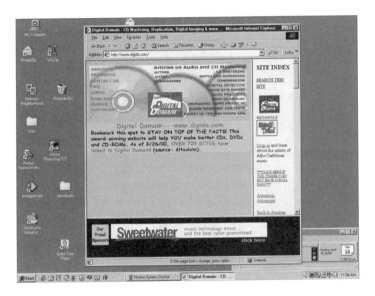

Digital Domain provides a thorough technical foundation in CD burning.

The Home CD Writer's Toolkit

To be a fully equipped home CD maker, you'll need the following:

- **A computer with a CD burner**   Be aware that most internal CD drives cannot burn CDs. You'll need a CD writer capable of burning those pits and lands.

- **Software**   There are numerous choices when it comes to CD-burning software, but Adaptec is the market leader. Also, the CD-ROM in the back of this book contains MusicMatch Jukebox, which is handy for burning CDs from MP3s.

- **Recordable media**   CD-R and CD-RW recordable discs are much like blank tapes. You might be thinking, "I'll just record over that old Wailin' Marvins CD that I'm tired of. It works with cassettes, right?" No, you can't reuse your old CDs. To burn your own CDs, you have to buy media that's specifically designed for recording.

- **Music or data files**   Oh yeah, I almost forgot—you need something to put on those bright new shiny CDs. There's a difference between preparing music files for CD storage and preparing data files. In short, music files must be Red Book standard: 44.1KHz sample rate, 16-bit, uncompressed stereo audio.

What Do the Experts Say?

Before you decide which CD-R hardware and software to buy, it's a good idea to read some product reviews. Arguably the top online source for reviews of technology products is ZDNet. To find information on recordable CD equipment, go to the main page (*http://www.zdnet.com*), click on Product Reviews, and then choose the CD-R section.

The ZDNet CD-R product review section.

For some alternative viewpoints, take a look at EMedia Pro at *http://www.emediapro.net.*

Another excellent source of product reviews is Sound & Vision. Visit them at *http://www.soundandvisionmag.com.*

Hardware—Or, How Much Is That Box in the Window?

If you're lucky, your PC came with CD burner. But if it didn't, buying an external unit doesn't have to blow the family inheritance.

Like everything else in CD burning, there are many choices and a fair bit of confusion.

Some CD-R units are intended as audio recorders only—you hook the recorder up to your home stereo and make copies from CDs, cassettes, DATs, or other audio formats. This is a viable option for a music group that wants to turn out its own limited quantity of CDs on a regular basis.

There are also CD-R units that you connect to a desktop computer. Personally, I find these to be much more useful. You can create new CDs from any audio or data files on your computer, and you can combine and edit these files any way you want. Plus, these units tend to cost less than the standalone audio-only CD-Rs.

CD-R units are completely different than CD-RW units. A CD-R unit can burn a disc easily and inexpensively, but you can't burn that same disc again. A CD-RW unit can write and rewrite a disc repeatedly.

You might think, "Well, then, I want a CD-RW unit." But that's not necessarily the best choice, for a couple of reasons. CD-R blank discs are cheap enough that you can simply use a new one if you want to rewrite a disc. And CD-RW discs won't play on many CD players. However, all CD-RW recorders can write to CD-R media. So ultimately, the biggest difference is price— CD-RW units are more expensive than CD-R units, but they offer more options. (Also keep in mind that all CD writers are CD players as well, so you get two for the price of one.)

When you go out to the local electronics store—or surf the Web—you'll be presented with a blizzard of choices. When you're shopping for a CD writer, there are a few questions you should ask:

- **Record once—or many times?** Is it a CD-R or a CD-RW? As mentioned, CD-RW units are more expensive and have more capabilities. But for many casual music fans, a CD-R unit is all that's needed.

- **Write speed?** How fast can it burn? Examples include 2x, 4x, 8x—the faster the better. But be aware that some 4x writers take longer than other 4x writers. If you're planning on burning a lot of CDs, this time difference becomes important. Read the product reviews to see how a CD writer's speed compares with its competitors.

- **Extra features?** What software and other features does it come bundled with? Many burners come with all kinds of goodies, including software packages for creating CD cover art.

- **Cost?** Perhaps most importantly, how much does it cost? In terms of the sound quality of the finished disc, there's not a lot of difference between the least expensive units and the most expensive units. So if you're willing to wait longer to burn a CD and the fancy extras don't matter to you, you don't need to buy the top-of-the-line CD burner.

A Fountain of Information

If you're looking for more information about burning CDs, I highly recommend Andy McFadden's CD-R FAQ Web site at *www.fadden.com*. It's a vast compendium of CD resources, and it's very well organized.

The section on CD writers, for example, contains a list of the best units on the market:

Plextor PX-R820T

Plextor PX-W8220T

Sony CRX140E (often labeled as HP 9100/9200)

Sony CRX120E (often labeled as HP 8200i)

| Sony CRX100E (often labeled as HP 8100i) |
| Ricoh MP7040A |
| JVC XR-W4080 (also labeled Creative CDR4224) |
| Teac CD-R56S |
| Panasonic CW-7501/CW-7502/CW-7582 (often labeled Matsushita or Compro 7502) |
| Sanyo CRD-R800S (often labeled as Smart & Friendly CD Rocket 8020) |
| Goldstar CED-8042B |
| Yamaha CRW-8424S |

This list is taken from postings at the site. There's nothing scientific about it, but it's a good starting point.

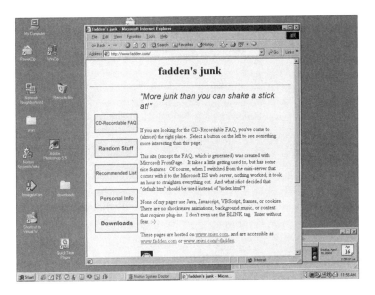

Visit the Andy McFadden CD-R FAQ site for new information about CD hardware—and just about anything else you can think of that's related to CD technology.

Software: Still More Choices

Virtually every CD writer comes bundled its own software, but this software has a reputation for being clunky and not fully functional. Although it might be adequate for basic uses, there are some other software packages to consider.

When you're shopping for the ideal CD creation software, look for a program that does it all. That is, you want a program that can write audio and data CDs and can also help you create a CD's artwork. With these programs you can create a "personal best" music CD, or you can use your burner for a method of date stor-age called *packet writing*.

With packet writing capability, you can add individual files to a disc, one at time, over the course of weeks or months. This is more flexible than Disc-At-Once (DAO) writing, in which you burn all the material to disc in one sitting.

There are two types of packet writing: variable and fixed. *Variable packet writing* is more efficient because the amount of space taken up on the disc varies depending on how large the file is. In *fixed packet writing*, the same size packet file is written to the disc each session.

Packet writing capability is useful for storing data. It's as if the CD is an additional hard drive, and many people use it as such. Packet writing allows you to drag and drop, move or delete files, and use the Save command to save files directly to your CD-R.

A single CD can contain both audio and data files. This is an example of a *multisession CD*. If you want to store your favorite Hank Williams songs with, say, a complete written biography of him, you'll need soft-ware that can write multisession CDs. Just be sure to put the music tracks on the CD first to ensure that all audio players can play them.

Some software allows a choice between DAO and Track-at-Once (TAO) recording. With TAO, the software tells the burner to write one track at a time and to turn off its laser while reading data for the following track. This gives the software more time to gather data between writing tracks and helps reduce writing errors. TAO places a two-second gap between audio tracks.

In contrast, DAO keeps the laser moving until the entire CD is written. Although DAO gives you more freedom over the gap between songs (two seconds might not be your ideal), it won't let you add tracks at a later date. DAO requires your burner to have an uninterrupted data stream for an extended period, so you'll need to quit all other applications first.

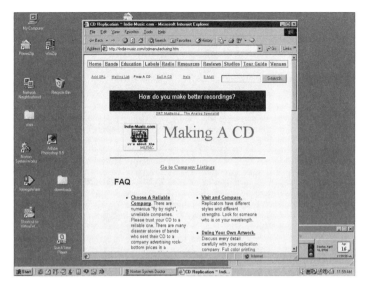

Indie Music has a good overview of how a band should shop for CD duplication services. If you're ready to make a lot of copies of an album, this is a good starting point. Visit the site's CD help section at http://indiemusic.com/cdmanufacturing.htm.

Many CD burner programs provide an option called Test Write. When you choose Test Write—a good idea, especially the first few times you run your software—the program runs through the entire process of finding, reading, and sending files to the burner. If the test runs into a problem, you have a chance to fix it without wasting a disc. (These improperly burnt discs are called *coasters*, which is about all they're good for.)

Some software allows you to burn a disc by creating a complete disc image file. If you want to do this, you're going to need a *lot* of space on your hard drive—enough to hold an entire CD, usually 650MB. This method takes a fully assembled copy of your files and burns it to the disc all at once. The advantage is that you're less likely to suffer from *buffer underruns*. This happens when your computer can't hold enough data in a short-term buffer and the data stream being written to the CD is interrupted.

Or, you can use the on-the-fly method. This is very popular because it makes it easier to rearrange your files and requires much less disc space. You simply give the software a list of what files to write and in what order, and then hit Record. If you have troubles with buffer underrun, try recording at a slower speed— 2x instead of 4x, for example. That way it's easier for the computer to keep its temporary buffer full.

What's the best program for CD burning? There are dozens of choices, but Adaptec's software has become an industry leader. If you're just getting started, try Adaptec's Easy CD Creator 4 Deluxe, or Adaptec's Toast for the Mac. If you're looking for alternative software—and there are a lot of good choices—make sure it's compatible with your burner.

Adaptec's software has become an industry leader in CD creation. Surf on over to http://www.adaptec.com.

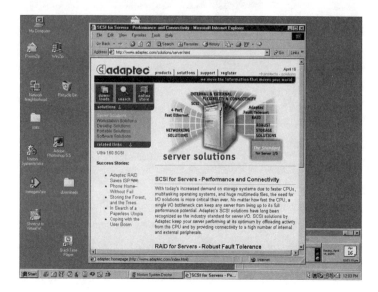

Recordable Media

Every blank CD comes with a rating indicating what speed it supports: 2x, 4x, etc. In the case of CD-RW discs, you can burn a disc no faster than its rating. So yes, you can use a 2x CD-RW disc in a 4x burner, but it will slow the burner down to 2x speed.

Burning a full CD (650MB) takes 74 minutes at 1x, 37 minutes at 2x, and 19 minutes at 4x. I'm guessing you see the pattern—doubling the speed cuts the time in half.

CD-R blanks are cheaper than CD-RW blanks, but you can get some good deals on CD-RWs if you shop around.

There are two types of CD-R blanks: one for audio and one for data. Audio CD-Rs cost more; not because they cost more to make, but because of the royalties that are added to compensate for the illegal copying for which they're often used. Most recorders will allow you to record audio using either type of disc.

However, if you have a consumer-quality standalone burner, you won't be able to use the less expensive data blanks to burn audio CDs. These discs have a specially encoded material to prevent them from being used for audio.

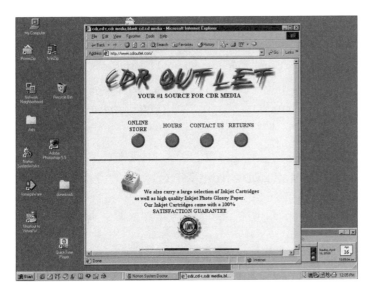

CDR Outlet is a huge online retailer of blank CDs. If you're ready to shop, check out the prices at http:// www. cdroutlet.com.

Important Things to Keep in Mind

CD burning is changing and developing faster than you can say "format conversion." Still, for the foreseeable future (maybe the next couple of years), there are some principles that apply to all burners and CD creation programs.

As mentioned previously, burning a CD requires an uninterrupted data stream to the blank disc. Depending on the speed of your burner, it may take more than half an hour to finish burning your CD. You may get bored and boot up your graphics program to start creating the album art. Bad idea. If you make too many demands on your computer, the data stream will be interrupted and your disc will be nothing more than a shiny (and silent) paperweight.

Before you click that Write CD button, get your hard drive ready. Empty the recycle bin and make sure you have enough space for temporary files. It's also a good idea to restart your computer just before you write a CD.

Use your CD software's Test Write option to run through the procedure without actually burning the CD. This ensures that your software will be able to read the files quickly enough to effectively write the CD.

If you have audio that's 44.1KHz, 16-bit, stereo, and uncompressed, that's considered Red Book standard audio and it's ready to go. No other format conversion is required. Simply select those files, click Start, and your computer will perform its magic.

If your audio isn't in this format, you need to convert it. You can find some audio conversion software at *http://mmound.about.com/ aa991129.htm*. Here you'll find a list Windows and Mac software to convert your files.

Can You Make CDs from MP3s?

Making CDs from MP3s has caused its fair share of confusion. Yes, you *can* make CDs from MP3s. In fact, there are two ways to do it.

To make a music CD from MP3s, you must convert the compressed data files to Red Book audio—44.1kHz, 16-bit, uncompressed stereo. First you must convert the MP3s to WAV or AIF files, and then you can burn them. (Certain software, like MusicMatch, can convert an MP3 and burn it to disc all in one step.) The music CD will then be playable in any standard CD player.

Or you can make a data CD from MP3s. With this method, you don't need to convert the MP3s to any other format, but you can only play that CD in a player that has MP3 player software (typically a computer). If you put that data CD in a regular CD player, you'll hear nothing but the sound of silence.

You might ask, "Why was 74 minutes chosen as the default length for an audio CD?" According to legend—and there's some disagreement about this—the famous conductor Herbert von Karajan (who had a contract with Phillips, an early pioneer of CDs) wanted the new format to be able to hold his favorite symphony, Beethoven's Ninth. This may just be a myth, but I take satisfaction in believing the reason is musical rather than technical.

MP3 Central pro-
vides links to help
you make CDs
from MP3s. Pay
them a visit at
http://www.zdnet.
com/downloads/
topics/mp3.html.

Burnin' with MusicMatch Jukebox

Okay, you already have CD writing software, maybe a good program by Adaptec or the software that came with your burner. So
why should you try MusicMatch?

There are three good reasons: 1) It's free—if you own this book,
you own MusicMatch. 2) It's particularly good at burning music
CDs from MP3s. 3) You can select a MusicMatch playlist that
you're used to listening to and burn it quickly and easily.

If I've convinced you, let's go step-by-step through burning a CD
with MusicMatch.

The first time you run MusicMatch, make sure there's an audio
CD in your CD drive—the program will perform a short test on
your drive the first time it boots up.

After the test, create a playlist of the music you want on your CD.
To do this, either drag-and-drop all the songs you want on your
CD to the playlist window or use the MusicMatch AutoDJ feature
by choosing File, Playlist, AutoDJ. This allows you to create
playlists based on your preferences.

When you're done with your list, click on the CD-R button in the top-right corner of your playlist window. You're asked to select whether you want to burn audio or data. If you choose audio CD, remember that your music must not total more than 74 minutes. If you choose data CD, you'll be able to fit a great deal more music on your disc, but it can only be played on your computer.

After you've specified audio or data CD, make sure you have a blank disc in your CD burner. When you're ready to burn, just click Create CD and MusicMatch does all the necessary conversions. It's really that easy?.

One of the really handy features of MusicMatch is its capability to burn music CDs from MP3s on-the-fly. Many CD creation programs make you convert MP3s to CD-quality WAVs, which is time-consuming and eats up quite a bit of disk space. MusicMatch does this MP3-to-WAV conversion all in one step.

Remember, as with all CD burning, you should close all other programs first. Don't surf the Web, and don't call Alaska using your Net telephony software. If the information being written to CD is interrupted, your blank CD-R will be useable only as a Frisbee.

If you want to create artwork for your jewel case (the little box that holds the CD), you can spend $29.99 on the pro version of MusicMatch. It's a pretty good deal, considering all the capability you get.

Wrapping It Up

So, now you're listening to a CD you made yourself—pretty neat, huh? Let the music play, and let's look at what you learned in this chapter:

- How digital audio technology is used to make compact discs.

- What to be aware of when setting up your home CD writer: hardware, software, and recordable media.

- How to create a CD using MusicMatch Jukebox.

PART VI

Get Famous
(Artists Only)

CHAPTER 22

Gather the Right Stuff

Modern advertising has proven that there's an audience for virtually everything. Using the near-science of demographics, advertisers have broken down the overall public into groups and subgroups: Men 18 to 34, women 34 to 49, pre-teens, Native Americans, college graduates, early technology adopters—the list is seemingly endless.

> For an extensive demographic breakdown of Internet use, browse through the Cyberatlas demographics page at *http://cyberatlas.internet. com/big_picture/demographics/*. It includes information about online media and music consumption.

We know that the general public is not one monolithic whole, and demographics tells us that each subgroup has its own preferences. The things that Southern Californian teenagers like to eat, talk about, listen to, and spend money on are much different than what's preferred by retired blue-collar workers or Alaskan civil servants. If you look at this in terms of music, the audience as a whole might not enjoy a given genre, but there's probably a sub-audience that is wildly enthusiastic about that genre.

So today's musician, armed with modern demographics, knows that reaching the right audience can give her a chance to find enthusiastic fans for her music. The fans might number in the millions or merely thousands, but somewhere there have to be people who like, say, Celtic music played with original instruments or spoken-word chants over syncopated timbale grooves. The audience is there; it's simply a question of reaching it.

And when you think about reaching a global audience, using tools just about anyone can acquire, the World Wide Web is the natural choice.

What You'll Learn in This Chapter:

▶ What makes the Web a tremendously powerful tool for promoting your music, regardless of its genre

▶ What items to include in your online promo kit

▶ How each of these items should be optimized for online posting

▶ How to get feedback from fans and reviewers, which you can use to market your music

The MP3 revolution has proved that fans of all kinds of music will dive into the Web like people lost in the desert who suddenly find an oasis. This global audience for music on the Web is in the tens of millions and growing rapidly.

> According to the online trend analysis firm CyberDialogue, the number of adults going online to access music-related content increased 48% from December 1999 to March 2000. The firm attributed some of this increase to news coverage of Napster.

There are people who download swing music, and others who download world beat music. There are Web surfers who swoon for classical music, and many who are hungry for MP3s of Elvis tunes. There are zillions of listeners who download modern rock and pop, and there must be at least thousands of people who download avant-garde jazz, New Orleans zydeco, and electric zither.

Did you know there were enough zither enthusiasts for a National Zither Conference? Take a look at the schedule of work-shops offered by zither virtuoso Gerti Huber at http://home. netcom.com/ ~kandm/confl.

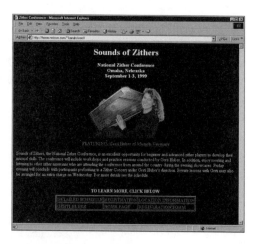

So let's put these last few thoughts together. Let's combine demographics, which breaks the audience into subgroups, with the Web's global, growing reach. When you combine these two concepts, you get one very powerful truth:

There is an audience for what you create, and you can reach that audience using the Web.

Is it easy? No way. Is it guaranteed? Definitely not. Have fortunes been spent in unsuccessful attempts to reach an audience on the Web? You bet.

But that doesn't obscure the central fact that the Web is a nearly perfect tool for the musician who wants to build an audience. Given the right tactics, the ability to learn from your mistakes, and plenty of perseverance, you *can* reach your audience on the Web.

It's as if the Web, with its many music fans and its ease of distribution, was created for musicians.

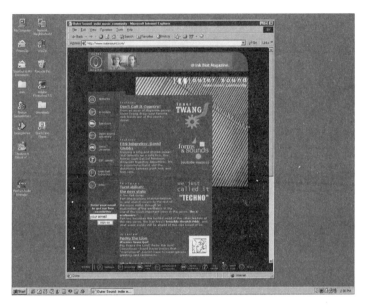

Outersound.com specializes in providing resources for independent, non-mainstream musicians.

Step One

They say that a journey of a thousand miles begins with a single step, and promoting your music on the Web is no different. It can be a long process, but you've got to begin somewhere.

The first step to promoting yourself on the Web is assembling what used to be called a *press kit*. But those days are long gone, so let's call it an *online promo kit*. This contains the materials you'll need to let your potential fans know who you are and give

them enough of a taste to make them want to come back for
more. These are the items that will help convince a music lover to
love *your* music:

- Music in several formats

- Photos

- Biographical and other background information

- Fan and/or reviewer response

- A list of links related to yourself or your band, especially
  sites that host your music

- Tour and performance dates

- Contact information that you can post publicly, like your
  email and post office box address.

Everything in your online promo kit must be optimized for placement on a Web site, so there are some things you need to keep in
mind when preparing each item. Let's rummage through your kit
and make sure each item is optimized for Web promotion.

Mojam.com is a
good example of
a site where you
can use your
online promo kit.
You can upload
your tour dates
and band info,
and you can be
listed along with
bands from across
the world.

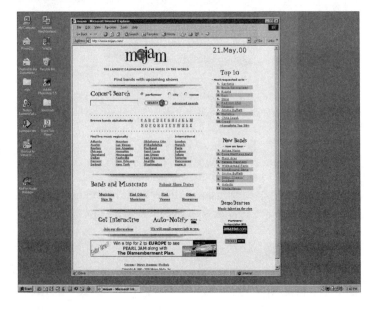

Music: Hit 'Em with Your Best Shot

Your goal is to turn a casual Web surfer into a lifelong fan of your music, and nothing does this better than a tasty music clip. The trick here is offer some of your most compelling songs, the ones that show you at your very best.

The attention span of the average surfer is short, so if you don't grab them with the first download, they probably won't come back for more. Take a hard look at your songs. (I know, you love them all, as you should.) Pick two or three songs you wrote when you were at your most inspired—and that you spent the most money on recording. Also, make sure they're the songs with the most intriguing beginnings. If you don't create passion in your fans in the first 30 seconds, they might not wait for that cool modulation at the end.

When you're deciding which of your songs to offer online, it's a good idea to get feedback from others. Are you posting *your* favorite originals, or the songs that most immediately reach an audience?

And don't worry about having your music stolen. To quote an expert on music publicity, "The problem for most musicians isn't that they're being stolen from, it's that they're not being stolen from *enough*." Let's face it, if you really want to get the word out about your creative efforts, you need to distribute some freebies. Have you ever heard of promotional copies? These are free copies of songs that the major labels hand out to important music trendmakers. In your role as a Web music entrepreneur, these people are the fans who see you on the Web. Heck, they're taking the time to listen to your music—they *deserve* a freebie.

Your fans might not know it, but you'll be playing the timeless game of making them fall in love with the appetizer and then charging them for the entrée. Don't offer your entire CD or song collection for free; just enough to convince your fans to shell out $14 for your CD.

(By the way, you don't need to have a CD to promote yourself online, but it sure helps. Contrary to popular belief, the Web music fan is willing to spend money. Not all online music is pirated— online shoppers spent close to $150 million on music in 1999.)

When you've decided which of your songs best promote you, you'll want to convert those little treasures into two Web-friendly formats:

- **MP3**   Converting your songs into this wildly popular format makes them easy and fast for your fans to download. Surprisingly little quality is lost, considering how small the files become. And there's an enormous installed user base of MP3 players just waiting to play your music. To find out how to rip MP3s, read Chapter 19, "Let 'Er Rip! Make CDs into MP3s."

- **RealAudio or another streaming format**   The major advantage of a streaming file is that it's instantly available to the curious Web surfer. He simply clicks on an icon and the music begins to play instantly. (Or at least it's *supposed* to. There are several things that might slow it down, but this situation is improving.) You can't expect someone who's never heard of you to wait even 45 seconds for your song to download, especially considering that many other bands are competing for that fan's attention. So making your music available for instant audition gives you an edge over MP3-only bands. To convert your files to RealAudio, go to Real.com and download the encoder/player. You don't need to spend $149 on RealProducer Plus, although it will give you higher quality. If you're just getting started, you can download the free RealProducer Basic. (You might also try the Windows Media Player, which seems to be growing in popularity.)

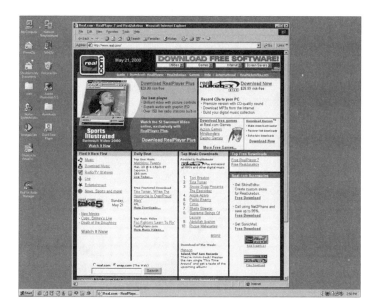

Visit Real.com to download software that will turn your music files into streaming audio.

Photos: No, That Cheap Polaroid Won't Do

In the image-driven age we live in, photos are of vital importance to any struggling band. Musicians sometimes grumble about "image over substance," but the fact remains that people are very influenced by visual imagery.

Think of your photos as a hook that reels in potential fans. Pick out your very best photos because you're probably only going to get one chance to grab that new fan. Show your best side.

And this brings us to a tough subject. Unless you're a professional photographer, don't try to take the photos yourself. A good photographer can make a frog look like prince. It's going to cost you anywhere from $75 to several hundred dollars to hire a pro (ouch!), but in the long term it's worth it. So put on your favorite outfit, polish your instrument, and smile.

When you've acquired these snazzy-looking photos, you'll want to turn them into digital files for uploading. Scan them with the best possible scanner and save them as .jpeg files. The .jpeg format is the best for displaying photos on the Web.

*Need some advice
on the best way
to scan a photo?
Spend some time
at Scanning Tips
Online at
http://www.
hsdesign.com/
scanning/
tipswelcome.html.*

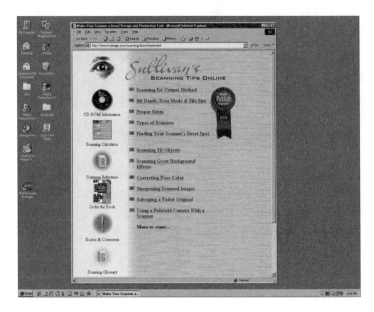

Biographical Information: To Know You Is to Love You

Although it's a task that many musicians recoil from, it's absolutely essential to have a written description of your music. As hard as it is, you need to find some adjectives to describe your songs. Why? Because text appears before anything else on a Web site, and you have only a few moments to grab the attention of that impatient Web surfer.

In addition, the most powerful advertising in the world is "word of mouth"—one fan recommending it to another potential fan. This can't be bought, and you'll never achieve renown without it. You can help shape this all-important word of mouth. If you post an online description of your music as "swing music with a '90s beat," someone who sees it and likes your music might just repeat it. And that's powerful.

So fire up your word processor and do the impossible: Provide a written description of your music. Make it colorful. Don't simply call it "rock." Call it "a double-edged concoction of indie rock with power pop, a dose of the Pumpkins but not so sweet, with the cool chic of Garbage."

Yes, I know, that example is way over the top. And no, your prose shouldn't be that purple, but make it lively. Give your band a description that will stick in a fan's mind.

In addition to describing your musical style, it helps to provide a short one-sentence (or one-phrase) description of the songs you'll post. Again, something that will create interest—you know your potential listeners. Describe your music in terms you know will move them.

You may also want to write out biographies of individual band members. Fans like to know band members as people. Give them little biographical details about your bandmates. No, he's not a guitar-wielding automaton, he's "Mick, the practical joker who only stops jamming to cause a little mischief." Make these little bios lively. The more real you can make them, the more fans feel like they know you.

By the way, if you're a musician who simply can't do this, don't feel bad. Some truly gifted musicians aren't good at this kind of thing. Don't feel shy about asking a friend or current fan to come up with some written ideas.

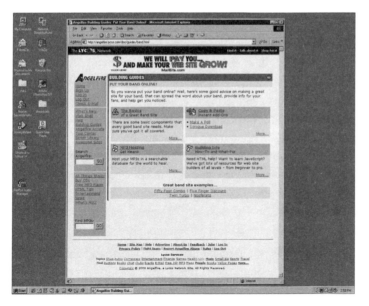

There are hundreds of sites that offer free Web pages to bands, but Angelfire's Bands Online is one of the most popular. It offers Web design tips and a How-To section geared toward the online musician. Toot your own horn at http://angelfire. lycos.com/ doc/guides/band. html.

Fan and Reviewer Response: An All-Important Tool

Fans like to see that their enthusiasm for a band is shared by others. Think of the times you've been to concerts. Doesn't the presence of other cheering music-lovers help you get excited about the group onstage?

You want to harness this persuasive power of group psychology for your online promotion. Or, put another way, you want to tell each potential fan that their good taste is validated by others who like you. So gather some quotes, as positive and descriptive as possible, from as many listeners as possible.

It's best if you can include quotes from publications or other respected sources. If you've ever been mentioned in a newspaper or magazine, even a brief mention, there's probably a way to use it.

Getting a reviewer to come to one of your performances is an art form all of its own. Unless you're a big-name act, reviewers usually won't show up without some prompting from you. So don't hesitate to send the local press and radio stations free tickets, t-shirts, CDs, and anything else that might get their interest. If the first invitation produces no results, try again later.

Can I let you in on the oldest publicist's trick in the book? There's a favorable clip in even the most negative review. Look at any ad for a movie and you'll see a list of superlatives: "Upbeat and imaginative," exclaims a major reviewer; "Hilarious," says this major magazine. However, if you stopped to read the entire review, you'd see some other comments, like "the story line is quite tired, but the acting is often hilarious." Notice that only the positive part of the review makes it into the advertisement. What this means for you is that there's something positive in virtually every press notice—so excerpt those positive comments. They're a very valuable part of your online promotion.

It's not quite as persuasive to have a fan's testimonial because, heck, it might be your sister. But if you don't have press clippings, or you have a quote from a fan that sums up your band in a really memorable way, include it in your online promotion. ("Like, wow, I mean, these dudes are awesome" is probably not a good choice.)

Whether you're including press quotes or fan quotes, pick the best four or five—that's about all you'll need. If there are some full-length rave reviews about you, you can include a hyperlink to the complete article.

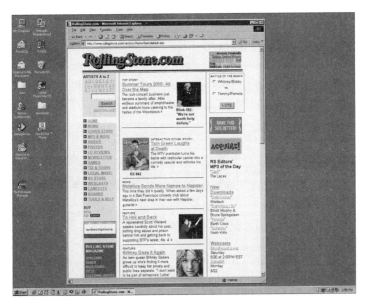

Upload your music to RollingStone.com and it might be chosen as an Editor's Pick, part of the site's service for unsigned bands. Hey, a plug from the Rolling Stone would look good in your online promo kit!

A List of Hyperlinks: Use the Power of the Web

An effectively promoted musician can post her music all over the Web. There's no reason to put your music in only one place in the great global music store known as the World Wide Web. When you take a look at Chapter 25, "Internet Record Labels," you'll see that many sites with big traffic numbers offer nonexclusive hosting deals. Take advantage of them and get your music into as many virtual store windows as you can.

When you put together your online promo kit, you'll want to gather a list of links to your online music. However, this doesn't mean you should list every link at every site that hosts your music. (There's no need to direct your fans at MP3.com to your music hosted by Amazon.com, for example.)

You also want to gather any promotional links. Maybe you're performing in a festival, or there's a rave review about your band on a newspaper's Web site. Or perhaps another well respected musician has posted some glowing comments about you on his Web site. Gather all these links, and verify that the URLs are still valid.

Some musicians also include *related* links, like a rock guitarist who provides a link to the Rock and Roll Hall of Fame or a DJ who links to famed producer Trent Reznor's page. These kinds of links aren't precisely promotional, but they demonstrate a shared interest between yourself and your listeners. Call it bonding between artist and fan.

If you're looking for a good site to link to from your band's home page, try MusiciansGuide. com. It covers virtually all aspects of the music business.

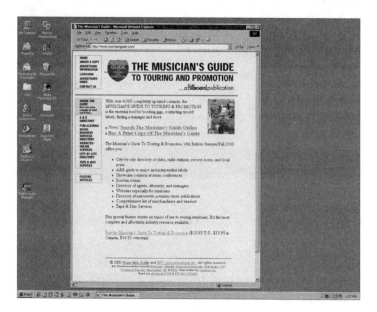

Tour and Performance Dates

Forget waiting for the local newspaper to announce your gig—you can do it yourself at the many sites that will host your music. (See Chapter 25.) When you announce your gigs on the Web, you can ensure *how* they're listed. So you can mention, "I'm playing at the Blue Parrot, and I'll be debuting a new set of songs I've just completed." Your listing can go on to describe your song list, your new artistic directions—anything you as the artist deem appropriate. In short, you're taking the control out of the hands of the harried newspaper editor and putting it where it belongs—with you.

It can also be helpful to include a short list of the most notable
venues where you've played. If you've jammed at the Blue Note
or the Hollywood Bowl, even if it was a few years back, make
note of it in your online promo pack.

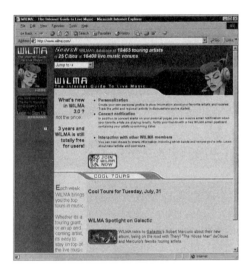

Wilma.com, a worldwide database of concert and club venues, is a good place to enter your tour information. The site offers schedules from over 16,000 live music venues.

Contact Information

You probably don't want to post your home address or phone
number on the Web. But you do want to provide an easy way for
your fans—not to mention booking agents and label reps—to get
in touch with you. Some bands provide a phone number with their
promotional material, but this adds the expense of an extra phone
line. If you need to keep your expenses down, a phone number
isn't a necessity. But make sure to list your email address prominently—and check it on a regular basis.

The Feedback Form

It takes some bravery to put up a Web form asking for fan feedback, but some musicians consider it an essential part of their
online presence. This form, created in HTML (the scripting language of Web sites), can be very simple or very elaborate. Either
way, its purpose is to find out how people respond to your music.

Taxi.com is a top resource that helps connect independent musicians with record labels, publishers, and film and TV music supervisors. You can list your contact information at this site.

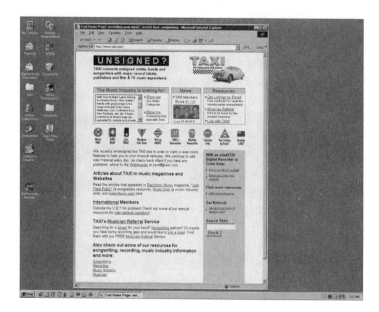

It can be highly educational to get feedback from your fans. And since they'll be filling out the form online and sending it to you via email, you may encounter some brutal honesty. Or, you may derive inspiration from the knowledge that your music has really touched someone. Most likely you'll get a little of both.

The questions you'll want to ask depend on your musical style and the approach you're taking. Many musicians like to use humor on their Web sites, so their material is tongue-in-cheek. Others take a scholarly approach and treat the art of making music with great reverence. Your questions should reflect your approach, but there's no single correct way to solicit listener feedback. Take an afternoon, put your ego up on a shelf, and write down some questions. The following list of questions is meant only to help you to create your own:

1. Which other bands sound like our music?

2. Did you understand and enjoy the lyrics?

3. Would you be interested in hearing more of our music?

4. What did you like the best about our songs?

5. What would you change about our music?

6. Do they have music on your planet?

Again, be fearless when you write your questions. Make it a task for the entire band. Or, if you're a solo artist, draft friends or family members. If you're not getting the response to your music that you'd like, it's helpful to know *why* before you labor in obscurity for years.

And more importantly, when you get a positive comment, you can add it to your online promo kit. Just make sure you ask the fan's permission before you post her comment.

You Too Can Be Criticized!

Most musicians harbor a secret desire to throw week-old tomatoes (or worse) at critics. And that's understandable. Critics, well… they criticize. And who likes to be criticized, especially when it comes to something as close to your heart as your music?

But you need critical response to your music, if for no other reason than to include it in your online promo kit. You want to be able to post plenty of comments like "'This band really cooks,' says Tom Bigguy from the *Dallas Morning Snoozer*." And ideally, you want to change the comments from time to time.

So let's add an element to your online promo kit: the reviewer solicitation email. This is a form letter, short and to the point, asking for feedback. The reviewers won't always come to you, but you can go (politely) pester them.

And let's widen the definition of *critic*. You certainly don't need to limit your quest for printable praise to traditional critics. Get quotes from renowned (or semi-renowned) musicians. Send your letter to a music professor or a music teacher. Send it to the owner of a club where you've played. Send it to *anyone* you think your fans might recognize. Get those positive quotes from anyone and everyone.

If you're just starting your band's publicity push, talk to a successful musician in your area who's been at it a while. What does she do to get reviewers' attention? Who are the press or radio people most likely to publicize a new group?

You can create a letter as a template and personalize it based on who you're sending it to. Give the recipient the Web address for your downloadable music files. Ask him to provide an honest opinion, and let him know that his comments may be posted online. Be friendly, write clearly, and double-check your spelling. And again, be brief.

If you're lucky enough to get some positive comments, send a short thank-you note to each recipient—and let him know when your next release is due.

Wrapping It Up

Your online promo kit is ready. You've gathered all the materials you need to reach the Web's global music audience. Congratulations—this is a powerful first step toward promoting your music. Let's pause and take a look at what you learned in this chapter:

- The Web is a vast collection of niche audiences, and building an audience is simply a matter of effectively targeting people who prefer your style.

- What items to include in your promo kit to help you reach this audience.

- How to prepare and optimize these items for online posting.

- Tips for getting those all-important testimonials from fans and reviewers, which you can use to demonstrate your music's appeal to new fans.

CHAPTER 23

Self-Publish with the Best of Them

At its most basic, the term *publishing* refers to the business of copyrights. A songwriter owns all the rights to a song until she signs a contract assigning those rights to a music publisher. According to copyright law, music is considered to be published if there has been an "offering to distribute copies of a work to a group of persons for purposes of further distributions, public performance or public display."

> Kohn On Music Publishing at *www.kohnmusic.com* is arguably the most authoritative online source of information about music publishing. The site covers everything from Webcasting rights to musicians' contracts.

Simply put, a publishing company buys the rights to a song and then promotes that song to the widest possible audience. This includes other musicians, TV, film, and advertising. In the media-saturated world we live in, more and more outlets for original music are appearing all the time.

Musicians love the part about having their songs promoted to a wide audience, of course. A music publisher can help an artist reach that all-important mass audience, and can put a few dollars in her pocket too.

But not all musicians love music publishers. Since publishers buy the rights to an artist's work (sometimes with a sizeable advance), the artist has to give up ownership of her beloved creations. Some of the bigger publishing companies provide artistic direction,

What You'll Learn in This Chapter:

► What it means to be published, and why many musicians are self-publishing

► How the Internet is fueling the self-publishing movement

► Important techniques for your own self-publishing efforts

► How to copyright your work

under which some artists may chafe. And publishers only continue to do business with a musician while her work is generating revenue, so songwriters are sometimes unceremoniously dumped from a publisher's roster.

> If you're looking for a publisher, avoid companies that offer to publish your work for a fee. Reputable publishers never charge artists to publish their work.

Probably the most common musician's complaint about publishers is "I can't get a contract with one." Publishers, who cease to exist without profit, necessarily look at an artist's work in a strictly commercial light. They won't offer a contract to an artist unless they feel sure that she'll generate revenue. This attitude clashes with that of musicians, who often view their work as a source of artistic and even spiritual fulfillment.

So an artist may put her entire heart and soul into creating a piece of music and be completely ignored by publishers. This is a common occurrence, as many musicians know. In fact, some musicians compare getting a publisher's attention to winning the lottery.

For musicians who dream of getting published, EMI Music Publishing is one of the first names to come to mind. Go to http://www.emisong.com.

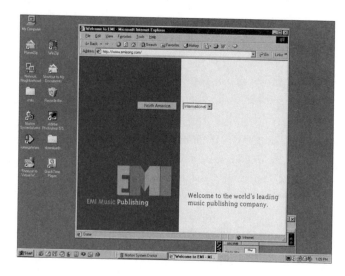

269

The Times, They Are A-Changin'

Distributing music without a publisher—self-publishing—used to be seen as fruitless. Yes, an artist could sell her own music, but too often it meant ending up with 600 copies of her album safely stored in her closet. She retained all rights and all artistic control, but she also retained most of the copies.

But take a look back at that phrase from copyright law that describes publishing as an "offering to distribute copies of a work for...public display." Let's say you want to distribute work for public display—without a publisher. Given some of the recent advances in technology, which of the following would you use to do this?

a. The Pony Express

b. Smoke signals

c. The Internet

If you chose c, you're aware of a movement that's profoundly changing the fortunes of musicians. (If you chose a or b, you need to look into having your time machine repaired.)

Artists everywhere are building their own Web sites in hopes of creating a direct musician/listener distribution chain all over the world. In self-publishing's most utopian ideal, an artist could record and mix a song in her own home, upload it to her Web site, and sell it to fans directly. No middleman to split profits with, no external artistic control, no printing, pressing, and shipping costs. Just an artist and her fans.

However, traditional publishers are in no danger of becoming extinct any time soon. They provide too many services, and they've built powerful distribution chains that are likely to surpass even the Internet's distributing power for years to come. And getting a huge audience to visit your Web site usually takes either a big name or big dollars, which are two things that still require traditional publishers.

But an artist doesn't need a huge audience to build a reputation or create income. In much the same way that bands point to success in local clubs as a way of enticing record labels to take an interest, having a popular Web site has become a calling card that's useful in attracting more attention. And even if a band's Web presence never results in a contract from a major publisher, it's a great publicity tool. A Web site is rapidly becoming a necessary part of any band's public relations arsenal.

Self-Publishing. com offers tips for musicians to promote themselves online.

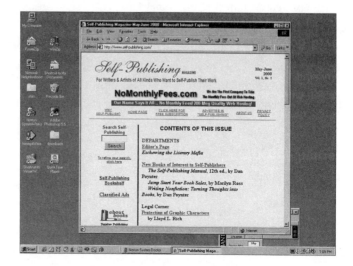

Building Your Web Site: The Foundation of Self-Publishing

If you've gathered all the materials for your online promo kit, as described in Chapter 22, "Gather the Right Stuff," you're ready to start building your band's Web site. To aid you, let's take a look at some other musicians' self-publishing efforts.

It helps to learn from the pioneers of this process. As you look at the Web sites of some big (and not-so-big) names, notice how they approach the following:

- What specific techniques do they use to promote themselves online?

- In what format do they offer music files?

- In general, how does the feel of the site reflect the band's musical approach?

Taking this survey approach to what other bands are doing on the Web is a great first step. "But I'm a musician," you say, "not a Web designer. What if I don't know the first thing about building a Web site?"

Unless you're passionately interested, I don't recommend dropping your guitar and picking up Web design software. Building a basic Web site isn't too hard, but your time is probably better spent writing songs or practicing with your band. So draft a friend who loves tinkering with computer software, or hire a college student. You don't need to hire a high-end Web design firm to build your band's site. Try the barter approach; there are many people out there with basic Web design skills. Trade your band's CD for some design work, or give your Web designer a free pass to all of your shows and mention her name onstage.

But even if you don't build your site yourself, you need to know how you want it to be laid out and what the general feel should be. You don't have to know how to use a hammer and nails to tell the architect you want your house to have five rooms and high ceilings. Think of yourself as the executive Web producer, overseeing the work as the site is built to match your vision.

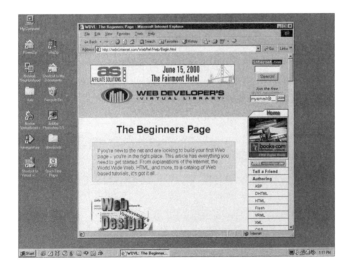

The Beginners Page is a good place to begin your education in Web site building. Hosted by Internet.com, it offers tips on how to embed sound in your Web page. Start learning at http://wdvl.internet.com/WebRef/Help/Begin.html.

Expose Yourself: A Web Presence Is Bigger Than a Web Site

Having your own Web site is central to self-publishing, but you want to have more than just a personal home page. You want to develop what's called a *Web presence*.

The strategy here is put your band in front of as many potential eyeballs as possible. There are numerous Web sites and Web communities that offer free sites to musicians, and you should take advantage of as many of these offers as you can. Keep your online promo kit handy (see Chapter 22) and surf through the dozens of good music-related sites, uploading your material to all the relevant sites that offer free exposure.

Take a look at Chapter 25, "Internet Record Labels," to find where to upload your band's marketing material and music clips to give them the highest visibility. Maximize your exposure by creating a free page on at least a half-dozen major sites, and put links on those sites back to your more extensive home page. Think of this process as creating your own web within the Web, developing pathways to your central site from as many locations as possible.

The Artist Formerly Known As Prince

The Artist is a leader in Internet self-publishing, being one of the first to distribute his albums online. His site ("funk owned and creatively grown") uses all the newest bells and whistles, and it requires the newest browsers and Flash (a multimedia plug-in that enhances a site's functionality).

The site is so focused on cutting-edge Web design that it's slow and cumbersome. As one of the pages says, "Takes a little while 2 download, please be patient." Although the site is visually attractive, its emphasis on design over content is good to avoid.

Throughout the site the Artist uses his own spelling: *2* for *to*, *b* for *be*, and the rather odd *ur* for *your*. At times it gives the site the feel of a 14-year-old's diary, as in this sentence from one of his philosophical treatises: "Many languages r brilliant in their attempt 2 CONfuse u." Although this seems half-baked to me, the Artist is using the site to reflect his unique individual identity—an important approach for any artist, whatever her style.

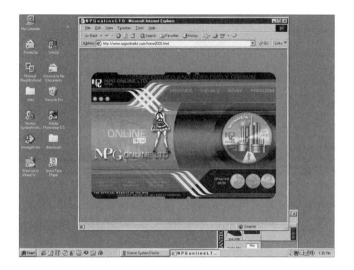

The Artist Formerly Known As Prince isn't known for his fondness for record labels. Expect him to remain at the forefront of Internet self-publishing at http://www. npgonlineltd.com.

The site is a complete environment for the Artist's fans. It includes downloadable songs, videos, his views on the music industry and other topics, and Artist-related news. An extensive online store lets you add items to your shopping cart as you browse (a baseball cap for $20, a *Prince's Greatest Hits* CD for $11, and so on).

One very effective technique that the site uses is letting the user choose the connection speed for the streaming RealAudio music clips. If you've got a 28KB modem, there's a stream for you, and if you have a 56KB or faster modem, you can make the music stream faster. This option costs more, but it's great for offering the instant appeal of streaming audio to everybody.

Beck.com

Beck uses a technique that's invaluable for any band on the Net: Users enter their email addresses and get updates and inside scoop "direct from Beck and BeckDirect.com."

Beck's quirky indi-
viduality is cap-
tured in his Web
page. It's a good
example of an
artist's identity
being accurately
represented by his
Web site.

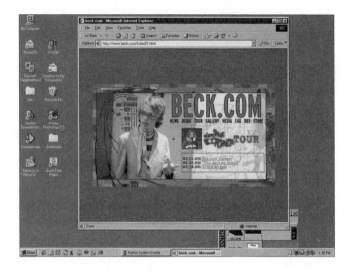

Although some fans feel pestered by mass mailings, and they should be used very carefully, they're a cost-effective way to reach a large audience of people who have volunteered their email addresses. If you send out mailings to your fans, make sure to personalize them. Write them in your own natural voice, making them "letters from a friend" rather then public relations releases. And whatever you do, keep your mailings as brief as possible.

The Beck store is a must-see if you're thinking about creating an online outlet for merchandising. You can fill your shopping cart with a banana girly shirt, a stripe knit hat, a turntable tee, or a pink scarf—all with the word *Beck* emblazoned on them. And of course, there's a big catalog of Beck CDs. The site even offers song clips from some of the CDs in RealAudio, including one album that hasn't been released yet.

Beck.com's most effective use of the Web is its presentation of Beck himself. There's a collection of information about him that even the most ardent fan would be hard-pressed to find anywhere else. What's Beck's real name? When was he born? Is he single? Where does he live? If that's not enough, there's a BBS (bulletin board service) where fans can read and write comments about old and new releases, lyrics, and band members. There's even a category called blackhole if you need to get something off your chest that isn't related to Beck.

This artist information and fan feedback section of the site is
something any musician can use. Give your fans information
about you as a person—there's a strong correlation between how
well your listeners know you and how well they'll like you.
(Unless you're in Oasis, that is.)

Hosting a BBS can be a traffic builder even if the topics aren't
about you specifically. A bluegrass musician can host a BBS
about fiddle techniques, or a solo performer can host a BBS about
audience participation. Be imaginative, and use the BBS (which
you can list in search engines) as another way to draw traffic to
your site and keep it there.

Radiohead.com

The Radiohead site is an important example for any self-publishing band because it takes a wildly creative approach to self-promotion. Forget concert photos and biographical
information—Radiohead.com is a work of art in itself.

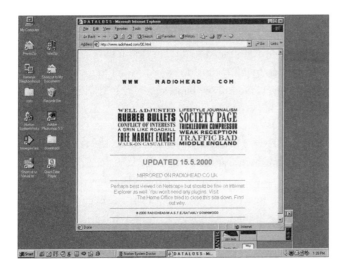

*Be prepared for
the unusual when
you visit
Radiohead.com.
The site is in a
category all
its own.*

Clicking on a link called Links Like Dots In Front Of Your Eyes
When You Get Old takes you to a Web page with patterns of
blinking dots—arranged in such a novel pattern that blinking dots
become interesting. Click on the link called Where We'd Like To
Go If We Had Time and see a broad array of non-music sites

favored by Radiohead members. Throughout the site are drawings that might have been done by 5th-graders, but with a decidedly adult perspective. You'll also find quotes like, "Try. Imagine the sound of crackling flames, of popping bones and blazing money. That's what you have to do."

If you think clicking on the Primetime link takes you to, say, a list of the band's most prestigious appearances, think again. It goes to a section called "Reproductive Capacity of Clones," which includes still more links to unexpected, offbeat locations. The word that best sums up the site is *surreal*.

In fact, there's little actual band information at the site, with the exception of a listing of tour dates and some information about getting tickets (in a section called Tickets Schmickets).

This off-the-wall approach certainly isn't for every band, but I've included it here as a reminder of the value of surprise. Visitors coming to your site will expect downloadable songs, band information, perhaps some links to related music sites—all important things to provide. But with Web sites proliferating daily, it's important to do something to set yourself apart. It doesn't have to be as strange as Radiohead's site, but if you have something unique to offer, by all means do so. You want to give that Web surfer who has visited many band sites a reason to remember yours.

Some Other (Not Yet) Famous Musicians

Most musicians aren't at the point where they can create a site like the ones you've seen in this chapter. But that shouldn't be a deterrent. It's important to have your own site even if your time and budget are limited. Although it's good to learn from these big-budget sites, you can also learn from sites built by musicians who aren't stars yet. Let's take a look a couple of these sites.

Emily Richards

Singer-songwriter Emily Richards' page is good example of a clear, easily accessed site. As soon as you get to the site, you'll see virtually all the promotional material in one view.

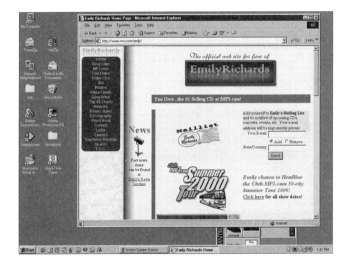

Emily Richards links her site at MP3.com, where she scores high with listeners, back to her personal home page at http://www.nvu.com/emily/.

At the top of the front page is the box to add your email address to the Emily Mailing list. Right underneath it is a link for her tour dates and a photo of her with Drew Carey and Dick Clark—it's always good to prominently display your career highlights. Underneath that is a photo of one of her CDs and—this is key— three places online to buy it: Amazon.com, CDNow.com, and Indiespace.com. To the left is a neatly organized list of links to the main points of interest: photos, bio, reviews, contact information, etc.

There's nothing revolutionary about the site's design, but it's completely effective as a promotional device. And it looks like it didn't take a lot of time, expense, or Web expertise to build.

The Ill Wind Ensemble

I've included the Ill Wind Ensemble in this survey because, like many other unsigned musicians, this Vermont-based group plays music that doesn't fit into an easily defined commercial formula. Or any commercial formula at all, for that matter.

The group "uses completely spontaneous improvisation to create an unusual variety of sonic textures." A typical performance features clarinets, reed pipes, PVC pipes, and numerous other instruments whose origins range from the local hardware store to India to Medieval Europe.

The Ill Wind Ensemble is the kind of group whose music does not fit into the commercial main-stream, so Internet self-pub-lishing gives them a much greater chance of reach-ing a large audi-ence.

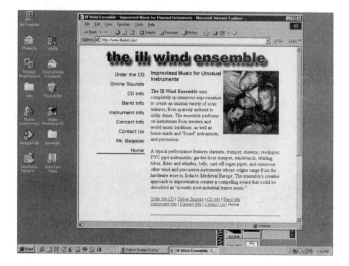

This sounds like a commercial record label's worst nightmare. An album by Ill Wind, while creative and highly musical, is as likely to get major radio airplay as your Uncle Herbert's drunken karaoke tapes. Are the kids going to rush out and buy the latest by Ill Wind? It's doubtful.

In a situation like this, it's particularly important to use the Web to bypass the commercial gatekeepers. Somewhere there's an audience for Ill Wind's offbeat music. It probably doesn't number in the millions, but it may well consist of thousands.

The ensemble's site a good example of effective Net self-publish-ing. The front page uses one of the most persuasive techniques of self-promotion, describing the group's approach in clear terms. You don't need to do this if the music you play is within the boundaries of the rock, pop, R&B, and country that currently dominate commercial radio. But if your approach is more than a stone's throw from the mainstream, it really helps. Don't make your visitors wonder what you're all about. They might not take the time to figure it out.

In addition to explaining the group's approach, the front page includes a quirky photo, contact information, and relevant links. All of this is visible without needing to scroll down. Bottom line: Their music may be off the wall, but their Web site is clear and easy to understand.

More Stops Along the Way

There's no lack of self-publishing musicians on the Web. This section looks at some other interesting musicians' sites. After you surf through these sites, look at your favorite band or artist's site to see how they promote themselves online. Musicians' Web sites are changing faster than you can say "Hyperlink."

Beastie Boys

http://www.beastieboys.com

Here these icons of crossover rap post RealAudio clips of their music and a timeline of the band's history.

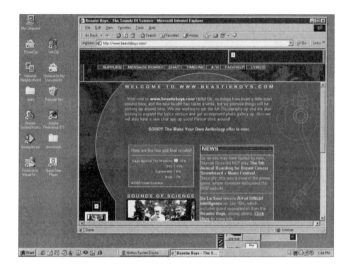

The Beastie Boys' site offers a time-line of the band's history, starting with their 1981 gig at someone's 17th birthday party.

Marilyn Manson

http://www.marilynmanson.net

There's more than enough attitude at this site. And although Manson cultivates a raw image, his site features some highly styl-ish design.

David Bowie

http://www.davidbowie.com

This is a Web site that's not afraid to be commercial. Set up an email address that ends in *davidbowie.com*, or order a credit card with Bowie's likeness on it.

Todd Rundgren

http://www.todd-rundgren.com

This pop balladeer's site includes a section called Subscription, which is his very interesting approach to eliminating the middleman in the music publishing business.

Sarah McLachlan

http://www.sarahmclachlan.com

This popular singer/songwriter's site features a link to Murmurs, a members-only fan site with a treasure trove of "Sarah Stuff," including photos, interviews, sound and video files, and fan artwork. This is an example of advanced Web marketing.

SarahMclachlan.com takes a straightforward but market-savvy approach to promoting the artist.

How to Copyright Your Music

So, you've embarked on a bold path: self-publishing. But what can you do to protect yourself? Without the help of a major publishing company, how do you clarify your copyright protection?

Fortunately, it's not that hard. Let's go through the process of securing the rights to your valuable creations:

- Record your song, even if it's just on your home tape deck. Or, write down both the music and words.

- According to copyright law, this music is now "fixed in a tangible medium of expression" and is automatically copyrighted.

- You own all the rights to this piece of music, unless you were composing under a *work for hire* agreement.

- Put a copyright notice on the tape or sheet music. It should look like this: © *2000 Artist Name*

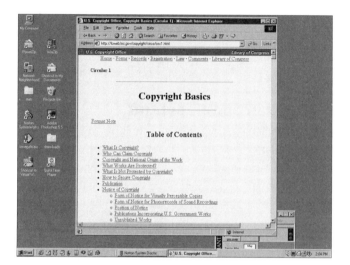

Visit the U.S. Copyright Web site at http://lcweb.loc. gov/copyright/circs/ circ1.html to get a complete overview of the copyright process.

That was pretty easy, wasn't it? It didn't cost a thing, it took about 10 minutes, and you didn't even have to leave home. But if you want to more fully protect yourself, you need to establish a public record of your copyright claim. To do this, you must register it. This is necessary if you ever want to file an infringement suit in court, and it's important if you ever want to sell all or some of the rights to another party. To formally register your claim, do the following:

- Download a copyright application form from the U.S. Copyright Office forms site at *http://lcweb.loc.gov/copyright/forms/*.

- Complete an application form for each work you want to copyright.

- Create two copies of the work, either on tape or sheet music. These copies aren't returnable and will be kept on file at the U.S. Copyright Office.

- Write a check or money order for $30 for each application.

- Put the check, the forms, and the copies of the music into the same envelope and mail it to

Library of Congress
Copyright Office
Register of Copyrights
101 Independence Avenue, S.E.
Washington D.C. 20559-6000

The Musician and Copyright

Any artist who's considering self-publishing should be well informed about copyright issues. Before you offer your work to the public, you need to understand the legal and practical issues involved. The following are some Web sites that will help you understand some of these difficult issues.

10 Myths About Copyright

http://www.clari.net/brad/copymyths.html

This site actually explores 11 myths about Internet-related copyright issues, but its author didn't want to change the title.

Copyright FAQ

http://www.mcs.net/~fishercg/copyfaq.html

This a clear and easy-to-read list of the most common copyright questions, which are answered by attorney Jeffrey P. Fisher.

Protect Your Band Name

http://www.music-law.com/bandname.html

Someone else might want to call themselves the Barking Dudettes. (Hey, that's a good name…I'd better go protect it!) Attorney Michael P. McCready provides advice on how to hang on to your moniker.

Protect Your Trademark

http://teas.uspto.gov/V1.21/index.html

If your band has a logo you'd like to protect, this form from the United States Patent and Trademark Office lets you register it online.

Music Law

http://www.miseryloves.com/law.htm

A detailed overview of copyright law by entertainment attorney Mike Beeman, geared specifically toward musicians.

Wrapping It Up

You've done it! You've taken your career into your own hands by self-publishing your music. All of your songs are registered with the U.S. Copyright Office, and you've successfully developed a Web presence to distribute your work. Let's take a look at what you learned in this chapter:

- The opportunities that self-publishing offers to musicians, and how these opportunities differ from those offered by traditional publishing.

- How the Internet's enormous reach and low entry costs make it the perfect tool for the self-publishing musician.

- A broad array of effective techniques for your own Internet self-publishing efforts.

- A variety of legal resources to protect your self-published music, including information about how to copyright your work.

CHAPTER 24

How to Get Noticed

I've seen it happen all too often: A band builds a beautiful Web site with great photos of live performances, a complete calendar of shows, and plenty of enticing music clips. They tweak the site until it's as perfect as they can make it. They get it all finished, sit back, and think, "Now *that's* a cool Web site." Then they go back to playing music. And the Web site? It sits undisturbed and unvisited, gathering the online equivalent of dust (cyberdust?). Oh, it will have *some* visitors: the band members themselves, the friends and family of the band...

That's just about where the list stops. The site's page views will break double digits (11 or more). Then it will be grouped with the other trillions of Web sites that hang quietly in cyberspace.

What happened to this Web site illustrates a basic truth: Musical ability doesn't always equal self-promotional skills.

What You'll Learn in This Chapter:

▶ How important it is to use online promotional outlets

▶ Some of the most effective ways to use the Web to reach an audience

▶ How you can use each of these techniques to best promote your music

▶ Web sites that will help you further explore online promotion

> If you're looking for a site that will host your band's Web page for free, visit Angelfire at *http://angelfire.lycos.com*. In addition to being a free service, Angelfire offers many helpful tools, like software for animating pages, and a library of HTML scripts to add to your page's functionality.

Many musicians are naturals at creating memorable melodies or wild riffs, but when they think about marketing themselves, it's as if a wet blanket gets draped over their brains. Their thoughts grow fuzzy and weak, and after a period of confusion they pick up their instruments again. This is nothing to be ashamed of, but it doesn't help build an audience.

But really making a career in music is much different than playing great music. A career in music is about reaching an audience (that is, making money), which requires constant promotion. Indeed, effective promotion is often just as important as good music in terms of reaching an audience. This fact causes musicians no small amount of agony, but it's very true. The basic equation goes like this: Good music + good promotion = success.

Look at Britney Spears, for example. She's certainly a pleasant enough performer, but there are thousands of young musicians with more talent than the midriff-baring pop star. What does Britney have that the others don't? A powerful, well-heeled publicity machine that promotes her in every way possible.

"But major labels have budgets that begin with a single digit and end with lots of zeroes," you say. And you don't have that kind of money (yet).

That's true, but there is an alternative. Let's go back to that neglected Web site. Fortunately, the online world offers multiple chances for self-promotion on a limited budget. Even if you can't afford an extensive radio campaign or an army of cardboard cutouts for every record store in America, you can promote yourself online.

> Among the best online marketing tools available are the file-sharing sites like Napster, Gnutella, Freenet, and Scour Exchange. Yes, you'll be sharing your music for free, but if you don't yet have name recognition, it's a great way to introduce your band to the public.

And while you can also spend big money on online advertising, there are plenty of effective Web promotional techniques that don't cost much. You just need to know where to find them and learn how to use them. So let's get going.

Search Engines

If you do nothing else in your online marketing efforts, make sure you submit your site to search engines. When it comes to getting free exposure, there's nothing that compares with being listed in these online guides. With the diffuse and chaotic nature of the Web, users rely heavily on search engines to provide a roadmap.

Without a listing in any of the search portals, your traffic-building efforts will always work against a handicap.

There are dozens of search engines, and the top ones get tens of millions of visitors a month. I've heard of sites building significant traffic with little more than a listing in a good search engine.

> Web search experts say that if you're searching for music files online, it's much more effective to use smaller music-focused search sites like Audiofind.com or Streamsearch.com than huge all-inclusive search engines like Yahoo.

You want to enter links to your sites in as many search engines as possible. This is easier said than done, though, because the top search engines are mobbed with submissions. You'll hear horror stories about people submitting link information repeatedly over a long period of time without ever getting a listing.

Indeed, getting yourself a good ranking on a search engine has become an artform all its own, and there are people who work full time on search engine placement strategy. To get advice from a top expert, visit Danny Sullivan's *SearchEngineWatch.com*. You'll find loads of information presented in easy-to-understand terms, and you can get a free appraisal of your own site.

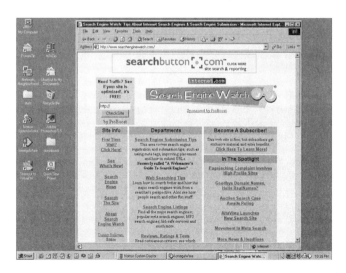

SearchEngine Watch.com, run by Web guru Danny Sullivan, is a top source of information about these all important Web portals.

One very important technique that search engine experts recommend is the proper use of keywords and meta tags. These are words and phrases embedded in your site that allow a search engine to properly list it. Many of the engines have *spiders*, software programs that continually crawl the Web and catalogue every site they come across. These spiders look for meta tags and keywords (among other things), so it's very important that you implement them properly.

Once you've built your site, you can use a two-part strategy to submit your links to the search engines:

- **Use a Submission Service**—These are online businesses that specialize in submitting your site to search engines. They've automated the process, so you can give them your information once and they'll submit it to hundreds of search engines at once. Two top submission services are Submit-It (*http://www.submit-it.com*) and Register-It (*http://www.register-it.com*). Both of these services will charge you, but it's worth it. (There's more on these services later in the chapter.)

Not only does Submit-It.com aid with search engine placement, but it also offers other online promotional help.

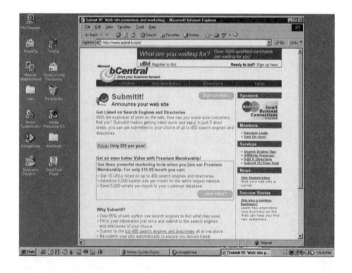

- **Submit Information Yourself**—It's a good idea to go to the most relevant search engines and submit your links yourself, even if you've used a submission service. Some experts disagree with this double-submission procedure, though,

because some search engines are sensitive to spamming—
repeated submissions. But there are a handful of search
engines that are so essential to building traffic that it's worth
submitting to them yourself. Just don't overdo it by submitting the same link again and again. Even under the best con-
ditions, it will take a few weeks (or longer) for your link to
appear.

Which sites are the most important to be listed in? Five of the
most popular search sites are Yahoo (the most popular site on the
Web, with 48 million visitors a month), Lycos, Excite, AltaVista,
and Ask Jeeves. If you're listed on these sites, you'll have a
chance to reach the majority of Web users.

In addition, submit your site to the top music-related search sites:

- **Audiofind** (*www.audiofind.com*)—Search for MP3s by artist
  or genre.

- **Imusic** (*www.imusic.com*)—Search for a specific artist.

- **Kerbango** (*www.kerbango.com*)—Good for finding Web
  radio broadcasts.

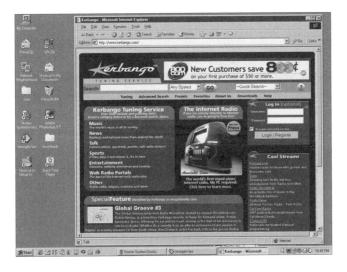

*Want to promote
your online radio
station? Make
sure it's listed at
Kerbango.com.*

- **Listen** (*www.listen.com*)—Find downloadable music in a
  broad variety of file formats.

- **Midi Explorer** (*www.musicrobot.com*)—Find MIDI files in many styles.

- **Scour** (*www.scour.net*)—This is a big one. Scour will find almost everything sound-related on the Web.

If you're a musician and you're interested in promoting yourself online, Scour is an important resource. It's an exhaustive music-related search engine.

- **Streamsearch** (*www.streamsearch.com*)—Geared toward finding streaming audio and video.

As broadband Internet use increases, search engines that focus on streaming audio and video, like Streamsearch, will become ever more important.

There are new music search services springing up all the time—
especially MP3-related services—so be on the lookout for new
ones.

Banner Ad Exchanges

Banner ad exchanges are among the most effective means of promoting a new site. All the members of an exchange service put
banner ads at the top of their sites that advertise other members.
A visitor to your site can click on the banner ad and take a look at
another member's site, and visitors at that site can click through
to yours.

One of the biggest of these programs is Link Exchange, a free
service offered by Microsoft Network's bCentral online promotion service that includes 450,000 sites. Users can choose from
several broad categories of Web sites that will show their banner ads.

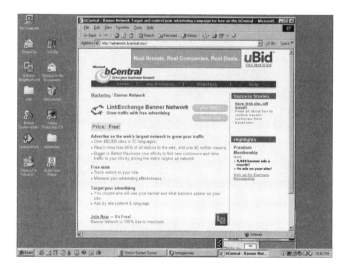

*Truly a great
resource for the
underfunded Web
site owner, Link
Exchange will
help you advertise
for free. Take a
look at http://
adnetwork.
bcentral.com.*

Or, Web site owners can spend some money and join bCentral's
programs that more aggressively promote members' sites.
Members can join the service at two levels, Premium Business
($19.99 a month) or Premium Pro ($499 a year). At the less
expensive level, the service offers 5,000 *impressions* of your banner ad a month. (An *impression* is when a user sees your banner.
It doesn't necessarily mean the user will click through to your

site.). At the more expensive level, your ad will be viewed by 10,000 Web users a month. (However, it's likely that only a small percentage of the users who see your ad will click through to your site.) In addition, both levels of membership will submit your site to search engines, check how your site is ranked on them, and enable you to send thousands of promotional emails per month to customers.

The downside of this program is that your site must include banner advertising for a site other than your own. This means giving up artistic control because you never know exactly which businesses will advertise on your site. But for a new site that's struggling to build traffic on a limited budget, these programs can be a major boost.

According to a recent poll by PC Data Online, 64 percent of online music consumers said that one of the Internet's chief advantages is exposure to new music and artists. As you promote your band online, keep in mind that there's a large and ever-growing Net audience for fresh musical talent.

Getting Hyper About Hyperlinks

Although an organized service like Link Exchange is useful, you want to create hyperlinks to your page on as many sites as possible. Be willing to trade links. Begin by asking sites that host music similar to yours if they'll put up a link from their site to yours. This process builds upon itself. As your site gains traffic, bigger music sites will be willing to trade links with you. Consider record labels (indie or otherwise), an online music store, or perhaps a club where you've played.

And you don't have to limit your link trades to music sites. Search the entire Web for possible connections to your site. As you surf around, constantly be on the lookout for sites to trade links with. The Web is full of sites run by people who are eager to build traffic and who would consider a mutually beneficial trade.

Some sites have "cool links" pages specifically for this purpose. You may want to build such a sub-page so it's easy to add a link.

This technique allows sites to offer link trades of varying values—they can offer a link from a deeply buried sub-page, or from a highly visible page.

You have little to lose by asking for a link trade, as long as you don't become a pest. It helps to develop a short email form letter, detailing the advantages of your site, that you can quickly personalize. Keep this form email handy as you surf so you can send it out on a regular basis. Be willing to use the phone, too, if you think you'll be able to get through to the site's decision maker. In the online age, this traditional means of communication continues to be persuasive.

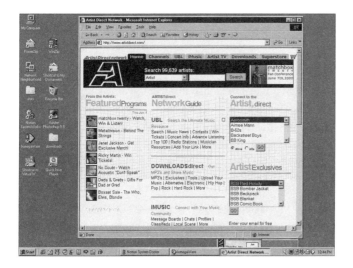

ArtistDirect.com is a sprawling collection of music-related sites—a good place to begin trading links with related sites.

The URL Heard 'Round the World

You want to spread your Web address with the zeal of a religious convert. (Well, just short of that, actually, but you get the idea.) Put *www.yourbandnamehere.com* on your business cards, album art, and invoices. Announce it onstage at your gigs, put it in the signature line of your email, rent a plane to fly overhead with it. Put it on your band's answering machine (and all the band members' machines), have it tattooed on your forehead…heck, write it into a song. (Okay, forget the tattoo thing.)

Farmclub.com is a hot phenomenon for unsigned bands. You can upload your music and get a chance to reach the site's considerable audience. Farmclub has its own TV show and a tie-in with AOL, and it gets coverage on MTV. It promotes over 100 unsigned bands a year on its TV show, and the site offers plenty of supplementary material about lawyers and publishing rights.

If possible, include a sub-headline with your URL. It's a lot more persuasive to see "redrocker.com: Alabama's Rowdiest Rockers" rather than just the URL by itself. And be careful not to create a backlash by putting your band's URL in inappropriate public places, like spray-painting it on public buildings or putting bumper stickers with it on other people's cars. Only put your Web address where it's ethical and sensible to put it.

What Is Opt-In Email?

There's been a lot of backlash in recent years against *spamming*, the sending of unsolicited junk email. You've probably gotten such junk emails, with titles like "How to Influence Everyone," "Stock Expected to Rise 7,000 Percent," and so on.

But there's an alternative called *opt-in email*. This is email that recipients have opted to receive. For example, a bluegrass fan might sign up for email about new bluegrass groups, or a jazz fan might submit her email address to a list about the newest top ten jazz cuts.

You can use opt-in email in a couple of ways:

- **Rent a mailing list**—Opt-in email services will sell you a mass emailing that goes out to a few thousand to hundreds of thousands of people. You can describe your recent release, mention your upcoming concert, and include the URL of your Web site. Since opt-in email recipients have volunteered to receive email on a given subject, they're less likely to see your email as spam.

- **Advertise on a mass mailing**—Thousands of email newsletters go out to millions of recipients a week. These newsletters are targeted to specialized audiences, such as Seattle-style grunge enthusiasts or Dixieland music historians. The people who write and send these targeted emails often include advertising blurbs, and you can buy ad space there. This enables you to reach a narrowly targeted audience that's interested in your genre.

There's no guarantee you'll get a large response, and even in the best cases the response rate is low. The industry standard for responses to traditional direct mail campaigns is 3 percent. I've heard of mass emailings that were very specifically targeted that reached an 8-10 percent response rate. But that can't be counted on.

Also, beware of unscrupulous operators in this market. Some of the services that offer to set up mass emailings for you are just organized spammers, and they'll cause great ill will among those who are pestered by your junk mail. Do some investigating before you decide to spend money on an opt-in mail service.

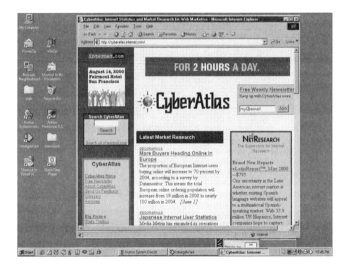

When you're ready to look into opt-in emailing, Cyberatlas.com offers many resources. It's also a good general resource for online advertising.

Talking Across the Online Fence: Bulletin Boards, Discussion Lists, and Chatrooms

Web users like to do a lot of things: download music, search for radio stations, look for cool photos, and read articles. But the most popular use of the Web is communicating with other Web users. Judging by the popularity of bulletin board services (also called BBS), discussion lists, and chat, Netizens have a seemingly inexhaustible desire to share their opinions and read those of others.

In case you're not familiar with these formats, discussion lists and bulletin boards are forums with comments, facts, opinions, and sometimes pure invention by anyone interested enough to submit them. Some of these services are run by moderators who decide what gets posted, but others are free-for-alls. You're probably familiar with chatrooms, which let users type and respond to messages in real time. This has become wildly popular; the number of online chatters typing away even as you read this probably equals the population of Delaware.

> Some musicians use a chatroom name that's the same or similar to their band name. Every time they post a comment, they're increasing their name recognition.

You can use this Internet phenomenon to your advantage. Find bulletin boards and chat sessions that are dedicated to your musical style. Unless your genre is ancient Icelandic folk music, you'll find dozens of relevant online discussions dedicated to it. (And you can probably find a few on Icelandic folk music, for that matter.) Once you're familiar enough with a bulletin board to know its feel and mood, make a relevant and interesting post. Add something that gets other members talking and thinking.

Think broadly. If you're a jazz guitarist, for example, you can join discussions on jazz orchestras, Dixieland, improvised music, music therapy, world music, and African American music, as well as chats about finding gigs, recording your own music, the business of music, and jazz online.

And—here's the promotional part—mention your Web site, recent release, or upcoming concert. If what you have to say is interesting to the other members, they may want to visit your site or download your music. At its best, this type of chat participation creates word-of-mouth marketing (chatroom participants are a talkative bunch, after all).

A major word of caution: If you take part in a chat or discussion list in a blatantly self-serving way, other members will tune you out faster than you can say "spam sandwich." It's okay to mention your music in the context of what others are talking about—online music fans welcome that—but make sure you're "listening to the rest of the band."

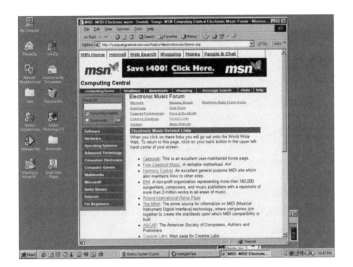

You'll find plenty of musicians to trade opinions with at the Electronic Music Forum. Share some vibes at http://computing central.msn.com/ topics/electronic music/bonus.asp.

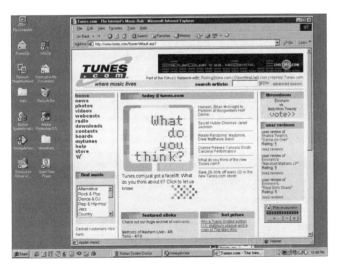

Explore Tunes.com to find links to music chatrooms and discussion lists.

Ready, Set... Type!

So, you want to find a chatroom where you can share your excitement about music in general and your new album in particular.

It's easy to do—there's a chatroom for everyone. However, being an effective chatroom chatter requires good typing skills. You don't have to be a professional secretary, but unless you can type a sentence reasonably quickly, other chatters might type right over you. In fact, they might anyway, given the sometimes chaotic nature of online chat.

So throw caution to the wind and look at some of these online chatrooms:

- **On The Moshing Floor** (*http://www.wtss.com/chat/*)—Christian alternative music chat.

- **Oz-Music Chat** (*http://www.oz-music.com/chat/public/*)—Australian music chat.

- **Fruits Of Music Chat Rooms** (*http://www.fruits.ch/cgi-bin/chat.cgi*)—Chat about Swiss electronica.

- **New Orleans Music Chat** (*http://www.talkcity.com/calendar/category/music.html*)—Do they still chat during Mardi Gras?

- **Classical Music Chat** (*http://www.classicalmusic.co.uk/chat.html*)—Talk about Beethoven with enthusiasts from all over the world.

- **Yerastica Hard and Heavy Music Chat** (*http://www.geocities.com/SunsetStrip/Towers/2238/Chat.htm*)—Discuss your favorite heavy metal band.

- **LAUT.BAR Chat** (*http://www.laut.de/lautbar/chat/index.html*)—This music chat is in German.

- **Alternative Music Chat** (*http://altmusic.about.com/mpchat.htm*)—Share opinions about R.E.M., the Smashing Pumpkins, and Garbage.

- **Indian Melody Music Chat** (*http://www.indianmelody.com/chat.htm*)—Discuss Indian music, ranging from classical to the latest film scores.

- **David McPherson, Senior VP, Sony Music**—This was a chat with an industry executive about the things that emerging artists need to know to break into the business. It happened in 1999, but check back at *http://chat.yahoo.com* for similar events.

AllRoadsLeadToRome.com

When you're developing your promotional strategy, keep reminding yourself of this important point: *A Web presence is bigger than just a Web site.* The Web is full of heavily trafficked sites that offer free Web pages to artists. These high-profile sites range from Amazon.com to MP3.com to Angelfire.com. Put up your photo and some music clips in so many locations that potential fans can hardly help but stumble across them. Link back to your central site from as many pages as possible. This is an inexpensive way to use the Web's interconnectivity to your best benefit.

The Bottom Line: Constant Effort

Although promoting your music online is affordable, you're not the only one who wants to reach the ears of an audience. Web promoters talk about the need to "rise above the clutter." In the battle to get noticed online, the advantage goes to the artists who never stop their promotional efforts. If your Web site reaches a high level of usage but you stop promoting it, your visitors may begin to fade away. If you spend 15 minutes a week in online promotion, you'll see a benefit. If you spend several hours a week, you'll see much more.

Enlist the entire band in the effort, or cajole friends into sending out emails and mentioning your new release in chatrooms. After a while, your marketing efforts can build on themselves as fans recommend you to other fans. (But that doesn't mean you can stop promoting. You can never stop!)

The online music world will be experiencing explosive change in the next few years, and new methods of self-promotion will develop. Keep looking for innovative ways to spread the word about your music, and start using them before they get adopted by the herd.

Wrapping It Up

So there you sit at your home computer, looking at your Web counter. Isn't it nice watching the number go up week after week in response to your self-promotion?

Before you launch your next online marketing effort, take a look at what you learned in this chapter:

- You learned that the phrase "build it and they will come" doesn't apply to Web sites. Promoting yourself is critical if you want to reach the rapidly growing online audience.

- You discovered some of the most cost-effective outlets for online promotion.

- You learned how each of these outlets works, and you also found some Web sites that will help you further explore online promotion.

CHAPTER 25

Internet Record Labels

I don't know about you, but when I think of the term *record label*, several things come to mind.

First, I always imagine record labels to be in large buildings in large cities. These companies have names such as Sony, Universal, or BMG, and their offices occupy several floors of a large skyscraper. Inside these chrome-and-glass skyscrapers are well-dressed men and women, sitting in big offices with fine, expensive furniture.

There are armies of secretaries. The secretaries are vital because they screen phone calls. This is important because—and this part isn't just in my mind—you can never get through to anyone at a record label. You can call the secretaries at "Major Label," but unless your name is "Big Star," the only voice you're going to hear is that of the receptionist.

What You'll Learn in This Chapter:

▸ How the Web is creating new types of record labels

▸ How these new labels function

▸ What deals artists can expect from uploading their music to a Web record label

▸ What you'll find at some of the biggest Web labels

> Not that long ago, there were many more major record labels. But through a consistent process of mergers and acquisitions, the number has shrunk to five. Some industry analysts feel that this has resulted in a music industry that's unwilling to take risks on new artists.

Maybe that's as it should be because the record labels—the big ones, that is—have enormous power. They have the distribution networks, they have marketing muscle, and they have the business expertise to turn a creative artist into a multimillion-dollar corporate product. If "Major Label" decides to make "Hometown Girl" a star, most everyone in America (or the world) will hear that person's name. If "Mr. or Ms. Big" answered the phone for every unsigned artist, "Major Label" would never get any work done, and no artists would become famous. So those secretaries, although frustrating for some, provide a very valuable service.

Many types of record labels exist. In addition to the "Big Five"—Sony, Universal, BMG, EMI, and Warner Music—numerous smaller labels exist. An example of an interesting smaller label is Rounder Records, which represents some great rhythm and blues artists. Many such "boutique" labels have catalogs that are more impressive than their bottom line. In addition, hundreds of smaller labels have low-budget contracts with a limited number of artists.

But regardless of how big or small it is, the goals of a traditional record label are basically the same. When an artist signs with a label, it promotes and distributes the artist as much as possible. In some instances, the label becomes a parent figure for the musician, providing artistic advice, shaping the artist's onstage routine, and setting up publicity and tours. In short, the label takes a little known or unknown artist and nurtures him into a successful (profitable) recording career.

The Recording Industry Association of America (RIAA) represents the record labels. It has been very active combating music piracy on the Web.

And Then Came the Web

The Web has a way of changing everything it touches, and record labels are no exception. Although the definition of a traditional record label is clear, the concept of an Internet record label is much less defined.

In fact, some of the sites listed in this chapter aren't, strictly speaking, record labels. But each in some way provides artists with services that the traditional labels provide.

Each of the Internet record labels listed in this chapter adds a new twist to the old label model. Each takes advantage of the Web's enormous power of distribution. It's as if the Internet, with its global reach, was invented for record labels.

Each of these Web labels takes advantage of the ease of digital copying. Instead of contracting a pressing plant, hiring a shipping company, and paying for a warehouse, a Net label can simply post an MP3 and request a credit card number.

Because Web labels have much less invested in the artists they host, they don't have to put up the enormous barriers to entry that the major labels do. In most cases, an artist needs only to upload some music files and a band photo to begin reaching fans. Only a few of these Web labels charge or do extensive screening.

> Almost anyone can start an Internet record label. At its most basic, it requires only a Web site, a small staff, and a marketing budget.

The downside, of course, is that the artists who post their music at online-only labels aren't going to benefit from the marketing efforts of a well-funded label. And that's a major drawback. In a world in which consumers are inundated with sophisticated advertising, those bands without a marketing budget are peddling up hill—up a very steep hill.

These Web labels offer access to a mass audience where previously none existed. As they continue to evolve, and the online audience grows ever larger, Web record labels will become an increasingly important resource for musicians.

This is just the beginning. According to Jupiter Communications, sales of digital music will grow to $147 million by 2003. Compare that with the $14 billion of music recordings sold in 1999. So the pioneers of this movement—Internet record labels—are in their infancy. There's no better time to get involved.

A Tour of Internet Record Labels

MP3.com

MP3.com's strong suit is its huge traffic numbers—the site itself claims six million visitors a month. Although this number isn't supported by the Web rating service MediaMetrix.com, the service does list MP3.com as one of the top 500 visited sites on the Web, which means it has a huge audience.

Thousands of unsigned bands have uploaded their music to MP3.com in hopes of gaining exposure.

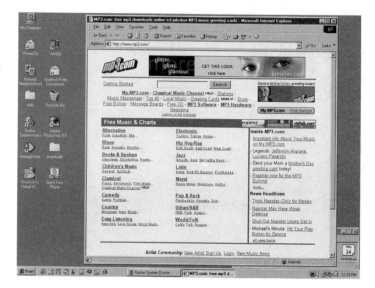

MP3.com's Artist Community provides several services for musicians. Its D.A.M. (Digital Automated Music) system gives the artist 50% of royalties from CD sales. When a fan orders an artist's CDs, MP3 covers the expense of CD manufacturing and shipping.

> MP3.com offers a no-risk proposition to new artists, and this has helped create enormous traffic at its site.

The D.A.M. program is a free service, and the simple non-exclusive agreement can be terminated by the artist at any time. In effect, the band seeking greater exposure has nothing to lose by posting its music on MP3.

Paradoxically, MP3.com's large traffic numbers can also work against a band seeking exposure. The site currently hosts the music from thousands of bands, so it cannot give high profile promotion to many acts. Anyone can sign up, which means that everyone does, so your carefully produced singles might be listed next to the kid from down the street who's singing a duet with his dog.

As with any of distribution method, simply putting your music out there is rarely enough—you have to advertise it, relentlessly. But MP3.com, similar to many of the top music sites, offers a poor man's alternative to this. It allows fans to vote for you—and if your band gets enough votes, it will be featured prominently on the site. This is the magic of Web music distribution—if your music has instant, powerful crowd appeal, you will command an enthusiastic audience. And you'll never need to convince a label executive of this.

IUMA.com

The online world is filled with snazzy business names such as Emusic or Riffage. In contrast, IUMA, the Internet Underground Music Archive, has one of the longest and most ungainly monikers. But this site, founded in the Web's infancy in 1993, has always had an aura of "by the musician, for the musician."

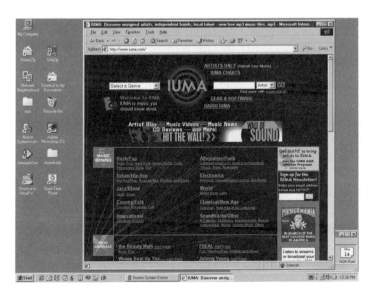

IUMA is a good place for unsigned bands to post their music.

You'll find every style and flavor at IUMA, from the blues of Dr. Oakroot to the experimental music of Stan Demski, from Ambient Electronica to Contemporary Christian. You can sample the music in RealAudio, and if you find something you like, download it in MP3.

IUMA offers a free Web site to musicians. Using the site's Artist Uplink service, a band can upload photos and MP3s of its music and build a basic promotional Web presence. The sites are no-frills templates providing band background, free downloads, and contact information.

To sell your music through IUMA, you need to send in five CDs or tapes of your album. For every CD/tape sold through the site, IUMA takes the first $5. You can set the album price yourself. So, if you charge $10, you will make $5 in profit.

IUMA also has a program that benefits musicians called "It's Your Damn Web Site." This program gives artists a percentage of the ad revenue generated from the banner ads located at the top of their IUMA-sponsored sites, amounting to about a dollar for every 415 page views the site generates. It takes a massive amount of traffic to create significant profit, but every little bit helps.

In addition to providing daily updates on how often your band's music downloads and Web page views, IUMA offers promotional advice to help you market yourself. This includes insider's articles by resident expert Sue Few, and tongue-in-cheek tips such as "Pay the local tattoo parlor to tattoo your URL on people's bodies," or "Visit quiet crowded places like the movies and opera and every five minutes or so, stand up and scream your band name and URL." This last tip goes on to recommend that band members stand in different parts of the theater to diffuse attacks by audience members—a good idea indeed.

Amazon.com

You can list your CD (or videotape, or self-published novel) with Amazon.com's Advantage program. Amazon.com will scan your CD cover art, encode two songs to provide samples for music shoppers, keep track of inventory, and ship your CD to customers.

The site requests two to five CDs to hold in its warehouse so that it can fill an order within 24 hours. Your band will have an Amazon.com page with space for customer reviews, bios, cover art, liner notes, and the all-important free MP3 downloads.

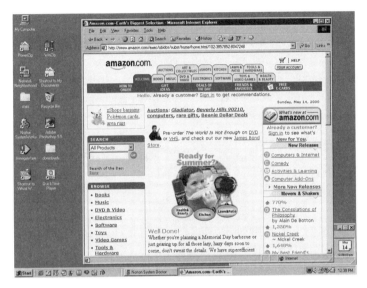

Amazon.com's Advantage Program isn't listed on its home page. It's most easily found by clicking on Site Guide at the bottom of the home page.

Amazon.com

You might be thinking, "Amazon.com—a record label?" Listen to the site's description of its Advantage Program: "Amazon.com is a complete promotion and distribution system for independent musicians." That's the classic definition of a record label.

The service is free to join. You set the retail price of your album yourself. If you make a sale, Amazon.com gets 45% of the sale price.

It's a plus to be able to say to your audience during a club date, "You can find our CD at Amazon." The site has a reputation for reliability and is very professionally run, not to mention having traffic numbers of more than 15 million unique visitors a month.

Of course, it doesn't mean that 15 million shoppers will see your album cover. If you're not actively marketing it, your music will be no more than the sound of silence for those millions of music shoppers. To promote you, Amazon offers a Marketing Resource

Center (accessible by members only) that offers guerilla marketing techniques to get the word out about your music. The site also
shares tips and success stories from member musicians who have
been able to reach an audience through Amazon.

Riffage

"Our mission is to revolutionize the way music is distributed by
using the Internet to allow musicians to communicate directly
with—and sell music to—their fans." So says Riffage.com, and
although it doesn't attract as many visitors as the largest music
sites, it lives up to its mission statement.

*Riffage.com
allows visitors to
access the site in a
variety of lan-
guages.*

Using MyRiffage, fans can rate and review the site's broad selection of indie bands, and create their own playlists. These recom-
mendations are viewed by other site visitors, creating a fan-based
marketing system that gives a boost to otherwise unknown bands.

> For musicians, one of the advantages of using Internet record labels is
> their non-exclusivity. A band can—and should—upload its music to a
> half-dozen or more Web music labels.

Riffage allows musicians to sell single MP3s as well as CDs
(although after quite a bit of browsing, I found only free MP3s).
The site provides a free Web page for musicians, many of whom

use the site's tour calendar to let fans know where they'll be playing. Riffage lets artists keep 85% of profits from sales of their album—an unusually high percentage.

Visitors can access the site in German, Italian, French, Portuguese, and Spanish. That might mean nothing to you (you're reading in English, after all), but think of the worldwide music audience.

Emusic

Emusic is a leader among Internet record labels. If you want to know what the label of the future will look like, visit Emusic.com.

Emusic.com has acquired an impressive array of music-related Web sites.

Founded in 1998, Emusic has dozens of strategic partnerships with online businesses, ranging from America Online to Yahoo!. Seemingly always in an expansion phase, Emusic acquired Tunes.com (which operates Rollingstone.com and Downbeatjazz.com), Cductive.com, and IUMA.com. Consolidating this family of music-oriented Web sites under one roof means that music distributed by Emusic is heard by millions of fans a month.

One of the thorniest issues confronting Internet music labels like Emusic.com, which charges for downloading music, is operating side by side with sites such as Napster, which is free.

This conglomeration of resources provides Emusic with a constantly expanding catalog of MP3s (they're legal) from Beck to Frank Zappa to They Might Be Giants, as well as thousands of indie bands like The Dillinger Escape Plan and the Slackers. Emusic has grown so large that it doesn't accept submissions from unsigned bands; it refers those artists to the IUMA.

Shopping at Emusic.com is a seamless experience, right down to the online shopping cart. The site offers more than 75,000 tracks for purchase—individual tracks for 99 cents each, or downloadable albums for $8.99. Use the site's search engine to shop by artist or genre, and click on the song or album title when you find something you like. You'll by given the opportunity to listen to a clip of the band (with RealAudio). If you like it, you can enter your credit card information, and instantly download it. Who needs to go to the mall?

Songs.com

Geared toward the acoustic singer/songwriter, Songs.com features CDs for sale by both known artists like Emmylou Harris and Janis Ian and lesser known folk/country/bluegrass musicians. For artists working on building name recognition, the site offers a variety of promotional services. So Songs.com is a combination CD store and independent artists' marketing tool.

An artist must become a member of Songs.com to sell her CDs on the site. Initial membership costs $190, of which $60 is an annual membership fee. As part of membership application, artists submit their press kit along with a CD so that Songs.com can screen for quality and focus. The site wants to stay specifically oriented toward the singer/songwriter genre. This entry fee covers the cost of a basic artist's home page, although if you want a more elaborate site, you can spend $290-600 or more. All the sites include song clips, biographical information, and artist's quotes as well as dynamically updated tour listings. Songs.com typically sells CDs for $14, of which the artist receives $9.50.

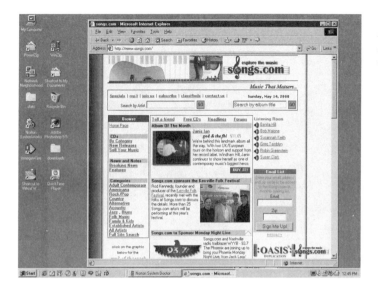

The singer/ songwriter meets the Web at Songs.com.

You might raise an eyebrow at the idea of charging musicians a membership fee to join. Indeed, this runs counter to standard procedure at traditional record labels, which sometimes give an advance to artists, and would never charge a fee to represent them. At a grassroots level, this fee-based membership helps focus and strengthen the site. Songs.com lists its roster at 300 musicians—a fraction of what a site such as MP3.com hosts. Because these 300 have paid, and presumably been screened, it helps narrow the field. The visitor—and potential shopper—at Songs.com doesn't know that all the artists at the site are good, but she knows that all take their effort seriously.

The artists benefit from not having to compete with the hordes. They also benefit from the site's marketing efforts. Songs.com promotes itself with sponsorships such as the Kerrville Folk Festival and Monday Night Live, a radio program broadcast from Jack Legs' Speakeasy in Nashville.

Garageband.com

"Should we give this band a $250,000 recording contract?" asks the front page of Garageband.com. If your answer is yes, you'll want to become a Garageband.com reviewer, and earn points toward music gear as you post reviews. The band voted most popular by the site's fans wins the big bucks recording contract. (Show me a traditional record label that offers unknown bands a chance like this.)

Garageband.com offers an advice column for bands by Ramones producer Ed Stasium.

The site has an ingenious method of determining popularity. It invites all visitors to fill out a form and become a reviewer. To provide an impartial vote, each reviewer is given two songs randomly selected from that reviewer's preferred genre, without the song's title or band name. When a reviewer submits her review, it's entered into the site's review computer, and the band's ranking is recalculated accordingly. If your band's creations strike a chord with the largest number of reviewers, you get the $250,000 contract.

> Garageband.com is one of the sponsors of the Online Music Awards, which is Webcast live every summer. To see an archived version of the show, visit Yahoo Internet Life at *www.yilmusicawards.com*.

Garageband.com claims its goal is to provide one such contract a month. There's also the possibility of other recording contracts. If your material is heard by one of the producers from the site's Advisory Board, he might offer you a deal on the spot if he thinks there's potential.

Although Garageband.com offers music from metal, hip-hop, folk, to electronic, it appears geared toward the indie rock band. Furthering this indie rock feel are sponsored chats with the likes of famed U2 producer Steve Lillywhite, and a column by Ramones ranging producer Ed Stasium in which he critiques a new band each day.

In a break with other Internet music distribution sites, Garageband.com sells no music. Its task instead is to "identify hot new artists to sign and promote with an effectiveness only the Internet can make possible."

SpinRecords.com

SpinRecords.com is a combination online store and Web record label. A visitor to the SpinRecords site will be offered not only music, but also opportunities to buy portable MP3 players and win a digital camera. In fact, to get through to the front page, you might have to click past a pop-up window that advertises something like the Pacific Beach Block Party, sponsored by SpinRecords (Win Free Stuff!) The online store at SpinRecords sells everything from skateboards to clothing to videos. You can stop by Rob's Horoscope service and take a look into your future (this one's free). In short, the site takes a decidedly commercial approach to online music distribution.

SpinRecords helps showcase bands with its many sponsored events.

There's plenty of music at SpinRecords too. You'll find just about any genre you can imagine—avant-garde jazz, spoken word, Celtic, as well as the old standbys like death metal and disco.

The site claims to offer an amazing array of artist support. In addition to selling your CD (you set the wholesale price, and they set the retail price), SpinRecords will put up your Web site with scanned art, music clips, and band information. You can also sell any other band merchandise through the site: t-shirts, hats, body lotion—you got it, they'll sell it.

In addition, the site offers help booking tours, and when possible, to send a video crew out to tape your group. SpinRecord's bands will be able to participate in one of the many promotional events the site sponsors, such as the Emerging Artists and Talent in Music (EAT'M) and LA Music 2000, which features acts from jazz to hip-hop.

Liquid Audio

Although LiquidAudio.com isn't a record label by the traditional definition, its mission is to lead "the convergence of music and technology to establish the Internet as a new medium for music distribution." Music distribution is precisely the focus of traditional labels—Liquid Audio simply takes it to the Web.

LiquidAudio.com boasts one of the largest online offerings of downloadable music.

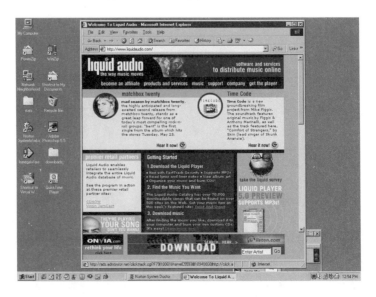

The site hosts an inventory of over 70,000 downloadable songs from more than 8,500 hundred artists. Some of these songs are offered as free downloads, and others are available for purchase through 750 online retailers, including CDNow.com and Amazon.com. Liquid Audio has formed alliances with more than 1,400 record labels.

Liquid Audio was formed in January 1996, which makes it an established company by Internet standards. Web music distribution is still in its infancy, and it's far from clear how it will develop.

The size and scope of Liquid Audio means that you'll find major label artists there. The sites offer tracks for sale by the likes of Matchbox 20, John Scofield, and Little Feat. If you want to surf through the sites with which Liquid Audio has retail affiliations, you'll find many major acts.

For the unsigned artist, the site offers a service called Liquid Platinum. A musician can join the program at various levels, ranging from $99 to $1395, depending on what services he wants and how much music he wants to upload. The program includes Web hosting, five simultaneous preview streams, and Liquid Pro software to encode songs. The artist receives 49 to 74% of the retail purchase price, depending of how the music is sold.

Joining the program is pricey, but it provides an artist access to the Liquid Music Network, the network of affiliations listed previously that extends throughout the Web. If you're only going to join one network, this is the one to be part of.

At This Rate, There Will Be More Labels than Bands

There are many more Internet record labels than those listed in this chapter. In fact, more and more "micro labels" are springing up on the Web. All it takes is a Web site, some music files, a modest marketing budget, and you can start your own. In addition, many sites do part of what a label does—for example, they promote bands, but they don't sell music. So, if you count these "almost label" sites, you'll see that the Web is an incredibly rich source for musicians.

Take a look at what's up in Norway and Finland at http://www.lysator. liu.se/~chief/scan. html.

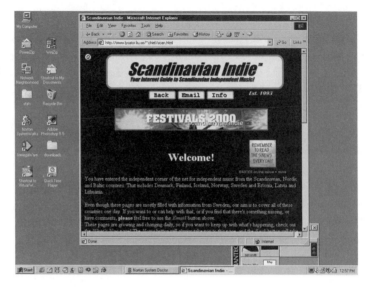

Many of these mini labels are worth investigating. Just because a Net label isn't one of the biggies doesn't mean it can't help you. A smaller independent label might not have the resources of a larger name, but it might be more flexible and more willing to focus on a band that's just begun building a fan base. So start surfing, and remember that the Web is opening new opportunities to musicians all the time.

Wrapping It Up

It's pretty nice, isn't it? You've finally gotten you're first record-ing contract—from a new Web-based recording label. Cool!

Take a break from getting ready to go into the studio to look at what you learned in this chapter:

- How the Web is changing, what it means to be a record label, and how Web-based labels add new concepts—like instant fan feedback and online commerce—to the traditional label business.

- What some typical compensation percentages are for musi-cians who sell music through Web record labels.

- What you'll find at some of the biggest Web labels, including all the most commonly used business models.

APPENDIX A

Online Resources for Finding What You're Looking For

Celebrity Web Sites

The Artist Formerly Known As Prince

www.npgonlineltd.com

The Artist isn't known for his fondness for record labels. Expect him to remain at the forefront of Internet self-publishing.

Beastie Boys

www.beastieboys.com

Here's where these icons of crossover rap post RealAudio clips of their music and a timeline of their history.

Beck

www.beck.com

Beck's quirky individuality is captured on his Web page. It's a good example of an artist's identity being accurately represented online.

David Bowie

www.davidbowie.com

This is a Web site that's not afraid to be commercial. Set up an email address that ends in davidbowie.com, or order a credit card with Bowie's likeness on it.

Marilyn Manson

www.marilynmanson.net

There's more than enough attitude at this site. And although Manson cultivates a raw image, his site features some highly stylish design.

Todd Rundgren

www.todd-rundgren.com

This pop balladeer's site includes a section called Subscription, which is his very interesting approach to eliminating the middleman in the music publishing business.

Sarah Mclachlan

www.sarahmclachlan.com

This popular singer songwriter's site features a link to Murmurs, a members-only fan site that provides dedicated fans with a treasure trove of "Sarah Stuff," including photos, interviews, sound and video files, and fan artwork. This is an example of advanced Web marketing.

Copyright

U.S. Copyright Web

http://lcweb.loc.gov/copyright/circs/circ1.html

Visit the U.S. Copyright Web site to get a complete overview of the copyright process.

10 Myths About Copyright

www.clari.net/brad/copymyths.html

This site actually explores 11 myths about Internet-related copyright issues, but its author didn't want to change the title.

Copyright FAQ

www.mcs.net/~fishercg/copyfaq.html

This a clear and easy-to-read list of the most common copyright questions, which are answered by attorney Jeffrey P. Fisher.

Protect Your Band Name

www.music-law.com/bandname.html

Someone else might want to call themselves the Barking Dudettes. (Hey, that's a good name… I'd better go protect it!) Attorney Michael P. McCready provides advice on how to hang on to your moniker.

Protect Your Trademark

http://teas.uspto.gov/V1.21/index.html

If your band has a logo you'd like to protect, this form from the United States Patent and Trademark Office lets you register it online.

Music Law

www.miseryloves.com/law.htm

A detailed overview of copyright law by entertainment attorney Mike Beeman, geared specifically toward musicians.

Software—Collections

AnalogX

www.analogx.com/contents/download.htm

This collection of shareware isn't as big as some, but it's interesting. Find applications that help you scratch like a DJ or do speech synthesis.

Midisoft

www.midisoft.com/html/free_software/free_dloads.htm

Offers plenty of low- or no-cost downloads of MIDI software, including the Midisoft Internet Audio Postcard Player.

MP3 Central

www.zdnet.com/downloads/topics/mp3.htm

A well-organized listing of MP3 shareware and MP3 news.

MP3 Fiend

www.mp3fiend.com

For the truly MP3-obsessed—download this MP3 search utility to aid in your never-ending search for fresh music files.

Multimedia/Audio—CNET

http://download.cnet.com/downloads/

This site displays a list of the top downloads. Or, choose from an extensive list. (Included is an interesting streaming utility called RadioSpy.)

Shareware Music Machine

www.hitsquad.com/smm/

This is it—the treasure trove. Not only is there a vast selection of shareware, but there are also links to the leading audio software developers.

Sonido Media

www.sonidomedia.com/tips/programs.htm

A good collection, including the ever-popular CoolEdit and the interesting MixMan Studio—good for DJs.

Synthzone Shareware Archives

www.synthzone.com/softarch.htm

This is a listing of lists of audio shareware—well put together.

Toolkit: Medley of Music Programs

www.zdnet.com/swlib/toolkits/music/tlk0597.html

Quite a nice selection of educational music shareware. Here you'll find Ear Power (an ear-training application) and Keynote Music Drills.

Software—Programs

ACID

www.sonicfoundry.com/PRODUCTS/ACIDFamily.asp

This software comes with hundreds of sound loops created by studio pros. You can mix and match, remix, and layer them until the music becomes your own.

Audio Magic Ring

www.hitsquad.com/smm/programs/AudioMagicRing/

Convert a sound file from WAV to AIF (or many other formats) with this Windows-based utility.

Band In A Box

www.pgmusic.com/products.htm

A library of music tracks composed in MIDI format. You can use them as a foundation for your own composing. Made by PG Music.

Barbatch

www.audioease.com

This Mac utility comes in handy when you need to turn an AIF sound file into a WAV, or vice versa. It can handle all the major formats, and some obscure ones too.

Bias Deck

www.bias-inc.com

A top audio editor for the Mac. Deck can do multitrack editing, effects processing, mixdown, and more.

Cool Edit Pro

www.syntrillium.com/

This 64-track recording and mixing software is a popular choice for Windows-based audio producers. Made by Syntrillium, which also makes Kaleidoscope, the screen saver that responds to music.

Goldwave Digital Audio Editor

www.goldwave.com/

This PC-based audio editor features real-time amplitude and spectrogram graphs, numerous effects, and multitrack mixdown capability.

Metasynth

www.metasynth.com

This sound utility for Mac users allows you to transform a picture into sound, or a sound into picture. It enables you to take digital information from one medium and apply it to another.

Media Wizard

www.filecenter.com/filecenter/details/1079.asp

This Windows sound utility allows you to convert sound files from one format to another, such as from WAV to RealAudio.

MusicMatch

www.musicmatch.com

One of today's top free software programs for MP3 and other audio file formats.

Noise Reduction

www.sonicfoundry.com/Products/ShowProduct.asp?PID=14

This handy plug-in removes snap, crackle, and pop from your sounds. It's also designed to analyze sounds and help you lessen hiss and reduce distortion.

ReCycle

www.steinberg.net/products/recyclepc.html

Having trouble with your loops and samples? ReCycle is an audio processing tool for loops and grooves. It can change tempo and quantize your samples.

Sound Edit 16

www.macromedia.com/software/sound/

A popular Mac-based editor that's bundled with the Macromedia Director authoring software. Capable of effects processing and multi-track editing and mixdown, and a favorite among the Mac crowd.

SoundHack

www.gmeb.fr/SoftwareCompetition/Softs96/SoundHack.html

Converts any sound file into virtually any other format. For the Mac.

Sound Forge

www.sonicfoundry.com/Products/ShowProduct.asp?PID=5

This has been a well-respected audio editor for years. The new version supports MP3 and multiple streaming audio formats. Windows.

WaveLab

www.steinberg.net/products/wavelabpc.html

A Windows-based editor that gives you real-time processing during playback.

Visiosonic

www.pcdj.com

The most interesting feature of this player/encoder for Windows is that you can play two MP3s at once and cross-fade between them like a club DJ. The PCDJ Mixmaster version is $29.99, and the basic version (which can't encode) is free.

Xing Audio Catalyst

www.xingtech.com

MP3 software with both Mac and Windows versions.

Instruction
AudioToday

www.audiotoday.com

A constantly updated source of sound-related news gathered from around the Web.

Broadband Guide

www.broadband-guide.com

Broadband Guide is an industry trade magazine that covers advances in telecommunications. This site is building an "ask the expert" section that will be a good source of information about audio and video over the Web.

The Compact Flash Association

www.compactflash.org

This nonprofit group is dedicated to maintaining the CF format.

Digital Experience

www.digitalexperience.com

A nearly encyclopedic compendium of reviews about sound cards and digital audio equipment.

Gamer's Guide To Sound Cards

www.gamecenter.com/Hardware/Roundup/Sound/

Hosted by CNET, this site is chock full of reviews and technical information. It's the site for people who realize that the way a game sounds is just as important as the way it looks.

Hyperreal

www.hyperreal.org/music

This site is geared toward the electronic musician, with emphasis on the DJ.

Home Recording

www.homerecording.com

This site is dedicated to helping the home audio enthusiast.

Latest Reviews—Audio

http://webdeveloper.internet.com/multimedia

These software reviews published by Web Developer's Journal are a good resource, especially if you're thinking about making a purchase.

Motion Picture Experts Group

http://www.mpeg.org

MPEG developed the standards that led to the MP3 compression technology.

The Personal Computer Memory Card International Association (PCMCIA)

www.pcmcia.org

A compendium of resources about the growing field of memory cards.

SampleNet

www.samplenet.co.uk/

Published in the UK, SampleNet is a top source of reviews and information about multimedia sound equipment, including sound cards, desktop digital audio software, and MIDI sequencers.

Simpletech

www.simpletech.com/flash/intro.htm

The Flash section of the Simpletech Web site provides plenty of background about flash storage.

Synthmuseum

www.synthmuseum.com

This site is a must-see for those interested in the early days of electronic music.

Synthzone

www.synthzone.com

A superb source of information about audio hardware. Check out the Owner and Service Manuals link.

The Tapeless Studio

http://tapeless.com/

An online magazine about computer-based audio recording. Includes reviews of pro audio hardware and software, and a discussion group with experts to answer questions about computer audio.

Tweakheadz.com: How To

www.tweakheadz.com/how_to articles.html

Knowledgeable advice on MIDI, sequencing, and sampling. Articles include "Secrets of Making Great Samples" and "Digital Audio Tips and Tricks."

Web Audio Workshop

http://nctweb.com/columns/web_audio_workshop.html

Tips on many multimedia sound topics, from "Executable Musical Postcards" to "How to Sell Your CDs Online." This site is part of Internet.com's Web Developer's Journal—a great resource.

Webmonkey

www.hotwired.com/webmonkey/98/17/index2a.html

If you want to find out about adding audio to a Web site, this is an important site to visit.

Worldwide Internet Music Resource

www.music.indiana.edu/music_resources

Organized by the Music School at Indiana University, this site is an exhaustive source of information about sound and music.

Internet Record Labels/Online Music Outlets

Amazon.com

www.amazon.com

Musicians can post their music for download at this Web megastore.

EMusic.com

www.emusic.com

Emusic.com has acquired an impressive array of music-related Web sites.

Farmclub.com

www.farmclub.com

Farmclub.com is a hot phenomenon for unsigned bands. You can upload your music to the site and get a chance to reach the site's considerable audience.

Garageband.com

www.garageband.com

This site offers an advice column for bands by Ramones producer Ed Stasium. It also offers a recording contract to unsigned bands.

Internet Underground Music Archive

www.iuma.com

A popular site that offers many resources for musicians.

Liquid Audio

www.liquidAudio.com

LiquidAudio.com boasts one of the largest online offerings of downloadable music.

Riffage.com

www.riffage.com

This music site offers a variety of languages.

Songs.com

www.songs.com

The singer/songwriter meets the Web at Songs.com.

Spin Records

www.spinrecords.com

SpinRecords helps showcase bands with its many sponsored events.

Important Sites

Artist Direct Network

www.artistdirect.com

This is a sprawling collection of music-related Web sites whose goal is to provide a direct connection between music artists and fans.

Broadcast.com

www.broadcast.com

The biggest collection of programming on the Net. From books on tape to the National Hockey League, watch and listen to it here.

Imagine Radio

www.imagineradio.com

This hugely popular site enables you to build your own Internet radio station (in other words, create your own playlist.)

Macromedia

www.macromedia.com

This is the developer of the leading multimedia software. Its applications have been on the forefront of multimedia sound. Here you can download the popular Shockwave plug-in.

Midiworld

www.midiworld.com

From composers to MIDI basics to synthesizers, this site has it all. Visit the MIDI Lab for some innovative compositional techniques.

Musicmaker

www.musicmaker.com

Here you can make your own customized CD. You pick the songs from a seemingly unending list, and they ship you a CD.

MP3.com

www.mp3.com

MP3 is the audio distribution format that's causing a major revolution in the music industry.

MTV.com

www.mtv.com

MTV.com is the most popular music site on the Web. The chat section includes Chat 24/7 with Audio, a leading-edge multimedia sound application.

National Public Radio

www.npr.org

One of the pioneers in streaming audio broadcasting, NPR offers a wealth of programming.

Pseudo.com

www.pseudo.com

Streaming media and hip-hop Webcasting—this is what the kids are dancing to.

Real.com

www.real.com

RealNetworks is the developer of the Web's most popular streaming technology.

RollingStone.com

www.rollingstone.com

The venerable music magazine's online presence is arguably more vital than its print version. Here you can download music, watch Webcasts, and read current music news.

Spinner

www.spinner.com

Spinner is one of the Net's biggest radio stations, with everything from country to jazz to New Age. A well-run site.

Tunes.com

www.tunes.com

This hugely popular site calls itself "The Internet's Music Hub" and generally lives up to the name. Download MP3s, watch Webcasts, read current news—Tunes.com offers something for every pop music fan.

Wired

www.wired.com

This online news source covers quite a bit besides Internet audio, but its coverage is superb. Make sure you visit the site's Webmonkey section—it's great resource for do-it-yourself Web audio projects.

Music Chat Rooms—A Mixed Selection

Oz-Music Chat

www.oz-music.com/chat/public/

Australian music chat.

Fruits of Music Chat Rooms

www.fruits.ch/cgi-bin/chat.cgi

Chat about Swiss electronica.

New Orleans Music Chat

www.talkcity.com/calendar/category/music.html

Do they still chat during Mardi Gras?

Classical Music Chat

www.classicalmusic.co.uk/chat.html

Talk about Beethoven with enthusiasts from all over the world.

Yerastica Hard and Heavy Music Chat

www.geocities.com/SunsetStrip/Towers/2238/Chat.htm

Discuss your favorite heavy metal band.

LAUT.BAR Chat

www.laut.de/lautbar/chat/index.htm

This music chat is in German.

Alternative Music Chat

http://altmusic.about.com/mpchat.htm

Share opinions about R.E.M., the Smashing Pumpkins, and
Garbage.

Indian Melody Music Chat

www.indianmelody.com/chat.htm

Discuss Indian music, ranging from classical to the latest film
scores.

David McPherson, Senior VP, Sony Music

http://chat.yahoo.com

This was a chat with an industry executive about the things that
emerging artists need to know to break into the business. It happened in 1999, but check back at the site for similar events.

MP3 Files and Software

AMP3

www.amp3.com

Like many big MP3 sites—and this one is huge—AMP3 features
many bands outside of the major labels. But you'll also see
Webcasts by the likes of Sheryl Crow and music news
from MTV.

Eatsleepmusic

www.eatsleepmusic.com

Visually attractive, hip site with many up-and-coming bands.
There are also many karaoke versions of pop songs by Prince and
Britney Spears.

Efolkmusic

www.efolkmusic.com

Pete Seeger would love this site: a good selection of folk, roots
rock, and bluegrass MP3s.

Electronic Music Forum

*http://computingcentral.msn.com/topics/electronicmusic/
bonus.asp*

Part of the Microsoft Network, this site has tons of resources:
thousands of MIDIs, MP3s, FAQ, newsgroups, and more.

Koan Pro

www.sseyo.com/kprobroc.html

Create and play ambient, interactive MP3s with the Koan Pro—
you don't have to be a musician to use it.

Lava

www.lava.com/

Lava is a plug-in that enables you to create and play back MP3s
with video and animation.

Maz MP3 Encoders

www.th-zwickau.de/~maz/mp3.html

There's plenty of shareware offered here. The most interesting is
Sound Limit 2.5, a shareware utility that can encode in a variety
of MPEG formats.

MP3 2000

www.mp32000.com

Although MP3 2000 can't claim to have everything that many other large MP3 sites have, it's very well-organized. There's also a well-chosen selection of MP3 news headlines.

MP3now

www.mp3now.com

A top resource for MP3s. You want it, they've got it: downloads, search engines, news, beginner's guides. This site appears to be a worthy competitor to the mothership, MP3.com.

Music Edge

www.music-edge.com

MP3 files and resources of all kinds—music, rippers, and hit lists. Music Edge has a lot to offer.

Official MP3 Music Webring

www.webring.org/cgi-bin/webring?ring=mp3;list

There's really nothing official about this gathering of Web sites, but it is a huge gathering of MP3s. Some of the sites are great, some aren't.

Pure MP3

www.puremp3.org

This is a network of sites, over 1,600 at last count, with two common themes: MP3s to download and a no-pornography policy.

Rioport

www.rioport.com

Created by the makers of the popular Diamond Rio player, this site offers free music in many different styles. After all, you need something to play on that Rio you just bought.

Shoutcast

www.shoutcast.com

This one is big: techno, jazz, chart-toppers. And all the MP3s stream if you have the Winamp player.

Streamworks

www.xingtech.com/video/streamworks/player

A good place to find good MP3 players.

WinAmp

http://winamp.com

The MP3 player of choice for Windows users. Don't forget to check out the personalized interface.

Wired Planet Player

www.wiredplanet.com

Wired Planet makes its own MP3 player.

Portable Players

Audiovox MP1000

www.audiovox.com

Diamond Rio

www.riohome.com

Frontier Labs Nex

www.frontierlabs.com

I-Jam MP3 Player

www.ijamworld.com

i2Go eGo Car

www.i2go.com

Lyra

www.lyrazone.com

MPMan F20

www.mpman.com

RFC jazPiper

www.jazpiper.nl

The Nomad MP3 Player

www.nomadworld.com

Pontis SP503

www.pontis.de/

RaveMP

www.ravemp.com/ravehome.html

Samsung Yepp64

www.samsungyepp.com/yepp64.html

Sony VAIO Music Clip

www.ita.sel.sony.com/products/vmc

Unitech Rome

www.mp-3.co.kr/

MP3 Portables—Information

Product Reviews: CNET—MP3 Players

http://home.cnet.com/consumerelectronics/0-1429220.html

Before you buy a portable player, take a look at these reviews of the top units.

Product Reviews: ZDNet—MP3 Players

http://www.zdnet.com/products/filter/guide/ 0,7267,6000954,00.html

ZDNet offers reviews of three top MP3 units: the Diamond Rio, Creative Labs' Nomad, and Nullsoft's MPMan.

Wearable Gear

www.wearablegear.com

This site is full of links about portable music players. You'll also find information about everything from new gadgets for mobile workers to articles about underwater keyboards. And don't miss the section on Beepware.

Newsgroups About MP3

alt.binaries.mp3.zappa

alt.binaries.sounds.country.mp3

alt.binaries.sounds.mp3.1950s

alt.binaries.sounds.mp3.1960s

alt.binaries.sounds.mp3.1970s

alt.binaries.sounds.mp3.1980s

alt.binaries.sounds.mp3.1990s

alt.binaries.sounds.78rpm-era

alt.binaries.sounds.mp3.alternative-rock

alt.binaries.sounds.mp3.bootlegs

alt.binaries.sounds.mp3.brazilian

alt.binaries.sounds.mp3.classic-rock

alt.binaries.sounds.mp3.comedy

alt.binaries.sounds.mp3.dance

alt.binaries.sounds.mp3.heavy-metal

alt.binaries.sounds.mp3.indie

alt.binaries.sounds.mp3.jazz

alt.binaries.sounds.mp3.latin

alt.binaries.sounds.mp3.reggae

alt.binaries.sounds.mp3.requests

alt.binaries.sounds.mp3

Online Stores: Audio/Computer Gear

Digital Camera Center

www.digital-camera-center.com

A good location to shop for SmartMedia Cards.

Supreme Video and Electronics

http://www.supremevideo.net

Mobshop

http://www.mobshop.com

800.com Electronics and More

http://www.800.com

Computers4Sure

http://www.computers4sure.com

WorldSpy

http://www.worldspy.com

More Audio Video

http://www.moreaudiovideo.com

TurboPrice

http://www.turboprice.com

Recordable CDs

CD-Recordable FAQ

www.fadden.com/cdrfaq/

A Web site with all the answers about CD-R. Very well done, and updated often.

CD-R Technical Directory

www.eciusa.com/cdr/techdic.htm.

The directory goes through hundreds of terms alphabetically, explaining CD terminology in an easy-to-understand style.

CD-R Hardware

www.cdr-hardware.com

CD-R Hardware is a complete overview of compact disc mastering and duplication. Good for the home user as well as larger industrial applications.

CD-R Outlet

www.cdroutlet.com/

Claims to have the largest selection of blank recordable media available online. I can't verify that, but it *is* large: CD-R, zip discs, DAT tape, jewel cases, and much more.

CD-Info

www.cd-info.com

Loads of information about burning CDs. Particularly helpful is the articles link—good background information about everything from disc packaging to the history of the CD-ROM.

DVD-CD-R Guide

www.zdnet.com/products/filter/guide/0,7267,1500164,00.html

Published by ZDNet, this is a good source of up-to-date product reviews.

Digital Domain

www.digido.com

This covers CD burning as well as DVD mastering. It also covers compression, jitter, dither, copyright, and quite a few other topics.

EMedia Magazine

www.emediapro.net/

An online magazine aimed at the interactive professional who produces optical disc technologies such as CD, DVD, and CD-ROM.

Glossary of Terms: CD and DVD

www.eciusa.com/cdr/techdic.htm

An ambitious effort, this technical dictionary covers hundreds of terms you'll need to know if you're going to create a CD or DVD.

Indie-Music.com: Making a CD

http://Indie-Music.com/cdmanufacturing.htm

A great resource for the band that's about to press a CD. This guide takes you through how to choose a company, pricing, artwork, and scheduling.

Making Your Own CD-R's: A Primer

www.digitalexperience.com/cdrprimer.html

This article takes you from the basics through the finished product.

Octave Libary: CD-Recordable

http://octave.com/library.html

Provides links to many frequently researched CD-R topics, but also provides some lesser-known resources, like finding CD-R software for Linux.

PC Technology Guide: CD-ROM/CD-RW

www.pctechguide.com/09cdr-rw.htm

A clearly written primer that provides in-depth coverage of digital recordable media.

Primer on CD-R

http://resource.simplenet.com/primer/primer.htm

Much more than a primer, this site travels far and wide over the subject of recordable digital media.

Self Publishing

Beginner's Page

http://wdvl.internet.com/WebRef/Help/Begin.html.

A good place to begin your education in Web site building. Hosted by Internet.com, it offers tips on how to embed sound into your Web page.

Search Engine Watch

www.searchenginewatch.com

Get your self-published material listed in search engines. Run by Web guru Danny Sullivan, SearchEngineWatch.com is a top source of information about these all-important Web portals.

Self-Publishing.com

www.self-publishing.com

Offers tips for musicians to promote themselves online.

Angelfire

http://angelfire.lycos.com

If you're looking for a site that will host your band's Web page for free, visit Angelfire. In addition to being a free service, Angelfire offers many helpful tools, like software for animating pages and a library of HTML scripts to add to your page's functionality.

Sound Search

Audiofind

www.audiofind.com

A searchable directory of MP3s and other sound files. Searchable by artist and genre.

CuteMX

www.cutemx.com

This site is designed to be easy to use.

Imusic

www.imusic.com

This music-oriented search engine focuses on finding music by artist.

Gnutella

www.gnutella.wego.com

Gnutella uses a distributed system for file sharing, making it immune to lawsuits.

Kerbango

www.kerbango.com

A search engine specifically for audio on the Web, it's particularly geared toward finding and rating radio station broadcasts.

Listen

www.listen.com

Listen will find downloadable music in a variety of file formats.

MIDI Explorer

www.musicrobot.com

A MIDI search engine that does of good job of combing the Web for files. You can group results by name or length.

Movie Database Search

www.imdb.com/search/soundtracks

This site has a search engine that locates soundtracks from a huge database of movies. Careful, though, because this is largely copyrighted material.

Napster

www.napster.com

This free-for-all file-swapping site gained 20 million users in about a year.

Scour

www.scour.net

Scour will find everything sound-related on the Web, with special emphasis on radio and movies.

Streamsearch

www.streamsearch.com

Geared toward finding streaming audio and video. Plenty of good movie trailers, too.

APPENDIX B

Napster and Beyond: File-Sharing Sites

Napster and other file-swapping programs are rapidly changing the music industry. This appendix contains the following:

- An overview of how Napster is leading a revolution from the dorm room to the boardroom

- A user's guide to Napster, including tips for advanced users

- A user's guide to Gnutella, a leading alternative to Napster

- A list of other top sites that help users share files

Napster, possibly the most popular musical phenomenon since the electric guitar, is under legal fire as of this writing. By the time you read this, the site may be shut down. Or, if it can defend itself in court, it may be bigger than ever. But whether Napster survives its legal challenges or not, the software it has popularized is creating enormous change.

The Napster revolution—and it *is* a revolution—is twofold. First, the site is revolutionary in that it gives users access to vast riches of recorded music—completely free of charge. If you want early Elvis or recent Pearl Jam, 1950s doo-wop or brand new hip-hop, Napster's file-swapping software helps you download it. Millions of PC users have made their music collections available to the public. It's as if the local record store threw open its doors and said, "Come on in and take whatever you want!" Except that no record store in the world is as well-stocked as the Internet. The fact that so much music is being distributed so freely has caused a major crack in the foundation of the music business.

But Napster has caused a second revolution. Consider this: Napster has in the neighborhood of 20 million registered users. This is an audience that many Web start-ups have spent tens of millions of dollars to attract. Indeed, many new online companies have gone to inordinate lengths to gather "eyeballs"—the ad campaign featuring gerbils shot out of a canon comes to mind. More than one online company has spent almost all of its war chest on one 60-second ad during the Super Bowl. But many of these Web companies have nowhere near Napster's user base.

Napster's user base of 20 million wouldn't be so amazing if its advertising budget weren't so small. Small? More accurately, almost nonexistent. Have you even seen an ad for Napster? No, because the company has never produced a major advertising campaign.

That's right. In about one year, Napster attracted 20 million users with an advertising budget that equals the cost of a Big Mac and fries.

If you hear a gasping sound, it's probably a record company executive. After all, a record company must spend millions to popularize an act. Was Britney Spears' popularity created through word of mouth? Definitely not.

> As of this writing, Napster is defending itself against a copyright infringement lawsuit. Expect many more legal disputes with similar sites as the uneasy relationship between the Internet and copyright gets ironed out.

20 million potential music buyers gathering in one place without spending a dime on the traditional music record labels is more than a just small cloud on the horizon. It's a perfect storm. What will happen to CD sales? What about retail music outlets? What about the labels' commercial formulas for creating successful artists?

Now the file-swapping craze has spread. There are a host of file-swapping sites (see the list at the end of this appendix), most with their own software, that go beyond Napster. For example, Freenet has no Napster-style centralized database, so there's no company to file a lawsuit against. Files are posted anonymously. There's virtually no way to remove that copy of the Backstreet Boys' recent hit, no matter how many lawyers the record company assigns to the case.

And Freenet facilitates the swapping of not only music, but also images and video. The Pandora's box that Napster cracked open can't be shut.

What the Napster free-for-all will mean for the recording business (and the film, video, graphics, and other publishing businesses) is impossible to predict. It's likely that businesspeople and artists alike are having meetings about that very subject even as you read this. But it's hard to say when they'll have answers to questions like "How do we make money from music when fans get all their music for free?" and "How do we prevent mass copying of our latest release?"

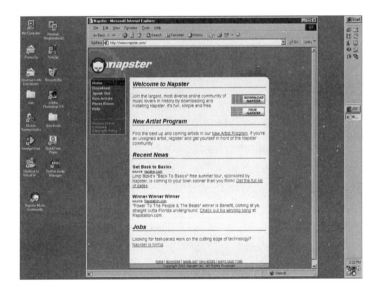

For a site with millions of visitors, Napster has a surprisingly bland front page. But when so many people are so eager to visit you, why spend money on fancy Web design?

How to Use Napster: Getting Started

Fortunately, getting up and running with Napster is pretty easy, and the following guide will make it easier still.

First, download the program, which is written for Windows users. If you're using a different operating system, look for alternative software in the Napster FAQ section. All of the software is free.

Mac users can use Macster to search for and download MP3 files from Napster users. To download it, visit *www.blackholemedia. com/macster/*.

After installing the program, you'll need to fill out a simple registration form that asks you the following:

- **Line Speed**   Choose the speed of your Internet connection, from 14.4 to a T3 line. If you have a really fast connection, like ISDN or T1, many other users will want to share your MP3s because it's easy to download from a hard drive with a fast connection. That's why some users select a slower line speed than they really have. They don't want their Internet connection clogged up with crowds of music-lovers.

- **Proxy Server**   You can leave this blank unless you're behind a proxy server. Most home users are not.

- **New/Existing User**   Create a login name and password, and put in your email address. Because so many millions of people have already signed up, many of the common login names are taken. Don't be alarmed if your first few attempts don't work just create one that no one else has already used.

- **Optional Information**   You can leave these fields blank. They're not necessary, so why fill them in?

- **Audio Information**   Select your audio player. If you've got an MP3 player that you're already using and are happy with, choose that. If not, you can choose Napster's player.

- **Share my MP3 files under folders** and **Save my new MP3 files in folder**   These choices determine where downloaded MP3s will be stored and whether you want to share your files with your fellow Napster users. If you choose the Music folder installed by Napster (the default choice), all your downloads will go there and will be available to the millions of other Napster users. If you choose not to share your downloads, select another folder on your hard drive as your download destination, and make sure that no folder is selected as the sharing folder.

Click Finish. Congratulations—you now have a Napster account. If you want to change any of your settings later (for example, you might get new MP3 software), you can go to File, Preferences.

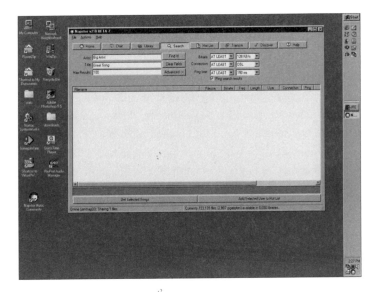

Plenty of people downloaded music from the Internet before Napster, but this file-sharing program has made it easy. The Napster dialog box is the program's central tool.

Can You Say Download?

Now on to the fun stuff—finding music. Napster makes developing an enormous music collection amazingly easy. (Some copyright lawyers would say it's *too* easy.) So let's get downloading:

1. Click on Search near the top of the main dialog box.

2. Enter a band or artist name in the Artist box, or type a song's name in the Song Title box. Enter information into both boxes for a more specific search.

3. Click on Find It!, or press Enter.

4. You'll see a list of song titles. Double-click on the one you want and it will begin to download.

Improving Your Napster Results: The Advanced User

When you're ready to do some serious downloading, click on the Advanced Fields option. You don't need to use any of these options if you don't want to, but they sure will make your Napster experience a lot better. Let's take a look at these advanced techniques.

By using some of the options in Napster's Advanced Fields boxes, you can greatly enhance your download capabilities.

- **Bitrate**　The higher the bitrate, the better the MP3 will sound. The most common setting is 128Kbps. It's not a good idea to download songs with a lower bitrate unless you just *have* to have that song and can't find it at a higher bitrate. However, if you choose MP3s with higher bitrates, such as 320Kbps, realize that they're larger files and will take longer to download.

- **Frequency**　This refers to the sample rate of the file. It's best to specify 44100Hz, which is also the most frequent sample rate for files found through Napster.

- **Ping Time**　This refers to how long it takes a data packet to travel from your computer to another computer and back. Choose a lower ping time to ensure that your downloads go faster. The lower the ping time, the better.

- **Line Speed**　The higher the line speed, the faster the download. Line speeds are listed with the fastest, T3, at the top. By specifying a higher line speed, you're choosing to download only from users with fast Internet connections. But remember, choosing only fast connections limits the total number of users with which you'll be sharing. If you know you'll be searching for music that's hard to find, it's worth choosing the slower Internet connections (and also the slower ping times).

The results of a song search. You can click on a song title to download it, or you can use the information from the song search to make your downloads easier and faster.

There's Gold in Them Hills: Downloading Songs

Let's go through downloading a song, and look at how your choices in the line speed and bitrate categories can help you.

The preceding figure shows the results of a Napster song search. This is a list of all the users that came up when I searched for a single song. Notice that some of the users have the song at

128Kbps, and some have it at 192Kbps. In this case, it's better to choose the version at 192Kbps because it will sound better.

View the list again and compare the line speeds. If you can download from a user who has a T3 line, that's faster than a download from a user with a T1.

To find the best results in each column, click on the column name. For example, if you click on Ping Time, the choices will be ordered with the smallest values on top. Click again and the list reverses, with the largest values on top. This comes in handy when you want to find the song with the highest bitrate.

You can also use Napster's handy colored dot option. Look next to the song titles and you'll see dots that specify line speeds: green for cable modems and above, yellow for 56k modems to ISDN-128k, red for 33.6 modems and below. Choose songs with a green dot when you can.

> Advanced Napster user's tip: After you've searched for an artist and found dozens of songs to download, it's easy to download more than one song at a time. Simply hold down the Ctrl key and click on each song title you want. Then click Get Selected Songs at the bottom of the search dialog box. You'll see the Transfer dialog box with a list of your downloads in progress.

Finding Friends in All the Right Places: Your Hot List

One of the truly ingenious things about Napster is that it helps you find music fans with tastes similar to yours. You like early Squirrel Monkeys, but no one else you know does? Among the millions in the Napster community, you'll probably find someone who's crazy about them. This function is called your Hot List, and it's a great way to share music with like-minded fans.

After you've done several music searches, you'll notice that some users appear repeatedly. These users probably enjoy the same music you do. You can add them to your Hot List in two ways:

- Select the user's name in the Search dialog box, and then click on the Add Selected User to Hot List button.

- Go to the Actions menu and choose Add User to Hot List. With
  this method, you have to type in the user's name. This is a particularly useful option if you have a friend you want to swap
  MP3s with.

Here's the great part of this system: Once you've added a user
to your Hot List, you can access his entire library of songs by
clicking on Hot List at the top of the Napster window. In the
far-left column of the Hot List dialog box, you'll see your Hot
List users, and Napster will tell you if they're currently online
or offline. If a user is currently offline, you can't access his
music. (This means he's doing something else instead of siting
in front of his computer. Can you believe it?)

Click on one of the users' names in the Online list. In the true
spirit of Napster, you'll see a list of every song in his library.
You can then download any of these songs you'd like.

> There are no MP3 files stored on the Napster servers; there's only a cen-
> tralized database of users.

Finding the Best Servers: Napigator

The millions of people logging on to Napster have clogged the
system's numerous servers. Many times you can't log on simply
because too many people are busy downloading at the same
time. To help you navigate around this problem, use Napigator.

Napigator helps music fans by listing alternative servers and
their associated usage statistics. This way you can find servers
that have optimal ping times and aren't clogged to the gills with
other users.

Even more helpfully, Napigator enables you to pick a server
based on a style of music. So if you're searching for trance
music, you can find a server with libraries full of every possible
type of trance music. And the genres are numerous. Jazz, rap,
indie rock, punk, big band, folk—if you've ever heard it, it's
probably there.

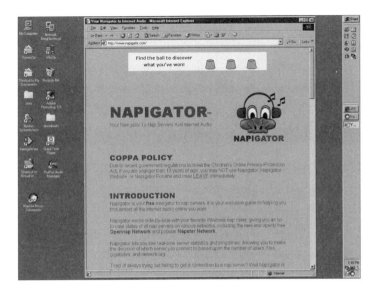

If you've had problems connecting because of overused servers, or if you'd like to narrow your search to a specific genre, give Napigator a try. Download the free program at www.napigator.com.

Napster's Leading Competition: Gnutella

This file-swapping program isn't as popular as Napster yet, but it's gaining fast. It also doesn't display quite as much file information as Napster does, but if Napster goes under, Gnutella will probably be the top choice for downloading music.

Although Napster and Gnutella are similar, there are two main differences:

- Gnutella is a decentralized system with no single server holding a database of information. Each computer (including yours) joins a connected ring of computers. This means that getting connected is a bit tougher, but it also means that Gnutella is virtually impossible to sue.

- Gnutella helps users find all sorts of multimedia files, including video, software and text.

To download the software, go to the Gnutella site at *http://www. gnutella.wego.com*. Fortunately, there's a version of the software written for almost every platform, from Windows to Mac to Unix.

When you get the software booted up, click on the Config tab in the upper-left corner to go to the Configuration menu.

Many of the choices in the Configuration screen don't need to be changed, but there are a few that are important:

- **Save new files to**   This tells the software where on your hard drive to put all the files you download. Make sure you choose a drive with enough space for all those large files you'll be downloading.

- **Path(s) to files**   Be careful when you select an option in this box. This specifies the folders that you'll be sharing with other Gnutella users. The program automatically shares anything in any directories under the folders you list. Remember, anything you share may be downloaded by millions.

- **Connection Speed**   This tells other users your Internet connection speed. This has no effect on your download speed.

Getting Connected: So, What's an IP?

Click on the gnutellaNet tab in the upper-left corner. You'll see an Add button with a box to the left of it. To get connected to the many other Gnutella users, you have to enter an IP address of an already-connected computer.

Finding an IP address is the most confusing and difficult aspect of Gnutella, but it's necessary because there's no central server. An IP, which stands for internet protocol, is the network address of a computer connected to the Internet. Typically, it's a rather odd series of numbers or letters.

There are two ways to find a suitable IP address:

- Go to the front page of the Gnutella Web site, where you'll find a list of IPs to use.

- Get an IP address from a friend who's already connected.

Once you find the IP address, type the number in the Add box and click Add. With a little bit of luck, you'll be connected to the network of Gnutella users. Don't be surprised if it doesn't work the first time. You may need to try the number later, or find a new number. This is quite a hassle, but it's part of working with a decentralized system.

You're Connected!

So, after some huffing, puffing, and calls to friends who are already connected, your Gnutella software has sprung to life and you can begin downloading.

Click on the Search tab in the upper-left corner to go to the search screen. Enter the name of a song, piece of software, or document in the Search box and click on the Search button. Be prepared to wait—the software has to search the network, and this might take some time.

After you see the search results, double-click on any title you're interested in. To check on your download's progress, click on the Download tab. If the download seems to be taking longer than it should (a not-uncommon occurrence), click on Abort Selected, wait a moment, and then click on Resume Selected.

To see what other users are downloading from your computer, click on the Uploads tab. Did you remember to move all your passwords from that shared folder?

One of the most interesting aspects of Gnutella is the Monitor screen. Click on the Monitor tab to find a list of all the search requests to your computer. If you see something interesting, double-click on it to add it to your own request list. But be aware that Gnutella allows users to search for all types of files, so there's probably going to be some material that's far from G-rated.

All in all, Gnutella is an effective file-swapping tool, but it's still working out the bugs. Expect some delays during this process.

More File-Swapping Sites

As file-sharing technology develops, file-swapping programs are helping people find more than music. Investigate the following file-sharing sites and you'll find Hollywood movie trailers, weird videos, graphics, text, software, all sorts of games, and more. Let's get surfing!

Spinfrenzy

www.spinfrenzy.com

Considering what a good MP3 search tool Spinfrenzy is, there hasn't been much hype about it. Download the site's software and you will indeed spin into an MP3 frenzy. The site's servers tend to be fast and steady, and the search results are extensive.

Scour Exchange

www.scour.net

Although Scour Exchange is one of the newer file-swapping programs, it's part of Scour, one of the oldest search sites. Scour has always been a great place to hunt for music, and now it's file-swapping utility helps you harvest a wide array of files—video and multimedia as well as music. Scour Exchange also has a hot list that lets you browse through selected members' file libraries. I've heard that there are a few bugs in the Scour Exchange program—not many files, problems connecting to servers—but with its connection to such a well-respected search site, these bugs will probably get ironed out.

Spinfrenzy is a great place to find MP3s.

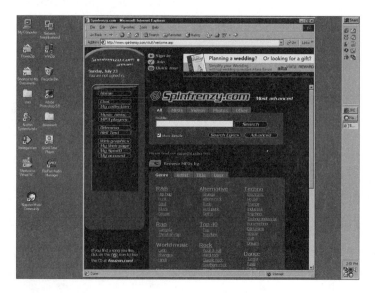

CuteMX

www.cutemx.com

Ease of use is CuteMX's selling point, but its clear and simple user interface doesn't mean it lacks features. This little-known file-swapping program is loaded with tools: a streaming player for instant audition of search results, hot lists, chat rooms, and a user-defined censoring program. The program allows you to finish your downloads later if your connection gets dropped. CuteMX is a must-download for the music fan.

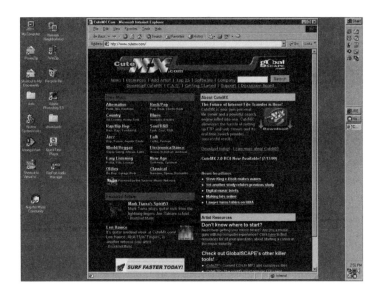

CuteMX is easy to use and provides good results for music searches.

Freenet

http://freenet.sourceforge.net

Developed by 23-year-old Irish programmer Ian Clarke, Freenet takes file-swapping a step further. It's designed for complete anonymity, so the identities of those who upload files are as unknown as the identities of those who download them. In addition, there's no centralized database like the one Napster has, so there's no one to sue. It's highly unlikely that the kind of court action for copyright infringement that has been brought against Napster and MP3.com can be brought against Freenet. The Freenet system has been designed so that it's virtually impossible to remove a file once it's been uploaded. And Freenet enables users to swap any kind of digital media, from video to text to music to graphics.

IMesh

www.imesh.com

Growing rapidly in popularity, iMesh helps users share any kind of digital files. You can specify if you're looking for audio, video, images, software, or documents, and then enter a keyword and search the desktops of all the other iMesh users. As of this writing, the iMesh software has been downloaded almost a million times.

But Remember...

In the excitement about Napster, it seems as if something fundamental has been forgotten: When you download music from Napster or one of the other file-swapping sites, the musicians don't get paid.

But bands like Pearl Jam and the Chili Peppers have big recording contracts, right? Who needs to worry about them? And anyway, record companies charge way too much for a CD, and they treat the musicians unfairly, so who cares about record companies?

Besides, CD sales have actually *increased* in the Napster era. Some say file-sharing programs are stimulating such interest in music that even the artists and record companies are benefiting.

These arguments have some validity. Record companies have been known to write exploitative contracts, and CDs are clearly overpriced. It's also true that a small minority of musicians have enough money to sit poolside and sip margaritas between album projects.

But—and it's a *big* but—that doesn't change the fact that musicians deserve to get paid to make music, and they can't do it if everyone gets their music for free. In addition, there's an army of lesser-known people who make their living from music sales, from studio engineers to the graphic artists who create album art.

Am I recommending that you don't use Napster? That would be pointless. Napster-style programs aren't going to go away. If anything, they'll proliferate.

No, it's not necessary to give up your Napster-Gnutella-Freenet habit. But here's a thought: Find a way to give back to the musicians you really enjoy. Perhaps you could download a few songs, and then go out and buy a couple of your favorite group's albums. Maybe you could explore Napster, and then go to a site like Emusic.com to buy a band's music on a per-song basis. There are plenty of ways to do it if you want to. All I'm saying is to give it some thought. Music wants to be free, but musicians have to pay for groceries.

GLOSSARY

Study Up! Here's a List of Helpful Terms

AIFF Audio Interchange File Format. This file format, was developed by Apple, is very flexible, allowing the specification of arbitrary sampling rates, sample size, number of channels, and application-specific format chunks that can be ignored by other applications.

Analog A method of sound recording and playback that uses a continuously variable physical phenomenon to reproduce another dynamic phenomenon. The cassette tape and vinyl record album are examples of analog recording media.

Amplifier A piece of electronic gear used to increase a signal level. Usually called *amps*, amplifiers are typically thought of as volume boosters.

Bit Short for *binary digit*. A bit represents either an "on" or "off" in a digital file. In digital audio, this term is often used to describe the quality of a sound file. The higher the bit number, the higher the quality of the sound. For example, 16-bit sound is far superior to 8-bit sound.

Batch encoder A software program that can convert large numbers of audio files to different formats.

Bright A term referring to pronounced high frequencies. A bright sound has a loud high end that gives it an aggressive quality.

CD-ROM Compact Disc Read-Only Memory, a popular format for storing large amounts of multimedia data. The CD-ROM format often includes audio.

CD-R   Recordable CD, achieved by burning data onto a special coating on the CD. A similar format is CDR-W, which can be erased and rewritten repeatedly.

Clipping   The result of overloading an amplifier to the point of distortion. Clipping can damage a loudspeaker's tweeters.

Compact disc   A popular digital audio storage media that uses the ISO9660 industry standard developed by Sony and Phillips. The CD was the first consumer digital format. It has a maximum playing time of 74 minutes.

Compression   Reducing a file's size. Various methods of encoding digital information can be used to reduce the size of a digital audio file by eliminating redundant or unnecessary information.

Constant bit rate (CBR)   An encoding method that varies compression quality to ensure a constant bitrate throughout an encoded file. This results in predictable MP3 file sizes. But it can also create lower-quality sound because a more complex musical passage isn't given the additional memory needed to faithfully reproduce it.

Decoder   Software that interprets files created by a corresponding encoder to reproduce the original audio. Decoders are more commonly referred to as *players*.

DAT   Digital audio tape. Although a DAT machine is tape-based, it produces sound as clean and noise-free as a disc-based digital player.

Decibel   In layman's terms, decibels (abbreviated dB) are a unit of volume measurement; a sound can be turned up or down by several decibels. In technical terms, decibels are on a logarithmic scale of relative loudness. In terms of a listener's perceptions, a difference of about 3 dB is a moderate change in volume, and 10 dB is perceived as a doubling of volume.

Digital audio   A method of sound recording and playback that uses ones and zeros to represent on or off states, replicating an audio signal. Digital audio is easy to edit and manipulate, it's free of the hiss of analog recording, and it can be stored on a computer's hard drive.

Distortion Anything that mars or alters an audio signal. There are many forms of distortion, and some are more noticeable than others. Distortion is often caused by sending too much signal into a recording mechanism.

DIY Abbreviation for "Do It Yourself." In audio, the most common DIY is building a home recording setup.

Dynamic range The range between the loudest and softest passages in a recording that can be reproduced accurately by an audio component. The greater the number of decibels between soft and loud passages, the wider the dynamic range.

Encoder Software or an algorithm that analyzes a sound file, isolates its defining attributes, and constructs a replica, usually in the form of a much smaller file.

EQ (Equalization) Sophisticated tone controls that can subtly enhance or drastically change a sound. EQ can change audio in several ways, such as making it sound fuller or brighter. Equalization controls include the frequency to be affected, the bandwidth, and the amount of boost (increase) and cut (decrease).

File-swapping programs Internet-based software that facilitates the trading of audio and multimedia files between many users. Napster is a file-swapping program.

Frequency The range of frequencies that make up sound. Measured in hertz, the frequency of human hearing is (at best) 20-20,000Hz. One hertz equals one cycle per second, and ten hertz equals ten cycles per second. The lower the number of hertz, the softer the sound.

Hertz (Hz) A unit of measurement in cycles per second, discovered by the German scientist Karlheinz Hertz.

Jukebox An integrated software system providing CD ripping, downloading, playlist organizing, online database connectivity, and playback of digital audio. RealNetworks and MusicMatch are two companies that currently offer jukeboxes.

Kbps Kilobits per second. In digital audio, Kbps used to describe the quality of MP3 files. Higher values produce higher-quality files that are larger in size and require faster connections for proper streaming.

Loops   Convenient audio segments that are rhythmically correct when played over and over. A single loop might be an eight-bar drum and bass pattern, for example.

Lossless   A digital compression technique that reduces the amount of data storage needed for a file but doesn't discard any of its information. The audio is identical before and after compression. MPEG-2 is an example of lossless compression.

Lossy   A digital compression technique that discretely discards parts of the audio signal in order to reduce the amount of storage needed. The popular MP3 format is a lossy compression method.

MIDI   Musical Instrument Digital Interface, a commonly used format for computer-based music composition. It translates musical performance into numerical data, which can be played back on MIDI-compatible sound modules. MIDI data can control many parameters of performance, such as pitch bend, volume, and note length.

MiniDisc   Sony's MiniDisc format places a maximum of 74 minutes of near-CD quality digital audio onto a 2.5-inch disc. The audio is compressed using Sony's ATRAC compression scheme.

MP3 (MPEG-1 Audio Layer 3)   The audio coding format defined by the International Organization for Standardization (ISO) as part of the MPEG-1 Audio Layer-3 specification. MP3 has become a popular audio compression format because it retains audio quality while greatly decreasing file size.

MPEG   The Moving Picture Experts Group, an organization that develops standards for the coding of moving pictures and associated audio. MPEG audio files can be either layer I, II, or III. The higher layer numbers add complexity to the format and require more effort to encode and decode. Typical compression rates are around 10-to-1.

RCA connector   Sometimes called phono plugs, RCA connectors are used primarily as low-level connecting devices between audio hardware like CD players, MP3 portables, and amplifiers.

RealAudio   The streaming audio format from RealNetworks, which was the first one available on the Web.

Red Book standard The formal standard for the audio compact disc. Red Book standard audio is 44.1KHz, 16-bit stereo.

Ripper Software that allows the user to convert files on a CD into a particular encoded format (often WAV) in one step, without ever leaving the digital realm.

Sample A digital snippet of a sound that can be triggered by a MIDI keyboard. A sample can be a drum or orchestral sound, a vocal phrase, or a sound effect.

Sample rate When audio is digitized, the sampling rate is the number of samples taken in a second. A high sample rate means that the quality of the recording is high. The most common sample rates in professional recording are 44.1Khz and 48Khz. Some users record audio at 22Khz to make the files smaller for Web use.

SDMI Secure Digital Music Initiative, a forum for music labels and Internet companies that are working toward standards for the secure distribution and delivery of digital music. The initiative aims to provide protection for copyrighted music and intellectual property without impeding consumer access to them.

Sequencer Software that records and plays back MIDI data.

Sound card A circuit board that typically includes an FM and/or wavetable synthesizer, an analog-to-digital converter chip for recording analog audio to a hard drive, and a digital-to-analog converter chip for playing digital audio from a hard drive. In short, a card that gives your PC music recording and playback capabilities.

Stereo The use of two channels to create a three-dimensional audio image.

Streaming Playback of digital audio, video, and/or animation as it arrives at your computer. Instead of waiting for an entire file to download, playback begins with the arrival of a certain amount of data, known as the *buffer*. This buffer provides a cushion so that inconsistencies in the Internet connection don't affect seamless playback. As of this writing, streaming is still in its infancy.

USB   Universal Serial Bus, a fast, high-capacity (up to 127 devices) serial connection protocol for computers. USB is becoming the norm on both PCs and Macs.

Variable bit rate (VBR)   An encoding method that provides high-quality playback by varying the bit rate over time according to the demands of the content. It's a relatively new method of encoding MP3 files that not all players support yet.

Waveform   A two-dimensional graph showing changes in voltage as a function of time. This is frequently used as a visual display of a digital recording.

WAV   A sound format created by Microsoft and IBM. It has a plethora of compression formats and is the most common type of computer audio file.

Yellow Book standard   The formal standard for storing data on a CD-ROM.

INDEX

Tell Us What You Think!

As the reader of this book, *you* are our most important critic and commentator. We value your opinion and want to know what we're doing right, what we could do better, what areas you'd like to see us publish in, and any other words of wisdom you're willing to pass our way.

You can email or write me directly to let me know what you did or didn't like about this book—as well as what we can do to make our books stronger.

Please note that I cannot help you with technical problems related to the topic of this book, and that due to the high volume of mail I receive, I might not be able to reply to every message.

When you write, please be sure to include this book's title and author as well as your name and phone or fax number. I will carefully review your comments and share them with the author and editors who worked on the book.

E-mail: internet_sams@mcp.com

Mail: Mark Taber
Associate Publisher
Sams Publishing
201 West 103rd Street
Indianapolis, IN 46290 USA

Install Instructions

Windows 95, Windows 98, Windows NT 4, and Windows 2000

If Windows 95, Windows 98, Windows NT 4.0 or Windows 2000 is installed on your computer and you have the AutoPlay feature enabled, the start.exe program starts automatically whenever you insert the disc into your CD-ROM drive.

1. Insert the CD-ROM into your CD-ROM drive.

2. From the Windows desktop, double-click on the "My Computer" icon.

3. Double-click on the icon representing your CD-ROM drive.

4. Double-click on the icon titled START.EXE to run the installation program.

5. Follow the onscreen instructions to finish the installation.

Read This Before Opening Package

This CD-ROM uses long and mixed-case filenames requiring the use of a protected-mode CD-ROM Driver.

By opening this package, you are agreeing to be bound by the following agreement: